Hard Times on Kairiru Island

HARD TIMES ON KAIRIRU ISLAND

*Poverty, Development, and Morality
in a Papua New Guinea Village*

Michael French Smith

University of Hawaii Press
Honolulu

94 95 96 97 98 99   5 4 3 2 1

Library of Congress Cataloging–in–Publication Data
Smith, Michael French.
Hard times on Kairiru Island : poverty, development, and morality
in a Papua New Guinea village / Michael French Smith.
p.   cm.
Includes bibliographical references (p.   ) and index.
ISBN 0–8248–1536–X (cloth : acid-free paper). — ISBN
0–8248–1581–5 (paper : acid-free paper)
1. Kairiru (Papua New Guinea people)—Economic conditions.
2. Kairiru (Papua New Guinea people)—Social conditions.
3. Subsistence economy—Papua New Guinea—Kragur. 4. Economic
development—Papua New Guinea—Kragur. 5. Kragur (Papua New
Guinea)—Economic conditions. 6. Kragur (Papua New Guinea)—Social
conditions.   I. Title.
DU740.42.S65   1994
305.899'9120953—dc20   93–41300
                                        CIP

Designed by Paula Newcomb

The interior ornament is adapted
from a wooden plate called *Waryangbungbung,* carved by
Borchem of Kragur Village, Kairiru Island.

Contents

Acknowledgments

I WISH TO THANK the people of Kragur village for the exceptional generosity and kindness they have shown me—patiently explaining their lives, and allowing me to eat from their gardens and sit by their fires. In particular, I thank those Kragur people who took me into their families and called me *taik* and *luk*. The hospitality of the staff and students of St. Xavier's High School contributed a great deal to my life and work on Kairiru island. I also thank the governments of Papua New Guinea and the East Sepik Province for their permission to carry out my field research.

I owe a great debt to Victor E. Smith and Margaret F. Smith. Throughout this endeavor they have provided unfailing support and encouragement of every kind. Theodore Schwartz has my gratitude for introducing me to Papua New Guinea and for his teaching and encouragement through the years.

The Institute for Intercultural Studies helped support my fieldwork in Kragur in 1981. The National Endowment for the Humanities and the Institute of Culture and Communication of the East-West Center provided a stimulating atmosphere for essential research and writing in the summer of 1991. James Carrier, Mary Taylor Huber, and Virginia Kerns all made valuable comments on my manuscript at various stages of its development.

I thank Julie Ecker Green for her word processing skills and Paul Martin for his map making expertise. Michael Pileng was an able research assistant during my work in Kragur in 1975–1976.

This book incorporates material that has appeared in other forms in the following sources:

"Bloody Time and Bloody Scarcity: Capitalism, Authority and the Transformation of Temporal Experience in a Papua New Guinea Village," from *American Ethnologist* 9:3 (August 1982), by permission of the American Anthropological Association.

"The Catholic Ethic and the Spirit of Alcohol Use in an East Sepik Province Village," from *Through a Glass Darkly: Beer and Modernization in Papua New Guinea* (Mac Marshall, ed., Papua New Guinea Institute of Applied Social and Economic Research, 1982), by permission of the Papua New Guinea National Research Institute.

" 'Wild' Villagers and Capitalist Virtues: Perceptions of Western Work Habits in a Preindustrial Community," from *Anthropological Quarterly* 57:4 (October 1984), by permission of *Anthropological Quarterly*.

"Business and the Romance of Community Cooperation," from *Sepik Heritage: Tradition and Change in Papua New Guinea* (Nancy Lutkehaus et al., eds., Carolina Academic Press, 1990), by permission of the Wenner-Gren Foundation for Anthropological Research, Inc.

Hard Times on Kairiru Island

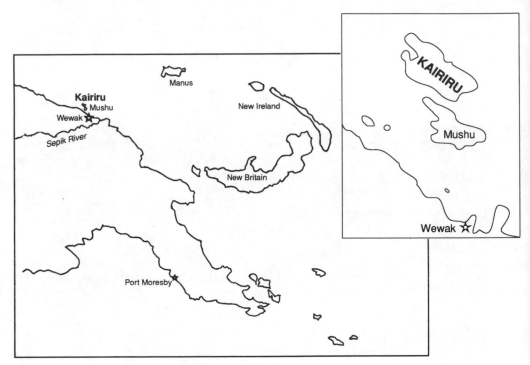

Kairiru island in relation to nearby islands and the Papua New Guinea mainland
(P. C. Martin)

ONE

Introduction: Hard Times, Goodness, and Visions of the Future

LOOKING OUT TO SEA from the open-air market in Wewak, the administrative center of Papua New Guinea's East Sepik Province, one can see two large islands. The nearer of the two, Mushu, is a low coral island. The high volcanic island just beyond is Kairiru (see map). Kragur village lies on Kairiru's northeast coast, one of several small communities scattered around the island's periphery. I first went there toward the end of 1975 to study the ways in which the extension of the modern capitalist economy was affecting the lives of people accustomed to living without all the things that are the stuff of daily life in the developed Western world. Life in Kragur proceeds without roads, electricity, telephones, or plumbing. More to the point, until relatively recently Kragur villagers knew little of such bedrock institutions of the economically developed world—whether it bills itself as capitalist or socialist—as money, buying and selling, employers and employees, wages, salaries, and the calendars and clocks used to measure time and organize labor.

The Sepik area—the East Sepik Province and the neighboring West Sepik Province—has long had the reputation of being one of the economically less progressive parts of Papua New Guinea. When passing through the national capital, Port Moresby, in 1975, I mentioned to an Australian acquaintance employed by the Papua New Guinea government that I was going to the Sepik to study social and economic change and that I was especially interested in people's responses to modern Western ways of understanding and organizing work and time. He wondered aloud why I

1

would choose the Sepik to study work and time, because, as he put it, in the Sepik "There isn't any." In fact, since shortly after the turn of the century, Kragur has been increasingly enmeshed in a new world of wage labor, the Western calendar, central government, taxes, schools, and churches; but although it lies near the Sepik region's largest urban center, Wewak, its inaccessability has slowed the pace of change. The new world is not yet taken for granted, and Kragur people devote considerable energy to trying to understand and master it.

Hard Times

Like many other coastal and island villages in the Pacific Islands, Kragur is strikingly picturesque. Terraced rows of thatched houses perch on a cliff above the sea, framed by stands of coconut palms and the lush green of the mountain looming above it all; but there is much discontent in this idyllic setting. Many Kragur villagers feel they are undergoing an extended period of hard times. I became acutely aware of this soon after taking up residence in Kragur, through talking with individuals and listening to the proceedings of public gatherings like one that took place a couple of days after Christmas 1975.

Kragur villagers are now nominally Catholics, but there are no extensive religious festivities in the village to mark the Christmas season. As in the West, however, Christmas has come to signal the end of one year and the beginning of another. There is a lull in the usual round of activities, in part because this is when many young men, and a few young women, who have left the village to work in urban areas or to attend school, return to Kragur on leave or school holidays. That year the Christmas season was also the occasion for a day-long meeting of the village men, including many returned migrants. They met in a newly completed thatched house not yet occupied by its owner and still fragrant with the scent of recently cut timber. Seated around the floor in the dim interior, smoking home-grown tobacco rolled in squares of newspaper and chewing betel nut, the men talked about what they could do to improve the lot of the village in the coming year.

The tone of the meeting was critical and pessimistic. In this holiday season, the return home of students and migrants was a source of chagrin as well as celebration. Garden produce, taro in particular, was in short supply, and the holidays were leaner and less festive than the villagers had hoped. The taro shortage was not a new problem that year, but many felt it acutely nevertheless. One older leader put this pointedly early in the meeting, suggesting that the gravity of the situation belied any festivities at all. "You celebrate Christmas, but I can't celebrate Christmas," he declared. "You talk about a happy Christmas. What happy Christmas?"

The village men raised a wide variety of issues besides the taro shortage. They spoke of the shortage of money nearly as often as the shortage of food. Both migrants and residents expressed concern over the declining village population and the problem of inducing young men and women—particularly young men—to remain in the village and ensure its future. While a young migrant, employed in Wewak by the Department of Public Health, spoke of the need to prevent disease by improving village hygiene, older men spoke vehemently of the needs to eliminate the practice of sorcery and to make certain that traditional magical knowledge be passed down to the younger generations before the death of their elders.

Most meetings in Kragur are conducted without the trappings of parliamentary procedure. The men—seldom are women present—discuss the issue at hand until they reach a consensus, which is usually shaped in large part by the views of a small number of more influential men. No votes are taken. Most accept the consensus decision, but there are often a few dissenters. Some speak up in the meeting; some hold their peace but grumble later; some register their opposition by silent noncooperation when the time comes to put a plan into action.

At this meeting, however, the influence of a contingent of literate, town-dwelling migrants was evident. One young man had borrowed a blackboard from the primary school in a neighboring village. He wrote across the top of it in Melanesian Pidgin, a lingua franca spoken in much of Papua New Guinea that binds together speakers of the country's hundreds of distinct local languages, *Wanem rot tru bai yumi i go longen long nupela yia?* "What course will we follow in the new year?" Kragur villagers are bilingual in Pidgin and the indigenous Kairiru language, which is also spoken on Karesau and Yuo islands, in the northern and western parts of Mushu, and in a few coastal mainland villages.¹ Kragur people often lace their Kairiru speech with a substantial amount of Pidgin and sometimes switch over completely to Pidgin, especially when they are discussing such contemporary phenomena as Catholicism, national independence, or money. (Unless otherwise indicated, quotations from villagers in this book are translated from Pidgin or a mixture of Pidgin and Kairiru.)

The young man solicited items for an agenda and chalked these on the board, although many adult Kragur men, and most adult women, are only marginally literate. During the course of the meeting the men voted on several issues. They passed a proposal that everyone should make greater efforts to boost cash production by planting more cacao seedlings; they defeated a migrant's proposal to systematize communal copra harvesting and marketing; and they approved a proposal to start an intervillage market for garden produce (although no one acted on it that year, or in succeeding years, to my knowledge).

Discussions of such specific proposals, however, were calm parliamentary islands in a sea of passionate debate of deeper issues. The issue underlying everything was whether Kragur would stagnate and decline or grow and prosper. One man complained of Kragur's lack of progress and blamed it on the moral fiber of the entire village, saying, "We, all of us, are lazy." Another compared the present adult generations unfavorably to those of the past, for, as he saw the problem: "Our fathers had bones! But you children are rubbish!" The leader of village Catholicism spoke with feeling of how the failure of other villagers to heed his admonitions and follow his example had thwarted his considerable efforts to improve the village. Many others complained that village leaders were not doing their jobs and were incapable of cooperating among themselves. A migrant of early middle age vividly expressed his concern: "Now, everything is going wrong. What can we do to make things right again? I don't think we can. If a ship runs aground on a reef and the people are drifting about, helpless in the sea, who will bring a boat and gather them up? I think the sharks will eat them all. That's what's happening to us!" Throughout the meeting speakers invoked familiar signs of village discord and declining morale. As one man declared: "Kragur is going to pieces! The village is full of illness and death, the people are nothing but skin and bones, the village grounds are covered with feces! Everything is falling apart!"

This book is about how Kragur villagers bring their view of the world to bear on adversity—how they understand the causes of hard times, and how they seek to overcome them. Kragur villagers have always had to face recurring adversity. The tide of illness advances and recedes. The success of subsistence activities cannot be assured; there have always been times of plenty and times of want. The first colonial intrusion and the rapid transformation of the village's social environment in succeeding years added new dimensions to villagers' perceptions of the quality of the times. Failures to surmount obstacles they have faced since long before the arrival of the first Europeans have now taken on additional significance because of what they imply about villagers' capacity to deal with new and unfamiliar problems. A poor taro crop or unsuccessful fishing not only means a poorer diet; it also reflects on villagers' capacity for effective work and cooperation, the quality of their leaders, and their ability to succeed in endeavors which for many represent the hope of the future, such as growing cash crops or running a charter-boat business. Failure to produce abundant food and to maintain a healthy and well-kept community villagers also experience as failure to stem the tide of migration to the towns by making Kragur the kind of place where young people want to stay. In addition, the new social order emerging in Papua New Guinea places novel demands on villagers and arouses new desires without providing the means for satisfying them. Villagers must now pay taxes. Beaten-bark loincloths or fiber skirts are no longer suitable attire, so they must purchase a few items of Western-style clothing. They feel the obligation to send their children to school to give them a leg up in the new world, so they must pay school fees. They acquire needs and uses for money without effort, but means of acquiring money are elusive.

If Kragur villagers feel they are living in an era of hard times, then, it is to a great extent because this is an era of tumultuous social change. They face a multitude of new problems, and familiar problems have taken on new significance in the light of the aspirations for progress that have been inspired by villagers' exposure to a new life that displays wealth, ease, and power heretofore unknown in the indigenous world. Kragur people are acutely aware of the yawning chasm that separates their material standard of living from that of the whites, sometimes referred to collectively as Europeans, who ruled them throughout the colonial period. They also see the distance separating them from an emerging Papua New Guinea elite who live in towns, working for wages and salaries and enjoying much of a style of life once reserved for whites alone. Kragur people are eager to narrow these gaps.

Progress, Development, and Goodness

When Kragur villagers speak of change and progress they often abandon the indigenous Kairiru language and shift to Melanesian Pidgin. To speak of progress in Pidgin one can say *kirapim ples* or, perhaps, *mekim ples i go het,* both of which mean, roughly, "to advance the village." New terms, however, are always being incorporated into Pidgin, many of them from English, the language of the modern educational system. Reading Pidgin newspapers or listening to radio news broadcasts in Pidgin, one now hears references to *divelopmen,* the government's plans to bring divelopmen to the rural areas, or the need to *developim*—that is, to develop— the nation's basic industries.

Some Kragur villagers have also incorporated this word for progress into their vocabularies, and many would agree that what the village needs is a good strong dose of divelopmen.[2] Indeed, like many other Papua New Guinea communities, Kragur has been very open to innovation and outside influences. Villagers have eagerly experimented with a new religion, schools, wage labor, and numerous new forms of technology, from bush knives to outboard motors; but their enthusiasm for progress or divelopmen must be taken with a major qualification. Prevalent notions of how the village can achieve progress or divelopmen, and what it would be like, are deeply rooted in indigenous conceptions of the inseparability of social and material well-being. Villagers are quite aware of the objective obstacles to more successful participation in the new economy—poor land, geographic isolation, chronically low prices for their major cash crops. Yet, in seeking greater success in Papua New Guinea's emerging market economy, they often approach the problem in much the same way they would approach more familiar problems of material welfare, such as poor fishing, poor garden crops, death, and disease.

To sum up what will be discussed in greater detail in coming chapters, Kragur villagers tend to assume that many problems of material well-being stem in large part from lack of correct and harmonious social relations (cf. Brison 1991). Since their social world includes the dead as well as the living, solving material problems also involves maintaining good relations with what Westerners would call the supernatural. Further, villagers tend to see material well-being as part of the basis of good social relations, as well as their product.

Villagers' long exposure to Catholicism has given their conceptions of social harmony and the supernatural some new dimensions, but it has done little to alter their basic views of the social and supernatural bases of prosperity. If anything, it has encouraged an indigenous tendency to analyze material problems in moral and religious terms. Hence, to many Kragur villagers the question of progress and development is a moral question; becoming developed is intricately intertwined with being good. This point of view has had a considerable effect on Kragur villagers' efforts in the direction of divelopmen, and it is not without its problems. For one thing, it can lead to painful doubt about one's own or one's community's moral worth when efforts to increase material prosperity founder.

It is important to make it clear at the outset that Kragur villagers are not concerned with their moral worth simply because it affects their material well-being. As I will illustrate in Chapter 3, they sometimes speak of material well-being as though it were important primarily because it fosters the harmonious and cooperative social relations that, in their eyes, constitute moral worth. One could say that they see moral and material well-being as having a circular and interdependent relationship. Even that, however, may be to impose too sharp a distinction, one that describes in terms of means and ends two dimensions of an integral whole. Villagers' treatment of moral and material issues suggests such an integral conception (cf. Schieffelin 1976:150; Kahn 1986:34).

An extensive discussion of how this view contrasts with the way the relationship between moral and material issues is construed in Western capitalist societies is beyond the scope of this book, I must address it briefly, however, for one of the key issues this eth-

nography examines is how the increasing influence of the institutions of such societies is affecting Kragur people's conception of
the moral and the material.

Anthropologists take pains to qualify the alleged "materialism"
of Papua New Guineans (Schieffelin 1976:150; Wagner 1981:26),
and it is just as important to avoid oversimplifying economic concerns in Western capitalist societies. Douglas and Isherwood
(1979:60) note the difficulty of applying to Western industrial
societies the anthropologist's "practically axiomatic" appreciation
of the role of material goods in carrying cultural meanings. When
they do so, however, anthropologists find that even modern Western materialism is a complex and often subtle thing. Douglas and
Isherwood call material goods "part of a live information system"
(10) necessary for the construction of "an intelligible universe"
(65). Sahlins (1976:170) argues that "The famous logic of max-
imization is only the manifest appearance of another reason, for
the most part . . . of an entirely different kind." McCracken
(1988) speaks of the importance of goods in modern Western
societies as "expressions, creators, and innovators of a range of
cultural meanings" (10), arguing that they perform such roles as
bridging the discrepancy between the real and the ideal (104–117)
and aiding in the construction of the self (24).

Some economists also qualify crude depictions of Western materialism. Power (1988) points out that the "folk" understanding of
what the economy is about in the United States, an understanding
some professional economists share with lay persons, equates economic activity with the pursuit of narrowly defined quantitative
goals. In fact, he argues, even in the modern West qualitative
objectives—such as the quality of community life—play a dominant role in economic activities. Power argues that Americans
appear "obsessively materialistic" in part because "the discipline
the instability of a capitalist economy imposes on individuals and
communities" limits opportunities to pursue a goal like community quality "through political or social means." Hence, people
"pursue it individually through commercial markets, for example,
by seeking to purchase a home in the 'right neighborhood' or by
moving to some other area entirely" (198).

Weber (1958 [1920]), of course, found moral and spiritual
motives behind modern capitalism's material expansion. The early

Protestants he described worked diligently not only to line their pockets but also to assure themselves that they were among the elect who would not suffer eternal damnation. Although the anxiety about one's faith and salvation Weber saw behind systematic commercial activity gradually became secularized, there remains the sense that "The earning of money within the modern economic order is . . . the result and expression of virtue and proficiency in a calling" (53–54). This certainly remains with us in the contemporary United States. As Katz (1989) illustrates, ideas about the moral roots of poverty still shape social policy in the United States. They also have profound effects on people's sense of self-worth (Sennett and Cobb 1972).

So, the people of developed Western societies are like the people of Kragur in that their material goods play complex symbolic roles and they find moral significance in prosperity. The nature of the economic system in developed Western societies, however, dictates that material goods often do not have the same significance they do in the indigenous societies of Papua New Guinea. The economies of these latter societies can be broadly characterized as gift economies (Mauss 1967 [1925]:31), in contrast with commodity economies (Gregory 1982:19). Mauss argues that where things—including human effort, commoditized as labor—are exchanged as commodities through purchase and sale, they are completely alienable; they bear no continuing relationship to the original owner and create no enduring personal relationship between the parties to the exchange. The important relationship in commodity exchange is the equivalence in exchange of the things themselves. In contrast, where things are exchanged as gifts "the objects are never completely separated from the men who exchange them; the communion and alliance they establish are well-nigh indissoluble" (Mauss 1967 [1925]:31). Writes Gregory (1982:19), following Mauss, "What a gift transactor desires is the personal relationships that the exchange of gifts creates, and not the things themselves." Accumulation is not the end of production and exchange, and the work of production is part of a fabric of personal obligation.[3] Personal relationships in a gift economy can be relations of domination as well as equality.[4] Nevertheless, since the things produced and exchanged are not conceived of as alienable but partake of the identity of the giver, they become part of the substance of human relationships. Hence, concerns about the quality of social relations and material concerns are not simply closely related, they are virtually identical.

Yet, while the distinction between gift and commodity economies helps one understand important differences among societies, we should think of these differences as relative, rather than absolute, as Carrier (1992:201–204) argues. Carrier points out that while "the modern West contains an elaborate system of transactions in which alienated individuals give and take alienated objects in monetary transactions in the market," one can find many instances of transactions that do not conform to this pattern. He draws from the literature examples of transactions in the modern West that have many of the personal, moral characteristics of gift exchange—in families, in a black market for stolen goods, in retail trade in which credit is based on personal relations of trust, and even in the "durable relations" that sometimes develop between large firms. Similarly, Apadurai (1986:11) argues strenuously against what he calls "the exaggeration and reification of the contrast between gift and commodity in anthropological writing." He holds that while commodities exist "with a special intensity and salience in modern capitalist societies," it is "definitionally useful to regard commodities as existing in a very wide variety of societies" (6). Thomas (1991:35–82) contends that anthropologists have neglected the importance of commodity transactions in precapitalist Pacific Islands societies.[5]

Gifts and commodities certainly coexist in contemporary Papua New Guinea. Gregory (1982) documents the rise of cash cropping and wage labor, but argues that while colonization promoted commodity production, "The gift economy . . . has not been destroyed . . . but has effloresced" (115). At the very least, then, a gift economy persists in Papua New Guinea with its own "special intensity and salience," articulated with a postcolonial commodity economy in complex ways.[6]

Whatever anthropologists may say, Kragur villagers themselves see striking contrasts between their indigenous forms of production and exchange and those of Europeans. Granted, villagers' ideas about their indigenous practices probably have been shaped in part by comparing them to European ways and seeing the differences thrown into sharp relief. Thomas (1991:203–204) even suggests that such comparison has led some Pacific Islanders to accentuate in practice the perceived differences, so that indigenous practice begins to look more like what the simplified gift/commodity dichotomy would lead one to expect.[7] Kragur people sometimes do exaggerate the contrasts between their ways and European ways, romanticizing indigenous practices and caricaturing European ones; but their exaggeration is also built on real differences encountered as problems in everyday life, as I will illustrate in later chapters. Gregory (1982:115–116) writes that "The essence of the PNG economy today is ambiguity." The concepts of gift and commodity help Western theorists to think about this ambiguity in terms of the meeting of two forms of political economy. The people of Kragur grapple with it in their own terms, and it is their terms with which I am most concerned.

Visions of the Future

Parry and Bloch (1989:18) argue persuasively that a noncapitalist society's encounter with capitalist markets and money does not necessarily throw its moral world into disarray. They hold that the extent to which this occurs depends on the nature of the noncapitalist society and its capacity to "tame" or "domesticate" capitalist influences. At the time of my research in Kragur, however, villagers had not succeeded in domesticating new economic forms, and their moral confusion was evident.

While the quality of social relations remains the focus of moral concern in Kragur, villagers' lives are complicated by new ideas about what makes social relations morally commendable. Exposure to the impersonal buying and selling of goods and services and work under capitalist discipline—hierarchically organized and regulated by the calendar and clock—is having a profound effect on villagers' views. The white society they have observed is strikingly prosperous in comparison with their own, and many must conclude that there is something fundamentally superior in the whites' characteristic way of producing and distributing material wealth. Although there is a strong tendency to assume that material superiority is the fruit of higher-quality, more harmonious social relations, just what harmonious social relations are has been called into question. Some have begun to wonder if impersonal buying and selling, frugality and accumulation—since they seem to be associated with European wealth—might not manifest greater virtue than the gift-giving and sharing of abundance traditionally considered the substance and the support of good social relations. Similarly, some see the temporally regular and highly coordinated white way of working, and of conducting virtually all activities, as a manifestation of an advanced form of spontaneous social harmony, and not as the fruit of a radically different form of human organization based on principles that contrast with those informing indigenous economic and political relations and the indigenous pursuit of material well-being.

Although many villagers have had considerable experience as wage workers in white enterprises and can make astute observations on the white way of life, they do not appear to understand fully how drastically their own lives would be changed if they ever succeeded in achieving a degree of development on the Western model. Their visions of development are often imbued with ideals springing from indigenous culture and society, some of which are quite at odds with the realities of life in the developed Western world. If they miraculously achieved a similar kind of development overnight, many Kragur villagers would be unpleasantly surprised by the attenuation of the ties of kin and community, the regimentation of daily life, and the class divisions that separate rich and poor in the developed world (cf. Gewertz and Errington 1991:14). Since many villagers seem to value prosperity in part because they feel it provides the foundation for harmonious social relations of a familiar kind, prosperity suddenly achieved at the expense of a radical social transformation would be a mixed blessing.

Instituting a more regular and coordinated way of organizing work and life in general in Kragur on the Western model would not necessarily mean realizing a higher form of spontaneous social harmony and unity of purpose. Rather, it very likely would result from further subordination to the demands of regional, national, and international markets and political institutions. Replacing gift-giving with commercial exchange might make it easier to accumulate capital to invest in commercial economic enterprises, which could increase village material prosperity. Yet, even if that prosperity did not end up concentrated in the hands of a few, it would not be the basis for a new era of greater social harmony of a familiar kind, for gift-giving is an integral part of that familiar ideal of harmony. If this new kind of prosperity were to nurture the growth of harmonious social relations, this social harmony would be of a new and unanticipated kind.

Choice and Constraint

F. G. Bailey (1971:298) suggests that economic change and development in small communities may require that people be "shaken out of the net of community relationships." He also argues persuasively that the dissolution of existing forms of community relationships does not necessarily lead to the demise of community life, but may also lead to the development of new forms of cooperation, more adaptive and perhaps more freely chosen. The question of choice is important here, for Kragur people seem to be moving toward a future that many of them perceive only dimly. This is common in all kinds of social change, even when people consciously seek change. In a discussion of "perceptions of development," Sandra Wallman (1977:13) comments that "From someone's point of view and in some respects, even 'successful' development is a double-bind—such that 'I got what I wanted but it's not what I meant. . . .' " If this comes to pass in Kragur, will it be because villagers chose unwisely or because they had little choice?

There is no simple answer to the question of choice. If I began my research in Kragur with any bias, it was toward emphasizing the power of the encroaching capitalist political economy to shape the course of change. I was also somewhat predisposed to find that Catholicism played a significant ideological role in the process of accommodating villagers to the demands of life in the new political economy. It would have been very difficult, however, to ignore the reflection and debate about change and the experimentation with ways of mastering the process of change that went on in daily life in Kragur, and the active role villagers were playing in forming their perceptions of goodness, social harmony, progress, and development. As Ortner (1984:143) points out, as anthropologists our "location 'on the ground' . . . puts us in a position to see people not simply as passive reactors to and enactors of some 'system,' but as active agents and subjects in their own history."[8] Further, my interest in Marxist approaches—which in part accounted for my appreciation of capitalism's power to bend to its needs non-capitalist societies and cultures—also inclined me to look for evidence of resistance to capitalism's incursions, covert and inchoate as well as overt. For example, for Marx, religion was not just the well-known "opium of the people"; it was also "the sigh of the oppressed creature" (1959 [1844]:263).

Nevertheless, it was also impossible to ignore the limits and influences on Kragur people's thoughts and actions over which they had no control. Chief among these were the unavoidable dominance of the new political and economic structure in the world surrounding them; the teachings of missionaries, government personnel, and European employers; and the fortuitous resonance between elements of the indigenous cultural tradition and Catholic teachings. Although I observed Kragur villagers exercising considerable autonomy, they were doing so under highly structured circumstances. As Marx also wrote, "Men make their own history, but they do not make it just as they please . . ." (1969 [1852]:15).[9] The challenge, then, is to deal with change and history as "a dialectical process . . . the product of the interplay between human action and structural constraint" (Comaroff 1985:1).

The significance of human action depends a great deal on actors' positions in the existing structure and their degree of power or authority. The position of an actor in a social hierarchy gives his or her actions their "structural weight," making them "more or less consequential for others" (Sahlins 1981:72). In Chapter 8, I will argue that those in Kragur who occupy new positions of leadership created in the postcontact era play a key role in a transformation of daily patterns of living that contributes to the development of new forms of temporal consciousness and new models of good social relations that are more compatible with life in the new political economy (cf. Smith 1982a). The relative power and authority of these leaders gives their actions more weight in shaping change than the actions of less influential villagers. No one in Kragur, however, wields significant structural clout in comparison with political and economic decision-makers in provincial and national capitals and international markets (cf. Gewertz and Errington 1991:14); and opportunities to move into positions of influence in the new political economy are limited by Kragur villagers' structurally determined "collective life chances" (Asad 1972:93). The dialectical process of history in this case, then, is also a dialectic "between the dominant and the subordinate in the colonial encounter" (Comaroff 1985:1).

Even people's freedom to think and act within the areas of indeterminacy left by a highly constraining structure may prove to be only a detour on the way to recreating and affirming the dominant structure. Actors' contributions may often lead to results they did not anticipate; or, as Wallman (1977:13) says, they get what they wanted but it's not what they meant (cf. Ortner 1984:157).[10]

The freedom to maneuver that Kragur villagers enjoy in forging an understanding of their new world also entails the possibility of creating more potent motivations for complying with the dominant political economy and stouter legitimations for it than could be imposed upon them from without (cf. Smith 1984). In saying this, I am not trying to sneak in the back door a judgment of the inevitable dominance of structure over actors' intentions, either as a general principle or as a conclusion about the Kragur case. Marcuse (1973:206–207) argues that the degree to which people can function as actors consciously shaping their destinies, and the degree to which society appears "as an independent whole governed by 'inexorable' laws," depends on specific historical circumstances and should not be assumed a priori.[11] Also, people's struggles within areas of indeterminacy—spheres of freedom to create meaning and to act relatively autonomously—often have ambiguous significance. They may have both innovative and reproductive potential, potential as both resistance and accommodation. Also, as Piven and Cloward (1982:143) observe in a study of the containment of class conflict in the United States, "social control is never complete, and never enduring. The very mechanisms that effect such control at one historical moment generate the possibilities for political mobilization at another." In other words, the jury is never completely in on the long-term significance of action "on the ground," for this is determined in part by shifting historical circumstances.

The products of Kragur people's exercise of autonomy within structured circumstances have potential both for impeding and for facilitating incorporation into the capitalist political economy, as I

will discuss in Chapter 9 (cf. Smith 1990). While greater incorporation is the likely eventual outcome of events, I do not want to
ignore countercurrents. As noted above, these may one day prove
more significant than we can anticipate. At the very least, they
give the march of events its distinctive character. Fernand Braudel
writes that "victorious events come about as the result of many
possibilities," and that "for one possibility which is actually realized, innumerable others have drowned," often leaving little trace.
It is necessary, Braudel argues, to pay attention to these drowned
possibilities "because the losing movements are forces which have
at every moment affected the final outcome" (quoted in Gutman
1973:580).[12] Losing movements also may not be completely
drowned but only submerged, living on as covert cultures of resistance to the dominant order (cf. Scott 1990; Terdiman 1985).

Postulating the historical relativity of the respective importance
of structure and agency and the importance of "drowned" possibilities in studying historical change highlights the need for observing
events on the ground—that is, for ethnography. As Marcus and
Fischer (1986:82) point out, "Without ethnography, one can only
imagine what is happening to real social actors caught up in complex macroprocesses."

This ethnography focuses on how, as Kragur villagers attempt
to cope with changes thrust upon them, their own thought and
experimentation contribute to the shape of change. My primary
concern is the still incremental movement toward redefining moral
behavior in practices of distribution and exchange and in the
organization and conduct of work and other daily activities.
Transforming behavior in these spheres would be a vital step in
the incorporation of Kragur into the capitalist political economy;
hence, the push and pull over these matters in the village is at the
center of the process of capitalist incorporation and resistance to
incorporation. To the extent that such a transformation is proceeding in Kragur it is not simply the result of the desire for greater
material prosperity acting as a universal solvent, washing away
older orientations. Rather, it is largely the unanticipated product
of the application of a familiar form of analysis to a radically new
problem (cf. Sahlins 1981:67) and the pursuit of a traditionally
valued goal, a goal that fuses moral with material concerns, in the
face of the potent influences and constraints of a new political
economy.

Methods and Conventions

In conducting my research in Kragur I made certain inquiries of a wide range of people and, like most anthropologists, came to rely in particular on the views and explanations of a small number of key informants. Some of these were people whom other villagers regarded as exceptionally knowledgeable; some were persons of exceptional influence; others were undistinguished. While some actors do carry more weight than others, cultures and societies get their shapes from the beliefs, opinions, and actions of their ordinary members as well as those of people of recognized knowledge and influence. In my presentation of life and events in Kragur in the chapters that follow, I identify common threads of belief, perception, and behavior; but I also note differences of opinion, instances of skepticism about commonly held beliefs, differing views of events, and a great deal of debate and speculation on the nature of things. Some of the lack of unanimity I describe here is a result of the great speed with which the world of Kragur villagers has been changing in recent decades. Villagers have been confronted with a profusion of new experiences, ideas, and institutions that have thrown those of their familiar world into contrast and forced on people the task of making sense out of it all. One cannot, however, attribute lack of unanimity solely to rapid change and radical disruption. It is also evidence of what Theodore Schwartz (1972:4) calls "the constant litigation of culture," which one may observe anywhere if not hampered by an overly homogeneous model of culture. Schwartz (5) writes of the "strong and distinctive personalities, the . . . diversity of approaches, the . . . multitude of small innovations and individual styles competing in the shaping of events." Such a view of culture is highly compatible with an emphasis on the active role that people play in shaping their histories. In dwelling on diversity and debate I hope to convey a sense of this active engagement.

Much of what I learned about all aspects of life in Kragur comes out of my efforts to understand particular events in which villagers were solving problems and making decisions—disputes, curing efforts, attempts to start businesses or improve the returns of indigenous subsistence techniques, and so on. Some events, such as efforts to cure illnesses through placating ancestral ghosts, have a much more "traditional" or indigenous flavor than others, such as establishing a fund for buying a boat with which to operate a charter passenger and cargo business. During the months I spent in Kragur I found not only that events of all kinds were intricately interrelated, but also that very few events, if any, no matter how traditional their ostensible focus, were not in some way colored by villagers' awareness of the problems of this era's massive social changes and did not in some way bear on villagers' efforts to cope with those problems.

I follow the anthropological convention of disguising to some extent the identities of the people I write about. Except when referring to deceased persons in the historical section, I have disguised individual villagers' names. Prior to missionization, a Kragur villager was generally known by only one name. Today villagers also have Christian names—like Stephen, Agnes, Benedict, Anna, Michael, Julie, Andrew, or Clara. Younger people often use their fathers' indigenous names as surnames in the Western fashion and their own indigenous names as middle names between the Christian name and the indigenous surname. Although many now address each other by their Christian names, they use their indigenous names at least as often. I refer to people here by indigenous names; but rather than using their own names, I use the names of deceased ancestors, absent migrants, or infants of the same patrilineal group.[13]

I conducted the research on which this book is based from November 1975 to December 1976 and in April and May of 1981. I have written much of this book, however, in the ethnographic present, that is, as though I were describing things as they exist at the moment. This has its problems, as Carrier and Carrier (1989:xii–xiii) point out. Chief among them is that the ethnographic present "lends an air of timelessness to the society the ethnographer describes," suggesting that things were much the same before and after the specific period observed by the author. Such an implication may creep in even when the author is explicitly concerned, as I am, with a process of change. Nevertheless, the ethnographic present is often easier to read, as well as to write. Also, while I do not wish to imply the "timelessness" of Kragur as I describe it here, neither do I wish to suggest that the problems Kragur people faced in the late 1970s and early 1980s are no longer important. Sadly, over the years letters from Kragur have told me of the deaths of many of the men and women who figure prominently in this account. Men and women too young to play central roles in village affairs when I last went to Kragur probably are now village leaders with ideas born of new worlds of experience. I doubt, however, that they have ceased entirely to wonder about the moral dilemma of development confronted by their elders. The peoples of the developed world, too, are still struggling to understand the relationship between material prosperity and their lives as social and moral beings.

TWO

The Setting: History and Geography, Kinship and Leadership, Food and Money

COLONIAL AND POSTCOLONIAL ACTIVITY in the Sepik region has been greatest along the coast and among some of the offshore islands. Yet, despite Kragur's proximity to the modern hub of the region, its location on Kairiru's north coast—without a hospitable landing site or commercial agricultural possibilities—has kept it comparatively aloof from the mainstream of political and economic change. After discussing this historical circumstance and describing Kragur's physical aspect, I examine some key dimensions of social structure, in particular the traditional system of leadership based on rights to important magical knowledge. Much magical knowledge pertains to food production and other facets of making a living, the topic I treat next. Villagers still produce most of their own subsistence, due to Kragur's comparative isolation from commercial markets and the limited scope for cash-crop production on Kairiru's north slope. Kragur people have very little money, and it plays a very small role in the distribution and exchange of goods and services within the village, my final topic. Despite the persistence of nonmonetary practices and attitudes, villagers are well aware of the increasing importance of money in the world around them. While they often criticize or joke about the importance of money in white society, many cannot escape a fascination with this new phenomenon and rueful envy of the new kinds of power and prestige that money brings.

Foreign Contact and Recent History

For generations Kairiru islanders traded with communities on other islands and the mainland, traveling by sail canoe as far as the Murik Lakes area—located on the mainland coast some sixty miles southeast of Kairiru—and Wogeo island, some thirty-five miles northeast of Kairiru. Tiesler's (1969–1970) documentary study reports that Kairiru islanders traded with Tarawai island (158); with the mainland villages of Kaiep (161), Turubu, Samap, and Kaup (160), lying along the coast between Wewak and Murik Lakes; with Karau (164), in the Murik Lakes area; and with Arapesh people on the mainland southwest of Kairiru (157). He also reports that Kairiru people acquired boat-building knowledge from Murik (160). Tiesler's map shows Kragur village (rendered Karakur) somewhat west of its present location, but it indicates no relations of any kind between Kragur in particular and other locales. Older villagers, however, remember the days when they sailed to Turubu for pots, to Murik Lakes for ornate baskets, and to Wogeo island for *galip* nuts (Tahitian chestnuts or canarium almonds), bringing tobacco in exchange.

Kragur people also told me that their grandfathers had traded with Tarawai and Walis islanders for metal tools obtained from Malay traders (or *Tenati,* as they are called in Melanesian Pidgin).[1] European explorers passed by, mapped, and named portions of New Guinea's north coast as early as the sixteenth century, but Malay traders had been visiting New Guinea in search of bird of paradise plumes and *bêches-de-mer* (sea cucumbers or trepang) long before any Europeans set foot ashore (Reed 1943). Although the Tenati did not come to Kragur, there are reports that they did business with Kairiru islanders at Victoria Bay, at the northwestern tip of the island, and at Yuwun, on the south coast. Reed (91) cites pre-1900 German reports of Malay influence on the nearby Tarawai and Walis islands, which, the German sources suggest, may be evidence of a long history, even centuries-long, of involvement in trade.[2]

Except for occasional sightings of foreign sailing ships on the horizon, this was the extent of contact with non–New Guineans until the beginning of the German colonial era. In order to safeguard its expanding trade in the region, Germany annexed the

northern coast of the mainland of what is now Papua New Guinea
with its adjacent islands in 1894. In the same year Great Britain
claimed the southern half, which became known as British New
Guinea and later as Papua, which it transferred to Australia in
1901. Initially, Germany placed control of its colony in the hands
of the New Guinea Company, formed in 1884 by German inves-
tors to establish plantations in the new territory. The German government took over administration of the colony in 1899, although
the company continued its commercial operations. Missionaries
followed close behind the New Guinea Company. In 1896, missionaries of the Society of the Divine Word arrived from Germany
in what is now Madang. Later that year they set up headquarters
on Tumleo island, just offshore about 140 miles west along the
mainland coast from Wewak. There and elsewhere the society established coconut plantations to produce income to support itself.[3]

Sometime between 1900 and 1909, Kragur villagers had their
first extended contacts with Europeans when, according to villagers' accounts, a mission vessel came to Kragur. Either then or soon
thereafter a handful of Kragur men were recruited to work for the
mission on Tumleo. One of these men, Viro, became deeply
involved with the mission. In 1908–1909 he traveled to Hong
Kong with Father Joseph Loerks—who later became bishop—to
pick up the first mission steam vessel, the *Gabriel*. Viro remained
a strong advocate of the mission's cause in Kragur until his death
following World War II.

In about 1905 Kragur took part for the last time in a major
intervillage raid, joining with other villages to attack the village of
Chem, which then stood less than a two hours' walk across the
island. From the point of view of Kragur and its allies, the raid
was a complete success. They decimated Chem's population, and
those who survived ran away to the south coast, where they established a new village on the beach, never returning to their old site.
One can estimate a date for this raid because a member of the
Divine Word mission, Father Konstantin van den Hemel, visited
the south coast of Kairiru in the course of a surveying expedition
in 1907 or 1908 and reported in his journal on the sad condition
of the Chem people living there. He estimated that the raid had
occurred one or one and one-half years before (van den Hemel
1907–1908; cf. Tiesler 1969–1970:175).

I also have van den Hemel to thank for the information that

between 1905 and 1908 the New Guinea Company recruited men from Chem as plantation laborers. As far as I know, during this period Kragur men worked only for the mission, although later they began working for secular enterprises.

In working for the mission, villagers were exposed to Catholicism as well as wage labor, so the ground was already prepared when the first indigenous mission workers, or catechists, came to Kairiru's north coast. The first catechist to work on Kairiru was a man named Brigil from one of the south coast villages. He had worked as a laborer on both secular and mission plantations, had been trained to teach basic Pidgin literacy and give religious instruction, and had worked as a catechist on the mainland before serving as one on Kairiru. Brigil established his first church in Surai, about a two hours' walk up the coast northwest of Kragur, in the mid-1920s. Other catechists followed Brigil, including another indigenous Kairiru islander, Michael Maraf. According to Kragur villagers' accounts, Maraf resided in Kragur for several years, enjoying the hospitality of the father of the present leader of village Catholic life. By about 1930 Kragur people had abandoned the most visible element of indigenous religious life, the men's cult (see Chapter 1), in favor of Catholicism.

In 1935 Bishop Joseph Loerks moved his headquarters from Tumleo to a site on Kairiru's south coast chosen for its ample harbor and fresh water supply. After World War II, the bishop's headquarters were moved to the mainland near Wewak. In the 1930s, however, mission activity on the island was increasing; priests began to visit Kragur and other villages periodically, and some Kragur villagers frequently made the trip to the south coast to attend mass. In 1938 several priests—six, according to current Kragur versions—visited the island's north coast and conducted a mass baptism of converts from Kragur and the nearby villages of Bou and Shagur. In 1939 the mission built a training school for indigenous catechists, St. Xavier's, on one of the island's rare expanses of flat ground a short distance east of the bishop's headquarters.

By this time Kragur men had begun to work for many employers other than the mission, and increasing numbers were leaving the village to work, some only briefly but some for many years. By 1942 some men had logged as many as a dozen years away from home as wage laborers.

World War II had direct and traumatic effects on Kairiru. Australia had displaced Germany from New Guinea at the outbreak of World War I and, following the war, continued to administer the colony as a "mandated territory," as former German colonies transferred to Allied control overseen by the League of Nations were called. In 1942, Kragur people saw the Australians expelled by the Japanese. Japanese troops occupied Wewak and surrounding areas in mid-1942 and established an encampment on Kairiru at St. Xavier's. Most European civilians had been evacuated when the war broke out, but most mission personnel had stayed on, and many of these were interned at St. Xavier's. Smaller bodies of Japanese troops were stationed in several Kairiru villages, about thirty in Kragur.

The years of Japanese occupation were hard. Kragur people lived in temporary dwellings in the bush for fear of Allied bombing. In order to conceal their own and the Japanese troops' whereabouts, they were often forbidden to light cooking fires. At one point, bombing ignited the abandoned village and burned it to the ground. Villagers could not garden, fish, or hunt regularly, and they often went hungry, particularly when the Allies cut Japanese supply lines and increased the pressure on local resources. The Japanese pressed able-bodied adults into service carrying cargo across the mountain from the main base at St. Xavier's. With the future in mind, they also established a school for village children, and many Kragur people still remember fragments of the Japanese language they learned there. A number of Kragur men were trapped in the town of Rabaul on the island of East New Britain when the war broke out and spent the duration there, forced to work for the Japanese.

In 1945 the war in the Pacific ended and Australia resumed control of New Guinea, now administered jointly with the former British colony of Papua as the United Nations Trust Territory of Papua and New Guinea. Kragur people were able to return to a more normal life, but not to life as they had once known it, for change proceeded rapidly. Access to schooling has increased steadily and dramatically since the war. The late 1940s saw the establishment of a Cooperative Society chapter on Kairiru and increasing government efforts to promote local cash-crop production. More recently, Australian rule has ended and Kragur has found itself part of a self-governing and then an independent nation, as of 1973 and 1975 respectively.

The development of schooling in Kragur deserves it own brief summary. Prewar schools taught by catechists were of limited scope and quality. They taught literacy in Pidgin but they did not teach English. Following the war, the mission reopened St. Xavier's as a catechist training school. Ibor, today's Catholic leader in Kragur, attended St. Xavier's and trained as a catechist. After he had completed two years and a few months of study, the mission sent him to the mainland Papua New Guinea Highlands, but in 1952 he returned to start a school in Kragur. The school was soon moved to Bou village, a short walk west of Kragur. With occasional lapses and many changes of personnel, the Bou school continued for several years, sending several Kragur young men on to study at St. Xavier's, which by then was expanding the training it provided.

In 1959 a teacher from the south-coast Kairiru village of Seraseng came to Bou and for the first time taught English to village children. Several successful Kragur men had their start in Bou school at this time, going on to attend high school and tertiary institutions and to find professional employment throughout Papua New Guinea. Finally, in 1972, Bou school joined the national secular school system.

Kragur's relative isolation from some of the main currents of colonial activity has been a significant fact of its history in this century. Today, making the sometimes difficult journey to Kragur, one can easily find geographic reasons for this isolation. Villagers themselves sometimes refer to Kragur and Kairiru's north coast in Pidgin as a *lus ples*—literally, a lost place or lost village. Such a designation would have made little sense in the precolonial era, when political, economic, and cultural influences were widely decentralized. In those days, no distant governmental, commercial, or ceremonial center regulated the affairs of Kairiru villages, and there were no such centers in the Sepik from which to be isolated. Larger villages, better able to defend themselves, undoubtedly exercised more complete political sovereignty than smaller, weaker communities; but, in general, villages probably enjoyed great autonomy. Since colonization, however, the colonial outposts, missions, and towns have become the centers of influence and events, and rural indigenous communities have been relegated to a periphery.[4]

The Sepik region itself was long a "frontier" (Huber 1988) at the edge of European activity in New Guinea. Until after World

War II the Sepik was primarily a source of indigenous labor for plantations and goldfields in more prosperous parts of the colony. Kairiru island was a backwater of this frontier. By 1899 the German New Guinea Company had small plantations or trading stations on nearby Walis, Tarawai, and even Mushu islands (Sack and Clark 1979:166, 180, cited by Huber 1988:109); but it had neglected Kairiru's rugged shores and steep slopes. Even scientific explorers and collectors seem to have avoided Kairiru. Many of the major collections of New Guinea artifacts made around the turn of the century are now housed in museums in Germany. When I examined these collections in 1984, I found a number of items—wooden plates, carved human figures—in styles reminiscent of objects I had seen on Kairiru, but nothing with a confirmed Kairiru origin. Chicago's Field Museum of Natural History also houses a major Melanesian collection, much of it from the north coast of New Guinea. Here, in an immense assemblage of artifacts, I found two canoe paddles and one six-by-eight-inch box labeled Kairiru, the latter containing a woven cord ornament, some shell rings, and two plain wooden combs. Artifacts from Walis, Tarawai, and Mushu, however, are plentiful in these collections (cf. Welsch 1989). Maps of the routes taken early in the century by Field Museum ethnologist A. B. Lewis and the German collectors Meyer and Parkinson show that, although they stopped at these islands, they persistently passed Kairiru by, perhaps because they tended to follow the routes already established by commercial vessels (Welsch 1992). Kragur itself is in one of Kairiru's less accessible locations, and even the arm of colonial government has not always reached it directly. According to patrol reports preserved in the National Archives in Port Moresby, both before and after World War II Australian patrol officers often had north-coast villagers come over the mountain to the south coast to meet with the officers on their periodic administrative visits.

This is not to say that colonial and postcolonial events have not had a profound effect on Kragur, for obviously they have. Much of the stream of events, however, has swirled around Kairiru and its north coast, disturbing them with powerful eddies but having greater immediate effect elsewhere. Japanese occupation and missionization have been the greatest deviations from this pattern, although mission commercial endeavors have been conspicuously absent on the island. Only a few miles have separated Kragur from

the main-traveled paths of explorers, businessmen, and government representatives, but these few miles have helped give Kragur's history and its present relationship to processes of social
change their distinctive flavor.

Island and Village

Kairiru island is approximately eight miles long and three and a
half miles wide at its widest point, rising to an elevation of about
twenty-five hundred feet at its highest point. Many clear, rocky
streams originate in its upper reaches and flow to the sea on all
sides. Below and slightly southeast of the island's peak is the lake.
Islanders say that the island itself is really called Tau and only the
lake was known as Kairiru until white visitors fostered the present
confusion.

There are few nonindigenous people on the island. St. John's
seminary school now occupies the site where the bishop's headquarters once stood. It has a small nonindigenous staff and serves
a handful of young indigenous men training for religious voca
tions. St. Xavier's is now a boarding high school for men, serving
other islands and the mainland as well as Kairiru. It is still staffed
largely by white members of Catholic orders, but the staff and
administration now include a number of secular personnel and
native Papua New Guineans.

Several small power boats owned by mainland and island villagers doing business as charter carriers of passengers and cargo call
occasionally at various points on Kairiru. The only frequent and
regularly scheduled transportation to the mainland is the St.
Xavier's boat, the *Tau-K*, which makes the round trip to Wewak
at least once a week, weather permitting. The *Tau-K*'s fare is
within the reach of many village people, so it has become their
principal means of travel to the mainland to buy or sell goods in
Wewak, visit kin, or begin journeys to distant schools or jobs.
Catholic mission light aircraft can land at St. Xavier's, but the
staff there and at St. John's only rarely travel to and from the
mainland by air.

A single-lane dirt road stretches along the south coast of Kairiru
for about five miles, but the only motor vehicles on the island
belong to St. Xavier's and St. John's. Most Kairiru villages are

accessible only by sea or on foot. The main north-south trail begins at the edge of the forest behind St. Xavier's and goes directly up and over the mountain. Switchbacks built by the Japanese occupation forces during World War II ease the ascent from St. Xavier's. Still, the two miles as the crow flies to the pass at the trail's highest point is a stiff climb for the inexperienced. After heavy rains, which are frequent, the red clay near the top of the mountain is like grease underfoot and sections of the trail collapse, leaving only narrow and uncertain footholds. Having reached the pass, one rapidly descends the same two thousand feet in the space of about a mile as the crow flies. About halfway down, the trail leaves the cover of rain forest, plunges past steep mountainside gardens and spectacular views of the sea and Wogeo island in the distance, and finally drops into Kragur, sandwiched between the precipitous slopes of the mountain and cliffs dropping thirty to forty feet to the narrow, stony beach.

Younger villagers think nothing of traversing the trail to the south coast for almost any reason, including the sports days held at St. Xavier's during the dry season. Middle-aged villagers make the trip with little hesitation should a need arise and often travel as far over bush trails to reach gardens, to hunt, or to cut timber. Few of the residents of Wewak, St. Xavier's, or St. John's, however, make the trip over the mountain or around the island by sea to Kragur. An occasional priest comes to offer mass at Bou School, public health service nurses come a few times a year to conduct infant health clinics, malaria control agents may come once a year to spray DDT on the inner walls of the houses, and census takers and tax collectors come to perform their tasks at Bou. Most of the time, however, Kragur and the other villages on the north side of Kairiru remain much to themselves, unless villagers go out rather than waiting for others to come in.

Within Kragur, the route between any two points is usually either up or down. The village site climbs from the cliffs to the encroaching forest in irregular terraces held back by walls built with the volcanic rocks that litter the village grounds. Kragur women keep the grounds relatively free of weeds and try to keep the stones under control. Crotons, coleus, other ornamental plants, and an occasional papaya tree or pineapple plant border the houses and pathways. The fifty or so houses and other structures in the village are built of bush materials. Frames of heavy timbers support roofs thatched with sago palm leaves, walls made of barklike palm flower sheaths or the leaf stalks of sago palms, and floors of split palm or bamboo. Dwellings are set up on posts two to four feet above the ground.

There is a clear space in the center of the village where people gather for many public events. Two weathered but ornately carved slit gongs—single logs laboriously hollowed out through a long narrow opening along the side—lie along its seaward edge. These drums, known as *garamut* in Pidgin, are used to accompany traditional singing and dancing and to call people to meetings. Today's village leaders, however, are more likely to call people together by banging on the village bell, an empty metal fuel cylinder left over from the war, that hangs from a coconut palm. Villagers often gather in the clear space for evening prayer meetings, assembling in front of a simple wooden altar containing a small statue of the Virgin Mary.

Just to the east of the main village, alongside the path to the men's bathing place, there is an unadorned thatched church building where village Catholic leaders hold Sunday services. The principal cemetery also lies at the eastern edge of the village. This too is a contemporary phenomenon, for in pre-mission times the dead were buried beneath the houses. The positions of houses having altered over the years, the streams and rivulets that sluice through the village during a heavy rain sometimes uncover the bones of past generations.

Koyeng, Kastom, and Kaunsil

Kragur is internally divided into nine named residential divisions called *koyeng* in the Kairiru language. In alphabetical order these are: Bomasek, Brangiau, Kragur, Ku, Nalwun, Shewaratin, Vanu Iviau, Vanu Rosh, and Yanglal.[5] According to some villagers' accounts, koyeng Kragur, from which the village takes its name, was founded by the first settlers on the present site. The koyeng are both spatial divisions and kinship divisions. The kinship foundations of the koyeng are groups of male household heads. While the male members of a number of koyeng can all trace common descent from a single male ancestor, in some cases koyeng are built upon representatives of more than one patrilineally defined "line" (in Pidgin, *lain*) without clearly defined historical connections. In one sense, it is the groups or clusters of groups made up of these men and their children and wives who are the koyeng, but the actual pattern of residence is more fluid. Kinship ties through women can also be the basis for a man's residence in a koyeng as a spatial division. A man may have more than one residence option, and which he chooses may depend on a variety of factors, such as disputes, obligations to his wife's kin, political alliances, or the availability of land on which to build a house or make a garden. No matter where they live, however, both men and women often speak of themselves as members of the koyeng in which their patrilineal kin predominate.

The koyeng are exogamous. Many first marriages are still arranged by the bride's and groom's elders; but even where the preferences of the young people themselves are a major factor, Kragur villagers, and other Kairiru islanders, practice what they call exchange of women between koyeng. That is, when a man takes a bride, his koyeng is obligated eventually to supply a woman to marry a man of the bride's koyeng. Both men and women sometimes marry outside the village, and if the spouse is from Kairiru an exchange is also expected.

There is a tripartite division among the koyeng. Most of the koyeng fall into either the group known as Lupelap or that known as Seksik. A third, smaller group called Kusulingyar includes only a single koyeng and fragments of two others. This three-part division is said to have organized both marriage and the activities of the men's cult in the past. The two main divisions are said to have been exogamous. Also, each division initiated the young men of the other into the men's cult. As Taunur, a knowledgeable older village leader, explains, "If your mother was from Lupelap, she married into Seksik, and later your maternal kin would take you to the men's cult house." I assume the Kusulingyar were fitted into this pattern somehow, although I obtained only vague accounts of this group's role. Apparently, the functions of the division of koyeng began to disappear when the men's cult was abandoned. Although now people marry outside their koyeng, the Lupelap and Seksik divisions do not appear to have been exogamous in recent decades. The divisions still have some influence, however. Kragur villagers sell their copra to the government Copra Marketing Board in Wewak and they have two separate accounts there, one held by a group whose membership roughly mirrors the Lupe-lap division and the other by a group that roughly mirrors Seksik. The Kusulingyar are rather evenly divided between the two. Similarly, groups of villagers who pooled their money to start two village trade stores in the late 1970s reflected this division.[6]

Traditional leaders on Kairiru are known in the Kairiru language as *ramat walap*—literally, big men. In Pidgin they are often called *man bilong kastom,* or simply *kastom.*[7] The longer version literally means "men of custom"—that is, those whose leadership is based on indigenous criteria and who are custodians of indigenous standards and knowledge. In the past there was undoubtedly a variety of routes to status and influence—prowess in war, for example, or success in interisland trade—just as today prowess in the modern educational system or the cash economy brings recognition. Those, however, who are now called ramat walap derive much of their power and authority from their possession of rights to large stores of important magical knowledge.[8] Magical spells are called *singsing* in Pidgin, but this also can refer to music, both traditional music and modern popular music. The Kairiru language distinguishes *bos*—magical spells, some of which are chanted or sung—from *ulai,* music without magical significance. Knowledge of a magical procedure includes knowledge of the relevant spell and the details of the associated ritual.

Ownership of magic is more than knowledge of spells and rituals; it is also the right to use the knowledge. This right is a form of intangible property resembling patent and copyright. Many kinds of material objects and knowledge in Kragur are freely available to anyone who cares to produce or acquire them, for example, digging sticks, axes, and other tools, and knowledge of the nonmagical aspects of taro cultivation. But, to possess or use a number of other kinds of knowledge and material objects, one must have what is called *tiptip* in the Kairiru language. Or, it can be said in Kairiru that one has *kes*—that is, a name or reputation for something. In Pidgin, one says that someone has a *nem* (name or reputation) or *stori* (historical claim or charter) for possession or use of something. The system includes many kinds of things. For example, not everyone in the village has the right to make or use the triangular-framed, long-handled nets used to scoop up spawning fish while the fisherman stands in the prow of a canoe. Very few have rights to one of the big sailing canoes once used in trading expeditions. While the form of such canoes was essentially the same, each had a different name. For example, Wagari, an older leader, has rights to a canoe called *Chilapwen,* and Sheltar, a deceased leader, had rights to one called *Urim Terakau.* Each named canoe sported a distinctive kind of decoration. The right to own and use such a canoe included rights to magical spells associated with canoe construction and sailing and rights to use particular harbors in distant villages where arrival in that specific canoe gave the owner safe passage and the right to trade with particular partners.

The most fundamental kind of tiptip is that to which one is entitled as the originator of something or the descendant of the originator. As Moke, an older kastom of some importance, puts it, "If you come first, you have tiptip." One also can be the first, at least within the village, by acquiring something elsewhere and introducing it to Kragur. In the case of at least some magical spells, human beings did not invent the spells, but acquired them generations ago from supernatural beings.

Rights of various kinds are usually passed from one generation to the next along partrilineal lines. The owner of something also can give someone else—either kin or non-kin—tiptip in an exchange of gifts, although the original owner retains his or her own tiptip. Hence, more than one person can hold rights to something. Rights to many kinds of things, however, are distributed very sparingly. This is the case with rights to magic for the production of important crops. Rights to such important magic sometimes pass from one koyeng to another in exchange, but when they do, they generally pass from one person of importance to another. So, Taunur of koyeng Shewaratin, owner of important fishing magic, acquired rights to canoe magic from Moke of koyeng Kragur; and Moke gave rights to canoe magic to Mangoi of koyeng Brangiau in exchange for rights to magic for growing tobacco. If one does not own important magic already, it is hard to become one of the elite who do.

Although rights to magic spread in this way, villagers are often well aware of who the original holders of tiptip are. In the case of important crop production and fishing magic, the original owners and their heirs have public rights and responsibilites for subsistence activities that they do not share with those who have only recently acquired rights. For example, those who possess primary rights to magic for controlling certain kinds of fish also have some authority over activities involved in catching the fish and distributing the catch and a degree of responsibility for the success or failure of those endeavors.

I was told that women as well as men could own important magical knowledge and play public leadership roles. Only one woman in the village, however, is said to be a woman of knowledge, and she plays no obvious public role. Some say there were more such women in the past, but they do not explain why they have no female successors. "All the women of knowledge have died," says Tarakam, a male kastom. "The rest of the women don't have mouths [that is, they don't play public leadership roles]. They just look after their families, because they don't have the stori for anything."

One effect of the tiptip system is that realms of public responsibility are divided among customary leaders. Some have primary responsibility for the magical husbandry of taro, while others are concerned with tobacco, yams, various types of fish, organizing curing activities, and so on. Some kastom are undeniably more influential than others by virtue of the breadth and importance of their magical knowledge and the vigor with which they pursue their public roles. Although their domains may be small and they look as poor and weathered as other mature villagers, the leading kastom have an undeniable air of aristocratic self-assurance. When they speak in public, they speak in tones of authority and with haughty oratorical style. In private one also notes their pride and self-confidence.

Some koyeng enjoy greater prestige and influence than others, primarily because their members can claim rights to more, or more important, kinds of magical knowledge. Since magical knowledge tends to be inherited patrilineally, there is some stability in this rough koyeng hierarchy.

New kinds of leaders were introduced in Kragur when the village joined the Local Government Council system in 1961. The Australian administration initiated the council system in the 1950s. In brief, it provides for voluntary establishment of Local Government Council areas covering numbers of communities. Each member village elects a representative to the area council organization—the village councillor, or *kaunsil* in Pidgin—who also functions as a village leader. Kragur belongs to the Wewak-But Local Government Council, which encompasses Kairiru and

neighboring islands as well as part of the mainland around
Wewak. Officials of the Wewak-But Council supervise the election
of a Kragur village kaunsil and a kind of vice kaunsil known as the
committeeman, or *komiti* in Pidgin, every three years. The
Wewak-But Council levies an annual head tax on adults for the
support of public works, such as building roads or maintaining the
council boat, the *Christopher,* which travels between Wewak and
the offshore islands, stopping periodically at Kairiru.

Villagers generally see these elected leaders as having a different
sphere of authority than customary leaders rather than as super-
seding them in any way. A majority of the men who have held the
office of kaunsil in Kragur, however, have had some claim to status in traditional terms, and this has aided them in the exercise of
their authority. The kaunsil sometimes acts as a conduit for information from the provincial government or as local mouthpiece for
government agencies—for example, the public health service. His
main responsibility, however, is organizing regular communal
work on such tasks as maintaining the main trails near the village;
keeping the village grounds clear of weeds, stones, and debris; and
replacing aging houses or privies. Much of this work—for example, communal house building—would be accomplished anyway;
but these are the kinds of external aspects of order that were dear
to the hearts of colonial administrators, and so they now have
become the special province of the only representative of external
political authority in the village, the kaunsil.

Making a Living

Kragur's primary subsistence crops include taro, sweet potatoes,
yams, and a variety of greens. Villagers also tend small stands of
sago palms in wet areas near stream beds high on the slopes of the
mountain. Sweet potatoes and the starchy food made from the
pith of the sago palm are sometimes more plentiful than taro, but
villagers generally consider taro their most important crop. It is,
says one customary leader, "the bones of the village." Villagers
practice slash-and-burn or swidden horticulture, shifting cultivation among garden plots left to lie fallow between use, then
cleared of regenerated bush with ax, bush knife, and fire. Most
gardens are located some distance from the village, and none of

any size is on level ground. Villagers use the trunks of trees cut in clearing the land to edge steeply angled terraces. Although metal bush knives and axes long ago replaced stone tools, the principal tool for planting and harvesting remains a simple digging stick.

Fish are the most important nonvegetable food, but fishing is limited by the seasons. There are two main seasons, which are given their respective characters by the southeast trade winds, from roughly May to October, and the northwest monsoons, from roughly late November to early April. The monsoon season is marked by greater rainfall, days of heavy clouds, and extremely high winds that sometimes blow down coconut palms and houses weakened by age. In its exposed position on the clifftop, Kragur has little protection from these winds. The monsoon season takes its vernacular name, *yavaralal,* from the monsoon wind itself, *yavar.* The season of the trades is known as *makatalal. Makat* is a generic term for fish, and this is the season of calm seas and the possibility of frequent and productive fishing.

Men occasionally hunt wild pigs and a variety of smaller game. People say that pigs are not as plentiful now as they were in the past because Japanese occupation forces killed so many of them for food. A few Kragur men bear deep scars from encounters with boars in the days they hunted them with dogs and spears. Today pig hunting is exclusively the province of the two village men who own shotguns.

Villagers sometimes supplement their diets with canned mackerel, rice, and other items purchased from tiny village stores—or trade stores, as they are known in Papua New Guinea. There were three of these in the village in 1975–1976. They were run by local men and occupied small bush materials buildings or partitioned corners of houses. All three did most of their business in canned mackerel and white rice. The most opulent of these stores also stocked three or four short shelves of such goods as kerosene for lamps, newspaper for rolling cigarettes from locally grown tobacco, and such less widely used items as batteries for flashlights and transistor radios, soap, sugar, tea, coffee, navy biscuits, and canned corned beef. During my stay in Kragur this store branched out into such items as towels, children's clothes, ready-made cigarettes, and bush knives.

Kragur people do not own or use many things that are not locally produced, although the locally produced material environment is not as rich as it once was. Villagers still build their own houses and make their own canoes, fishing nets, and smooth, well-balanced wooden handles for their axes and other metal tools. A few men still carve wooden combs or fashion glossy, sharp-toothed coconut-meat scrapers from shell. Women still laboriously knot both purchased and handmade cord into the stretchy, resilient net bags, called *bilum* in Pidgin, used to carry everything from babies to enormous loads of coconuts. Most households still have some ornately carved wooden plates, some decorated with a distinctive sea turtle motif, and perhaps a heavy taro pounder ornamented with a stylized human figure. There are also the weathered slit gongs and the hourglass-shaped hand drums with heads of lizard skin, called *kundu* in Pidgin, that the men bring out on special occasions. Many more such carefully crafted objects of mundane or special use graced the village in years past. Much decorative religious art was destroyed or allowed to decay when the men's cult was abandoned. The fire that destroyed the village during the war took with it innumerable plates, drums, clay pots acquired in trade with mainland villages, and much else. As recently as the early 1970s, artifact merchants from Wewak visited Kragur and purchased many carved plates, taro pounders, and other objects at absurdly low prices for resale at enormous markups to tourists or artifact dealers. As some villagers tell it, this visit came around tax time, when people were badly in need of ready cash.

Although some villagers still have the skills to replace ornate drums, plates, and other handcrafted articles, changing times have turned their attention elsewhere. Some locally made items have been replaced over the years by commercially manufactured counterparts. All families, for example, now own aluminum cooking pots, enameled metal plates, and metal tools. Many also own kerosene lamps, sheets or blankets, perhaps thin mattresses or woven mats, and flashlights. A very few have transistor radios. Most of these items are old and worn. Everyone also owns a few items of European clothing. Only one man, one of the oldest in the village, wears the traditional loincloth, although his is made of a piece of cloth rather than the beaten bark used in the past. Today men customarily wear shorts or what is called in Pidgin a *laplap,* a calf-length strip of cloth wound around the waist. Women usually wear a loose blouse and a cloth skirt or a laplap, having long ago abandoned the traditional fiber skirt. Seldom does anyone wear shoes or even the rubber thongs popular in town. Like their other manufactured possessions, villagers' clothing is usually faded and worn.

Kragur people look poor. They certainly have very little money. I estimate that in 1980 per capita income was less than twenty kina (K20), at that time equivalent to about twenty-five U.S. dollars. Villagers do not spend much of their time in moneymaking activities. A survey of time allocation I conducted in 1976 (see Appendix) found that, on the average, village men spend about eight hours a week and women about four hours a week in moneymaking activities, primarily producing copra. In contrast, both men and women spend about twenty-five hours a week gardening, making sago, fishing, building or repairing their houses, or in some way satisfying their material needs directly. (Women also spend many hours a week on cooking and other household tasks, to which men contribute very little.) There were good reasons for lack of enthusiasm for copra production in 1976. The price paid to local producers had plummeted by more than 50 percent over the preceding two years (Papua New Guinea Copra Marketing Board) and the country's major newspaper, the *Papua New Guinea Post Courier,* carried items with headlines like "Collapse Faces Copra" (May 1976:1). What money villagers earned bought less than it had five years before. As of December 1975, the Papua New Guinea consumer price index had risen 63.2 percent since 1971 (Hiri February 1976:12).

Even were the price of copra to remain high, it would not be a golden opportunity for Kragur. I have already noted the lack of regular transportation between Kairiru and the mainland (cf. Philpott et al. 1974). In addition, Kairiru's land is generally unsuitable for agriculture, including tree crops and grazing (Haantjens, Reiner, and Robbins 1968; Territory of Papua New Guinea, Department of Agriculture, Stock and Fisheries 1969). All the islands offshore from Wewak lag far behind other parts of what used to be called the Wewak Sub-District in the number of coconut palms per capita, largely because of "limited and unsuitable ground" (Territory of Papua New Guinea, Department of Agriculture, Stock and Fisheries 1969). Villagers have been disappointed by their years of effort planting coconut palms and processing copra. Although production picks up whenever prices rise, they entertain little hope that copra production will ever bring them a major economic breakthrough.

The most common way of earning money, aside from copra, is selling garden produce in the market in Wewak, at a small market near St. Xavier's, or to St. Xavier's itself. Villagers usually undertake such sales only to meet specific immediate needs for cash. When I visited Kragur in 1981, for example, one family had moved temporarily to the other side of the island to work for several weeks producing sago for sale on the mainland in a crash effort to earn enough money to pay their son's high-school fees.

I will look more closely at villagers' forays into local business ventures in Chapter 7. Fortunately for most, however, they do not have to rely for money entirely on their own meager earnings. Kragur men have been leaving the village to work for money ever since the first decade of European contact. Such migrants return home with some savings or send money back periodically. The scale of migration is impressive. In 1976 Kragur had a resident population of about 214, but about 92 villagers above the age of twenty had left Kragur. Only fifteen or so had merely moved to other Kairiru villages to live with kin; a few were attending tertiary schools; but most had left the village to work for money or to be with spouses who were working for money. Almost 60 percent of these were under forty years old. This accounts for the hourglass age distribution in the resident village population, where about 87 percent are either under twenty or over forty. Many of those who leave Kragur do so only temporarily, returning after a few years to make their homes in the village. Some, however, appear to have taken up permanent residence elsewhere. This is more clearly the case for the few young men, and the smaller number of young women, who have graduated from high school, teachers college, technical school, or university.

Gifts and Money

Despite the export of young people to work for wages and salaries, the use of manufactured goods, the presence of village stores, and a great interest in money, the fundamental rhythm of economic life in Kragur is not yet that of earning and spending, buying and selling. Rather, the rhythm is still that of a gift economy

(Mauss 1967:31), or what is sometimes called an economy based on reciprocity (Sahlins 1972:185–275). What this means in Kragur at the most mundane level is that daily life is characterized by the informal flow of food and mutual aid between households linked by kinship ties. A household enjoying a momentary surplus shares with other related households without being asked, and households temporarily in need ask other related households for assistance. Toward evening, when the major meal of the day usually is prepared, women and children pass back and forth over the stony paths, appearing at open doors and windows to hand in plates of taro, rice, or other cooked food, or to ask quietly if there is any fish or taro or sago to spare. More than one man proud of his fishing prowess told me in private of how sometimes there would be barely enough left for his own family because he had been so generous with his catch; but in public such giving and receiving take place without comment or display. As Marvin Harris comments, "One can tell if a life style is based on reciprocity . . . by whether or not people say thank you" (1975:124). In Kragur, people often do not. Etiquette calls, not for verbal reciprocity, but for doing what is expected when one is oneself in a position to give.

To a certain extent, a kinship tie with someone entitles one to ask for and be given food or other goods. When Kragur people give in this way, they hope and expect eventually to receive something roughly equivalent in turn. However, from the standpoint of one's reputation—and, as will be discussed later, one's health and well-being—it is better to give generously without commensurate return than to enjoy the largess of others. To be a prolific producer and a generous giver is a mark of good character. Those concerned with their good names are careful not to sully their reputations by seeming too concerned with what they receive in return. Being a giver rather than a receiver is a key aspect of status. On one occasion an older customary leader of considerable renown remarked to me that I probably had noticed that he never asked me for anything from my store of supplies—rice, canned mackerel, sugar, coffee, soap—as so many others often did. "I'm too important," he explained concisely.

The association of giving with status is most evident in giving on a grand scale, in such events as feasts commemorating deceased kin. The largest of these are the feasts called *warap* in the Kairiru language and *krismas* in Pidgin. The heir of a ramat walap gives a warap to validate his claim to following in his kinsman's footsteps as a leader.[9] A warap is not given for someone of lesser importance; but a warap given in the name of a prominent leader is said to commemorate all the kin of the leader who have died in recent years as well. As Ibor, Kragur's Catholic leader, puts it, "One big name covers the small ones." Although the last warap to take place before I first went to Kragur relied primarily on purchased rice and beer, a more traditional event would be based on taro. Months in advance the sponsors of the event—the heir of the ramat walap and his close kin—would enlist the aid of one of the principal taro magicians to oversee cultivation of a large taro garden in which all village families, not just the close kin of the ramat walap, could have plots. At the warap, the sponsors distribute the taro and other food and tobacco contributed by their close kin and other villagers to invited guests from other villages. The guests consume some of the food on the spot and carry the rest—net bags of taro and bundles of sago and tobacco—home with them. The guests themselves bring gifts of food, and the sponsors of the warap later distribute this among those who helped accumulate food to present to the guests.

I have not witnessed a warap. When I last went to Kragur in 1981 there had not been a warap since about 1971. According to villagers' accounts, the participants end up with about the same amount of food they put in. The sponsors, however, gain the greater share of the glory, not for possessing wealth, but for their ability to amass and distribute wealth.

Overseas trade was probably a somewhat different matter. Hogbin (1935:401) writes of Wogeo overseas trade in the 1930s:

> The transactions can hardly be called barter as the goods are not exposed and examined, but the returns expected are rather more rigidly fixed than is usual in pure gift exchanges. Thus, if a man hands over a parcel of nuts and requests that he be given tobacco he definitely expects a bundle of a certain size. . . . It is true that if he considers the return gift inadequate he has no direct redress, but in the future he will avoid this particular [trading partner] and make an agreement with someone else.

Wogeo trading voyages took place infrequently, often at intervals of years, and the trading canoes, too large for normal use, would be "left to rot on the beach" (404) when a voyage was completed. This may describe the nature of Kragur overseas trade at the time as well, since Kragur took part in the same trading circuit. Villagers' accounts do make it clear that trade took place in the context of personal relations between specific individuals (cf. Strathern 1988:161). Trading partners assured each other of safety and hospitality in their respective villages and partnerships could be passed from generation to generation (cf. Hogbin 1935:398).

Modern money now enters into the circulation of goods and services in Kragur, but largely on villagers' own terms. Contemporary commemorative events for the dead now may include rice, beer, hard liquor, and other items purchased with earnings from copra production or the contributions of migrant kinsmen employed in the cash economy. Like taro, fish, or sago, money is also subject to the requirement that one share one's bounty with kin. Of course, villagers use money to purchase goods in Wewak or pay taxes or school fees. Within the village, however, they use money only to purchase goods at the trade stores. They do not use money to buy goods other villagers produce or to compensate other villagers for their labor. Reciprocal assistance among kin supplies most needs for labor beyond that which single households can muster. Villagers accomplish large tasks, such as house building, communally, although the owner of a new house is expected to make the major contribution to the communal meals that end each day's labor and the feast that marks the house's completion.

Premonetary customs and attitudes are still very much alive. Decades ago Kragur villagers would have had little with which to compare them. Since colonization, however, they have had comparative foils in the early colonial enclaves, the growing urban areas, and the many Western commercial, administrative, and religious outposts. Occasionally, older villagers contrast their indigenous way of life with this new world and say that, while other people have coins and bills, food is the money of Papua New Guinea. They also perceive, however, that money is not only different in form and substance from taro, pigs, or fish, it is integrally associated with different kinds of relationships among people.[10]

Kragur villagers have learned much of what they know about money from observing its use among white colonial and postcolonial administrators, missionaries, and employers. Some of their perceptions of the role that money plays among the people of foreign societies border on caricatures of the commercial spirit in social relations, although this exaggeration also conveys insight. From their observations some villagers have concluded that among Australians and Americans one must pay even a brother or a sister for food or lodging just as one pays at a hotel (cf. Carrier 1992:198). Comparing such practices with their own ideals of unstinting mutual aid among kin and generous hospitality to strangers, these observers find little cause for envy (cf. Linnekin 1983:244; Thomas 1990:139–140).

Nevertheless, they are also painfully aware that it is those with the most money who enjoy the most power, security, mobility, and prestige in the larger world that now encompasses Kragur (cf. Burridge 1969:41–46). As one middle-aged man puts it: "Money makes you a man. If you have nothing, like me, you'll be rubbish forever. If you have a hundred or a thousand in the bank, then you're a man."

Interest in money in Kragur is intense; but villagers' efforts to emulate the new standards of wealth that the foreign community and the small indigenous elite display have been repeatedly frustrated. For most Kragur people, money remains an elusive and problematic thing. Discouragement in his voice, an older man plainly states the lesson experience has taught him and his fellows, "We don't understand the ways of money."

The explanations that politicians and bureaucrats offer for national economic problems and the slow pace of rural development eventually reach Kragur. Villagers sometimes find them difficult to understand; they almost inevitably find them unsatisfying. This is not simply for want of Western education. Villagers view the disparities of wealth and power in the world and within Papua New Guinea from near the bottom of the heap. Things look different from this vantage point, and messages from more comfortable elevations often fail to ring true. So, while they doggedly pursue new commercial ventures as best they can, villagers also continue to argue and speculate about the ways of money.

Events in 1976 brought some of villagers' concerns about the origins and deeper nature of money into the open. Shortly before national independence in 1975 it was announced that Papua New Guinea was to have its own currency and that everyone was to begin exchanging their Australian currency. In order to discourage procrastination, the national administration enacted a timetable for currency exchange such that the longer one waited to exchange

Australian currency, the less Papua New Guinea currency one received. A number of Kragur villagers found this quite unsettling, as it suggested that money had no inherent value. What kind of stuff could it be if it could be arbitrarily deprived of its worth by a distant power? The source of money's value remains a mystery to many, and some older villagers regard this mystery as being like the mysteries of their own society—that is, as an esoteric magical and religious question. When they found my explanations of the ways of money unsatisfactory, some of my acquaintances simply assured me that the elders of my society had not yet divulged to me the deeper secrets: "You're young. They haven't told you yet," they said.

For most villagers, however, just what role money should play in daily social relations is a more immediate problem. They have seen the prosperity of those who live by money and they have seen that their social relations—buying and selling, payment of wages, and obvious concern with an immediate equivalent return when goods change hands or services are provided—are strikingly different from those prescribed by indigenous ideals. Like their observations of the impressive productivity of the white way of working, this raises questions about the social basis of prosperity and the adequacy of the prevailing morality to meet the challenge of new forms of wealth and new levels of material well-being.

THREE

Social Relations and Material Well-Being

To understand the Kragur concern with good social relations and their inseparability, in villagers' eyes, from material well-being, one must consider a crucial dimension of worldview in Kragur: the tendency to see the world as governed by animate and conscious beings and forces. This way of seeing things has been called a personalistic view of the world, in contrast with a view in which blind, impersonal forces dominate. The personalistic view is most apparent in small-scale preindustrial societies like that of Kragur. The contrasting view is epitomized in Western scientific thought, although many Westerners are not deeply instilled with the probabilistic, impersonal worldview of science and often interpret events in personalistic terms. They ask "Why me?" when personal crises strike; they blame national crises on national moral failings, the pernicious influence of some minority, or the schemes of enemy nations; they blame the poor for their poverty and praise the rich for their wealth. When things go wrong in businesses and other organizations, managers often look first for inadequate employees rather than for weaknesses in the nature of the organization (cf. Deming 1982:102–110).

Nevertheless, in places like Kragur the personalistic view meets with fewer challenges than in the modern West and is more compatible with some of the society's characteristic features. It should be apparent that a personalistic view is highly compatible with a gift economy in which material goods are valued as means of creating personal relations and even, as Mauss contends, partake of the identities of those who exchange them. A personalistic view is also particularly compatible with the nature of life in a small-scale, geographically and socially restricted world like that of Kragur villagers. As seen from Kragur, the world has narrow limits, and I will argue here that life in such a small world contributes to the pronounced development and influence of a personalistic view.

From a personalistic standpoint, the natural world responds to human emotion and expression; it is not merely the object of technological action. The strength of this orientation in Kragur helps account for the tendency to see material well-being and social relations as closely interdependent. One can easily see this tendency in the way Kragur villagers explain a wide variety of events. While they may not agree on a single explanation for an event, those they suggest are all likely to invoke in some way the quality of relationships among people or with humanlike supernatural beings. This way of looking at the world has an inherent dark side—a readiness to find human actions or motives behind chance misfortune, a readiness that is heightened in a social world containing many objective dangers and tensions. Partly because of the uncertainty of their social world—both its observable dangers and the fears engendered by a tendency to see other people behind misfortune— Kragur villagers value good social relations. They value them because they see them as the basis of health and prosperity, but they cannot be taken for granted. Yet, as I argue in the final section of this chapter, they also value good social relations in themselves; and they value material well-being not just for itself but also because they feel that it helps them achieve good social relations.

A Small World

Perhaps the most striking feature of the world as viewed from Kragur is that it is small. Villagers' views of the scope of the world vary; schooling and travel have broadened the outlooks of many, especially the young. It is safe to say, however, that most resident villagers and the more poorly educated migrants have a view of the geographic and social world that is decidedly limited in comparison with that of many educated Western people or better educated and more widely experienced Papua New Guineans.

In addition to being limited, the world as seen from Kragur is localized. For some villagers the known local world is not only the center of things in an emotional or an orientational sense; they also speak of it as the actual historical and geographic center of things. Older villagers commonly say that Kairiru was the "first place" and that the neighboring islands and the mainland came into being after Kairiru. They sometimes find evidence for this in the fact that on Mushu island and the mainland, shells, sand, and other debris of the sea floor are found even far inland and at high altitudes. In contrast, Kairiru, as appropriate to the "first place," is solid earth and stone.

Some villagers claim not only that Kairiru is the first land mass but also the locale of the creation of the first human beings, whose progeny spread to populate the known world. Kairiru myths speak of many topographical features of the mainland as the incidental products of Kairiru-centered events. Myths that account for the origins of various other features of the present world also display this localism. A story of the origin of the moon that Taunur told me, for example, concerns events near a place on the south side of Kairiru island called Lumawauk.

When villagers tell such stories or speak of how Kairiru was the "first place" they usually simply ignore the questions that their recently expanded knowledge of the world might raise. For example, did Kairiru exist before Australia and were the first inhabitants of Australia simply descendants of the first human inhabitants of Kairiru? The cosmology embodied in traditional accounts developed in the context of a very limited known world and quite naturally took only that into account. If I pressed them to relate traditional accounts of the world and its origins to the larger world of which they are now aware, villagers usually disavowed having any opinions. Some villagers did ask me, however, what people in America thought about human origins.

Kragur people in the past went on trading expeditions to points on the mainland as far away as the Murik Lakes area. They sailed northeast to Wogeo island to trade and must have been at least aware of nearby Koil and Wei islands and perhaps the islands of Blup Blup, Kadovar, and Bam farther to the east. They certainly knew the islands of Tarawai and Walis to the west of Kairiru. They did not, however, go into the interior of the mainland. According to present accounts, the horizon beyond Tarawai, Walis, Wogeo, and the eastern islands was the end of knowable space on Kairiru's seaward sides. People seem to have conceived of the world as a watery place punctuated by islands, *bak* in the Kairiru language. Villagers often describe past geographical knowledge by saying that their parents or grandparents thought that beyond the horizon "there were no more islands." The mainland, larger than any known land mass and with unknown limits, was differentiated from other land masses by calling it *bak tenang,* or "island mother," even though Kairiru was believed to have originated first.[1]

In the past, many Melanesian islanders saw the world as a large expanse of water, ending at the horizon, and centered on one's own island. Schwartz (n.d.) attributes such a view to Manus islanders, and Hogbin writes of Wogeo in the 1930s that "The local notion is that the earth is like a huge platter with raised edges and the sky above a shallow upturned bowl. At the center of the platter, beneath the highest point of the bowl, is Wogeo itself. . . . Radiating outwards are the other islands and the moon and the stars" (1970:27–28).

In the past, social as well as technological factors severely restricted mobility. Chronic warfare and hostility made it impossible to wander far from home in safety except within the limits set by kinship ties and networks of trading partners. Mobility has increased enormously in the decades since European contact. Pacification brought the possibility of greater mobility within the immediate world of villages, islands, and the mainland, and wage-labor opportunities took some Kragur men as far away as Hong Kong and Australia as crewmen on mission and commercial ships. Increasing first- and second-hand experience of a wider geographic area has expanded and refined geographic notions. The idea of a round world, however, remains novel to many of those with little or no schooling and the insular picture dies hard. One young woman, for example, asked me if after one reached America there were more islands beyond. Many younger villagers with more schooling, however, are competent with maps and have a more accurate view of world geography than their elders, despite their sometimes narrower first-hand experience.

The effective geographical world of Kragur villagers has expanded, but it remains small. Mobility has increased and continues to do so, but it is still limited. Although many men travel widely as wage laborers, back in the village horizons again contract. Only one resident villager traveled beyond the Wewak area during my stay in Kragur in 1975–1976, an older man who visited his son in Port Moresby at the latter's expense. With regard to travel closer to home, I asked a sample of villagers—thirty-five men and women, about 38 percent of those between primary school age and sixty-five years old—how often they had been to Wewak since the previous Christmas, a period of about ten months. I also asked whether they had ever had business in or simply entered a selection of stores, offices, and other establishments there. There was great variation within the sample. A few men had been to Wewak several times. The kaunsil and Ibor, the Catholic leader, had been on the average once a month, but these two are exceptional. A few older men had not been to Wewak at all that year, and many had been only seldom. More women than men had not been to Wewak during the survey period, and one woman surveyed had never been at all.

Once in Wewak the range of most villagers is limited. A large percentage of the town's commercial establishments and government offices remain unpatronized or unexplored. This is partly because villagers have no use for the goods and services offered in some establishments. The many illiterate adult villagers, for example, have little use for the bookshop or the stationery store. Nor do most villagers have money to spare for luxuries like the local movie theater. Patterns of movement, however, also betray the de facto segregation of town life. This is not the separation of black from white as much as the separation of whites and elite Papua New Guineans, such as provincial government employees, from the urban and rural poor. In the Wewak Hotel it is no longer forbidden for "natives" to drink at the inside bar. In general, however, the only indigenous people who do so are the urban elite. Rural visitors to town or blue-collar workers prefer to drink on the cement terrace that opens onto the street, although the prices are the same.

Whatever the causes, villagers still see the world as a relatively small place. The village is small, as are other known villages, the island is small, the most accessible town is small, and the limits of mobility for resident villagers are narrow. Geographic limits are also social limits, especially where the technology of communication is rudimentary. Hence, the Kragur social world is also small. The 1976 government census of Kairiru villagers appears to count nonresident as well as resident villagers; it reports 419 Kragur villagers, while I found just over 200 in residence. Even the greatly inflated government census count yields only about 1,700 islanders (not counting the staff and students at St. Xavier's and St. John's). Most of daily social life, however, takes place largely within the even narrower confines of the village and its surrounding lands.

The Personalistic View

Life in such a small world probably contributes to the dominance of and helps render plausible the idea that the world is governed by animate and conscious forces sensitive to human emotion and expression rather than impersonal, "natural" forces such as weather systems, geologic faults, or viruses.[2] Descriptions of such a view are common in the anthropological literature from Tylor's discussion of "animism" (1873) to the present. Referring to Melanesian peoples, Wagner (1981:87) speaks of "anthropomorphic or sociomorphic explanation," Schwartz (1973:156) writes of "a cosmology of animate and personal causation," and Gudeman (1986:134), drawing on Fortune (1932), describes supernatural agents as "metaphors of human will." Diamond (1974:144–146) and Schwartz (1972:33; 1973:165) use the terms "personalism" or "personalistic explanation" to describe this orientation toward the world. These terms recommend themselves because they suggest a contrast with a view of the social and natural environments as impersonal and disinterested. They also suggest the tendency to see relations with the entire environment as analogous to or influenced by relations among persons, and the tendency to see events that befall one not as chance occurrences but as caused by or aimed at oneself, that is, as having specific personal reference.

The societies in which such an orientation dominates have had little exposure to modern scientific views in which the physical world is one of impersonal natural laws; but lack of a scientific perspective in itself cannot explain the highly developed influence of a personalistic view. Diamond (1974:144–146) suggests that such a view is especially influential in places like Kragur because "all significant economic, social, and ideological functions" take place within or among "kin or quasi-kin groupings" and because of "the intensity of personal life." Schwartz sees the scale of societies as more fundamental than the role played by kin groups and relations, although the features of scale he emphasizes also bear on "the intensity of personal life." In small-scale societies, the social world is one of what Schwartz calls small "face-to-face ratios" (1972:33). The smallest face-to-face ratio would be one-to-one; that is, everyone is known equally by everyone else. This is approximated in a small community like Kragur. One finds extremely large face-to-face ratios in modern mass societies. Here, although a public figure like a national leader, a newscaster, or a movie star is well known by millions, who constitute the high side of the ratio, those millions are anonymous to the well-known figure. Most members of such a society understand that it is the politician or the celebrity who is the center of attention and that attention does not flow back.

Small-scale spheres of social interaction and typically small-scale notions—for example, the idea of an omniscient supernatural being, like God or Santa Claus, who is aware of each individual's behavior—do persist in large-scale societies (Schwartz 1972: 33; 1973:169). Yet, the crowds of unknown people that surround one and the knowledge that distant bureaucracies do not know one individually provide a social environment consistent with the idea of impersonal forces without human attributes. In such societies, typically small-scale notions have to coexist with a view of nature as moved by disembodied forces—gravity, natural selection, and so on—which operate quite without any personal, human attributes.

In contrast, the view that oneself or one's group is "the center of malign or benign attention" (Schwartz 1973:169) has a stronger social basis in the nature of life in small-scale societies. The idea that the entire environment is somehow conscious of and sensitive to human actions and emotions, that events are the result of human or humanlike awareness and reaction, is particularly consistent with experience of a social world in which all are well known to and highly aware of one another. In such a world every person can be a center of attention, and the interpersonal ramifications of one's own and others' actions are relatively direct and obvious.

Further, the people of many small-scale societies typically live in worlds that are geographically as well as socially limited, and they use technologies that require immediate involvement with the physical environment, which thus becomes intimately known and imbued with human significance. Cut down to human scale, the world is well suited to interpretation in personalistic terms.

It must be kept in mind that the contrast between impersonal and personalistic views is not a contrast between rational and irrational views of the world. Impersonal interpretations of events can be pushed too far as easily as personalistic interpretations. In the movie *The Godfather,* mobsters distance themselves from their violent deeds by claiming it is just business, not personal; in capitalist societies it is easy to forget the human decisions behind "the invisible hand" of the market and their human consequences; social scientists are often guilty of reducing individuals to pawns of abstract systems. Also, particular personalistic interpretations can have their own validity. As Diamond (1974:146) notes concerning personalistic views of illness, "the belief that people can make other people sick contains its obvious truth . . . and is not only the result of scientific ignorance."

Explaining Events in Kragur

People do not find it necessary to explain all that happens in their daily lives; but when they pause to consider the causes of out-of-the-ordinary events they reveal a lot about their views of how the world works. In explaining things ranging from straying pigs to serious illness and crop failures, Kragur people exhibit a highly personalistic view, a deep conviction of the inseparability of the social and the natural worlds, the human and the nonhuman worlds.

Lost Pigs, Sorcery, and Accidents

After his brother Sheltar died, Taunur looked after the son, Yabok, and daughter, Kamasho, he had left behind. One evening Yabok—at this time a young man studying for the priesthood and home briefly on holiday—returned to Taunur's house, hungry. Finding that Taunur and his wife, Mwairap, had not prepared any food yet, he went to the house of another close kinsman to eat. That same evening Taunur's pig, Tau Moin (Woman of Tau), which wandered freely through the village and the nearby bush, did not return as usual to be fed and to spend the night under the house. The pig finally came home sometime the next day; but Yabok told me with some amusement that Taunur had been worried that he had angered his dead brother, Sheltar, by not taking better care of Yabok, and so Sheltar had caused the pig to wander off as a mild sign of his displeasure.

His many years of Western education not only have made Yabok skeptical about spirits of the dead; they also have rendered him less likely to assume that events are somehow aimed at people. Taunur, however, is like most other Kragur villagers in his tendency to look for human or humanlike motives and actions behind what a skeptical Westerner would call natural or chance events, like the temporary disappearance of a pig or its coincidence with failure to feed his adopted son. Like many other villagers, Taunur also is likely to explain these human or humanlike motives and actions in terms of states of social relations, in this case his and his wife's neglect of their obligations to Taunur's dead brother.

The use of sorcery as an explanation is a good illustration of the difficulty of thinking of events as the products of purely impersonal, mechanical causes, or as accidents, or as simply "bad luck." Sorcery is much feared in Kragur. Many villagers are careful to throw discarded betel nut or cigarette butts into the fire so that sorcerers cannot act against them via the saliva that adheres to these objects. Sorcery is called *poison* in Pidgin, while what is called poison in English, a toxic substance introduced into a person's body, is called *kif* in Pidgin. The distinction, however, is a fine one, for as one older villager, Tarakam, explains, sorcery performed with a cigarette butt and kif are basically the same, "because my saliva is on [the cigarette butt]." Villagers fear alleged sorcerers within their own community as well as in other villages. No one in Kragur openly admits knowledge of sorcery, which must be inherited or purchased like other important kinds of knowledge. Those in the village most often suspected of having or using such knowledge are men of high status who possess rights to a variety of other kinds of esoteric knowledge as well (cf. Stephen 1987). Sorcery is believed to cause pain, illness, and death, either directly or through influencing events. As Taunur told me, if someone is bitten by a snake he is unlikely to die unless he or she is a victim of sorcery. Someone does not die from a snake bite just because by chance they met a snake on the path; they die because they have been rendered susceptible to harm or put in harm's way by sorcery. Taunur's brother Sheltar died when a homemade dynamite charge, used for stunning fish, went off in his hand. Everyone recognizes the need for skill and caution in bombing fish; nevertheless, many thought that Sheltar had been ensorceled. Had he not dynamited fish before without mishap? Why did his skill fail him this time?

Villagers have an excellent working knowledge of much of their natural environment. They fish, hunt, and garden skillfully and successfully. They also avoid physical danger as much as they can. Villagers were quick to warn me, for example, not to sit directly underneath heavily loaded coconut palms and to avoid walking through palm groves when the monsoon wind was bending the trees and shaking loose the dry nuts. Exceptional ill or good fortune, however, generally calls for an explanation, more often than not involving human or humanlike actions and motives and the state of social relations. Several years before I first went to Kragur, Morap, then a young boy, was walking along the top of the cliff overlooking the bay below the village. As he passed beneath a palm tree, a coconut fell, striking him a glancing blow on the head and causing him to fall from the cliff-top thirty or forty feet to the boulder-strewn beach below. Those who rushed to help him found him unconscious, but he soon revived and they found that he was uninjured. Had he been killed or broken several bones there probably would have been mutterings of sorcery; but, since he survived unscathed, his exceptional good fortune became the focus of explanation. I do not know what explanations villagers offered at the time of the incident. During my stay in Kragur, many suggested that the intercession of God or the Virgin Mary had saved him. Some villagers also mentioned another incident in which a boy fell a great height from a palm and was unhurt and said that God or the Virgin Mary had interceded in both these events because of villagers' loyalty to the Catholic God and the Virgin. As I will discuss in Chapter 4, villagers' ideas about what it means to be good Catholics include ideas about proper forms of social relations. So, the popular explanation of God's or the Virgin's intercession in these cases is, essentially, that it was a reward for maintaining good social relations among villagers as well as with these powerful supernatural beings.

Spirits of the Dead, Food, and Health

As the examples I have given illustrate, supernatural beings are also part of the Kragur social world. The dead are perhaps the most ubiquitous and figure in explanations of many kinds of events. To many villagers, of course, they are not "supernatural," but a taken-for-granted part of the world. While the dead can be helpful in daily life, they also can be dangerous when activated by the anger of their living kin, acting on whose behalf, whether the living consciously will it or not, they can ruin people's gardens or bring them failure in fishing or hunting. One villager told me that he is usually very successful in fishing both because his dead mother guides him to good fishing spots and because he always distributes a large part of his catch to other people. This not only pleases his dead mother, it also fends off the anger of others that could ruin his fishing. Another says, "If you catch some fish and give some to others, especially the old people [who can't fish for themselves], it's as though the dead see you and say, 'You're a good man, you share with everyone.' " Generosity is also good policy in gardening. Explains a respected taro kastom, "If when you get food from your garden you share with everyone, you'll always have good crops."

Failure of subsistence efforts caused by the dead kin of angered living persons is called *suak* in the Kairiru language. In fishing, it may not even be necessary to fail to distribute one's catch to bring on suak. I was told that, in the past, someone going fishing would not tell others for fear they would wonder, "If this man catches some fish, will he give some to us or will he eat them all himself?" Their dead kin might treat such suspicion of impending selfishness in the same way as anger at an accomplished wrong and act accordingly. Anger also can bring about suak in other kinds of subsistence endeavors. Ibor, one of two village men who own shotguns, told me how he had gone hunting for wild pigs one day; although he had come across signs of at least three, he had not gotten a shot at any of them. Apparently the kaunsil had recently called everyone to help process Ibor's and his brother's copra on a day when many had not expected it. Consequently, said Ibor, "Ol man i tok tok long mi." That is, they grumbled angrily about him, so he now was having no success in hunting.[3]

The dead also appear prominently in explanations for illness. Here, also, the dead do not act independently, but as partisans of the living: the root of illness caused by the dead is unresolved anger or grievances among the living. In Pidgin it is said that such illness occurs because "man i gat tok"—that is, someone has a complaint or grievance—or "man i gat wari," or "man i gat kros" —that is, someone is worried or angry. Thus, such illness is sometimes referred to as *sik bilong wari* or *sik bilong man i gat tok*. The dead kin of the person who harbors the anger intervene on the living's behalf and cause the person against whom the anger is directed, or one of their kin, to become ill.[4]

Illness caused by the dead also is called in Pidgin *sik bilong graun*, that is, "illness caused by the ground." As one villager is fond of phrasing it, "The ground kicks you." Or it may be said that "graun i gat tok," that is, "the ground has a complaint or grievance." Used in this way, *graun* refers to the collective dead of the kin group. In the past those dead were literally in the ground of the living, for their remains were interred beneath the houses of their close kin. One villager expresses quite clearly the idea that the dead attend both to the anger of the living and to their petitions on behalf of the victims of illness, saying "all our dead mothers and fathers are in the ground and they hear. [If a person is sick] we ask the ground to loose its hold on him."

The anger of the living does not necessarily cause illness, however. Anger is only dangerous if it is not made public so that it may be eradicated, whatever dispute or grievance is at its root resolved, and the involved persons reconciled. The dead act upon anger that is not dealt with by the living. "If I'm angry with you," says one villager, "if you are aware of it, we'll shake hands and it will be over; but if you aren't aware of it, the dead will make you ill and give you pain." The person who does something that could arouse anger in others need fear illness only if his act becomes known. Villagers do not see the dead as omniscient moral watchdogs, but merely as partisans of the living. The degree to which the anger of the living is justified does not seem to affect the zeal of the dead on their behalf.

Despite the danger of hidden anger, many grievances are never aired until an illness occurs that implicates them in its cause. It may be that villagers believe some anger is simply too inconsequential or too transient to arouse the intervention of the dead. There is at least one skeptic who professes to give no credence at all to the theory of illness caused by the dead, saying "I have a dead mother, a dead father, dead grandparents and ancestors. Plenty of times I've been angry and just sat in my house and no one became sick. The ground doesn't have ears to hear you, the ground can't make someone sick." It is probably apparent to villagers that they can ignore much anger and many grievances without danger. The only sure test of which grievances may result in illness is whether or not illness does in fact occur. (It is possible, of course, that in some instances people hide and nurse their anger in the hope that it *will* eventually result in illness.)

Curing illness caused by anger via the intervention of the dead involves identifying and resolving the relevant dispute or grievance. One of the customary leaders who has tiptip for this function calls all the adult men of the village to gather near the house of the sick person. Even the professed skeptics show up and the assembled men devote from a few hours to an entire day to publicly voicing any anger they harbor against the sick person or members of his or her family. The leading men of each koyeng tend to dominate the proceedings, often acting as spokesmen for other members of their kin groups, men as well as women. Although the aim of the proceedings is to eliminate interpersonal anger, for the cure to work men must voice their grievances with the full complement of emotion. Although the grievances may be old and stale, one must speak as if the anger were fresh in one's blood. Whatever else this may accomplish, it is surely cathartic, perhaps for the listeners as much as for the speaker. A number of different grievances may be aired during a single curing session. Villagers claim that when they hit upon the one responsible for the illness the sick person will begin to show signs of improvement. If the patient does not show improvement during the session or soon thereafter, say during the night or the following day, the men will hold further curing sessions and continue to search for the relevant grievance. If they have no success they eventually may decide that the illness was not caused by the dead, or they may simply assume that someone is refusing to reveal his anger.

As the following case illustrates, setting relations right with the dead by patching up the quarrels of the living can be a complicated business.

An unmarried man, about nineteen years old, was suffering from extreme nausea and diarrhea. A day-long curing assembly concluded that the following events were responsible for his illness. The patient's mother is from a nearby village. A Kragur man, with no close kin ties to the patient, had invited several men from that village, including one of the patient's mother's close kin, to harvest one of his sago palms. When they cut the sago palm it took another sago palm down with it in its fall. The owner of this broken palm, also of Kragur, demanded compensation from the group from the neighboring village, but they put him off. So, the patient's father promised to pay the ten kina for which the owner of the broken palm was asking. But he delayed payment for some weeks. Hence, the assembly concluded, the owner of the palm had become angry and his anger had resulted in the illness in question. The patient's father and the Kragur man who had invited the sago-cutting party agreed to pool their resources and pay the owner of the broken palm in order to terminate the grievance and cure the illness.

As in many other cases, however, the initial diagnosis had to be discarded because the illness continued unabated. A second curing assembly was held, and it reached a new conclusion. The patient is a member of the koyeng of a kastom known for his ownership of rights to much important fishing magic. When applying magic the practitioner often must observe certain ritual restrictions. In this case, the kastom recently had been performing magical procedures during which he and the other members of his koyeng were supposed to have observed a taboo on sexual relations. The magic had met with little success, and it came to light that the patient had broken the taboo. The assembly decided that some villagers blamed the young man for the failure of the magic and still harbored their anger. It was decided that this must be at the root of the illness. The patient's father again paid compensation, this time to the fishing kastom, as a form of public apology rather than to make good any material loss. The young man began showing signs of improvement soon thereafter.

Any opportunity for generating grievances always brings the danger of illness. For example, such ostensibly festive occasions as feasts at which men get happily drunk and conviviality is the order of the day never occur for their own sake but always in connection with the fulfillment of some social obligation. They can be occasions for great anxiety, for if the conduct of the affair offends someone, illness may result. On the afternoon preceding a large feast that he had arranged in commemoration of deceased kin, an older man commented to those with whom he sat smoking and chewing betel: "If you do something like this you have to do it right. If you do things wrong . . ." And, as he paused, another man completed his sentence: " . . . someone will get sick." All present nodded solemn agreement.

Taro, Kastom, and Cooperation

In the Kragur view, rents in the fabric of good social relations also can affect material well-being directly, without the intervention of ghosts or Catholic supernatural beings. The poor taro crop of the year prior to my first arrival in Kragur is a case in point. This was a topic of much discussion in the village, both in public gatherings like the one held just after Christmas and in private conversations. Villagers put forward a variety of explanations for the problem. One young man suggested to me that the soil in the gardens might be depleted, and an older man suggested that people simply had not spent enough time making and caring for gardens because of the demands made on their time by copra growing and work for the village kaunsil. Most agreed, however, that in some way the problem was caused by antisocial behavior, either the failure of village leaders to cooperate among themselves or otherwise to act in a public-spirited way, or the failure of the other villagers to cooperate with the leaders.

The customary leaders, or kastom, bore the brunt of the blame. Particular kastom own rights to use the magic for protecting taro from disease and insect infestation and for ensuring large and healthy tubers. The kastom with primary tiptip for taro magic also have authority to organize a centralized garden in a single general location where all villagers have a plot regularly tended by the taro magicians. All villagers do not own land in any single area, but some can temporarily use land that belongs to others, providing they do not plant coconut or betel palms or other crops that occupy the land for more than a single season. Such a collective garden had last been organized in the middle or late 1960s in preparation for a warap for a deceased kastom of great importance. Many rank-and-file villagers said that in recent years the taro kastom had not cooperated among themselves to initiate a centralized, collective garden or to organize regular visits to scattered gardens. Some kastom did not agree that the latter was their duty. Gardens are located all over the mountainside and, according to one of the principal taro kastom, he and the other kastom with knowledge of taro magic can be asked to visit gardens to remedy illness, but not simply to increase the quality of the crop. Some of the rank and file, however, saw the situation differently.

Several villagers, sitting by their fires late at night and lowering their voices, suggested that the failure of the kastom went beyond this and that some actually had used their magical knowledge maliciously to decimate the taro gardens. A kinsman of one of the taro kastom had died the previous year, and many suspected this kastom of magically lashing out at all and sundry in his grief and sorrow.[5] Villagers spoke of this as though it were understandable and not unusual, although it had gone too far in this case.[6] Others, including one of the principal taro kastom himself, asserted that the kastom as a group had urged the people to make a centralized garden and to work harder in all their gardens, but the villagers had not heeded their advice. A few of the rank and file suggested that this may have angered some of the kastom, goading them to magically despoil the taro. A few others, however, argued that people had ignored the advice of the kastom because in the past when everyone had cooperated to make large collective gardens the produce had been dissipated in feasts honoring the deceased kin of prestigious leaders. According to one of the taro kastom, a collective garden should be made only for such occasions of ceremonial feasting and distribution. Nevertheless, many villagers spoke of a large, centralized garden as a remedy for the lack of taro for daily consumption.[7]

There was no single accepted explanation for the taro shortage. Individual points of view varied widely, but the large majority felt that in one way or another the fundamental problem was in the fabric of social relations: neglect of public responsibilities, failure to cooperate for the common good, a general lack of harmony and unity of purpose. The role of magic aside, all the talk of failure to cooperate sounds quite plausible to an outside observer; in some way, lack of cooperation may have contributed to the problem. The point, however, is that the same basic theme runs through villagers' explanations of this problem as one finds in explanations of straying pigs, miraculous good fortune, hunting and fishing success, illness, and other events and circumstances: maintaining good social relations, whether it be among human beings or with supernatural beings with humanlike motives, brings material well-being and prevents material misfortune.

The Dark Side of the Personalistic View

Maintaining conflict-free social relations is never easy; and life in a small, close-knit community presents special obstacles. Life in Kragur takes place in a social world that is not only small but, in part because of its limits, intense. Interdependence is great, personal contacts are frequent, privacy is rare, anonymity is impossible. This "intensity of personal life," as Diamond (1963:94) calls it, is part of the social basis of a personalistic view. It also, he suggests, gives rise to "unusual sophistication and subtlety about people." This may sound rather attractive to residents of modern urban and suburban communities where we must strive to avoid anonymity and often know each other only in our narrow public roles. The intense personal life of a small-scale society, however, can be wearing for one not accustomed to it. While living in Kragur, I found that one of the pleasures of my infrequent trips to Wewak, itself hardly a place of faceless crowds, was to wander in public places without meeting people I knew and being asked where I was going or what I was doing. (A common greeting in the Kairiru language is *koliek piye*, "Where are you going?")

I believe even villagers find their small-scale social world a strain at times. Families sometimes build second houses near their gardens. Although these are usually smaller than village houses, they are furnished with all the amenities—clay fire platforms, bamboo shelves, shady verandas—and often boast carefully tended borders of ornamental plants and striking views of the cultivated slopes, the surrounding forest, and the sea in the distance. People build such garden retreats not only to save time when there is much work to be done, but also, some told me, so that they can occasionally escape from the noise of dogs and children, the frequent public gatherings, and the lack of privacy of life in the closely packed village. As F. G. Bailey (1971:5) writes of small European peasant and post-peasant communities: "It is very hard to mind your own business if you live in a village. It is hard even if you were not born there and have come to live in the village as a stranger. It is impossible if you are local born and bred. . . ."

Life in societies where everyone knows everyone else and is bound to everyone else in a multitude of social relationships creates friction, and this friction can generate unpleasant heat as well as soothing warmth. Diamond (1963:94) points out that the intense personal life of small-scale societies often produces "dangerous sensitivity" as well as "sophistication and subtlety." This is the negative aspect of a personalistic orientation: a readiness to see others' motives and intentions as self-interested, even malicious. To know people well is to know their weaknesses as well as their strengths. Even without such a jaundiced view, however, a tendency to interpret events in terms of human actions and intentions —that is, in a personalistic way—is likely to contribute to a climate of mistrust. In such a world, as A. I. Hallowell (1955:145) writes of the Ojibwa of northeastern North America, "if something does go wrong, it is somebody's fault."

There is no place on earth where things do not go wrong, but the daily uncertainty of life and health is greater for people who live at close quarters with the natural environment without advanced technology. Infant mortality is common in Kragur. Although traditional modes of treating serious illness exhibit inchoate psychological sophistication, they are extremely inefficient by modern Western standards. Daily life is filled with opportunities for physical misfortune: a canoe capsizes during a fishing expedition; a man is nearly fatally gored by a wild pig while hunting; a felled tree pulls its neighbor down on top of a man clearing his garden; an ax slips and deeply gashes a woman's leg; a man is severely injured when he falls from a tree while harvesting betel nut; a small cut on a woman's leg becomes infected and, in the absence of antibiotics, becomes a debilitating tropical ulcer. Misfortune calls for explanation—or, to use the metaphor of illness, diagnosis and treatment—in a way that uneventful times or good fortune do not. There is much misfortune to explain in a community like Kragur, and a tendency to explain it in terms of human actions and intentions contributes to a suspicious view of one's fellows and the humanlike entities in the environment.

The combination of a personalistic view having an inherent dark side and a risky relationship with the natural environment puts a strain on social relationships and helps account for Kragur people's preoccupation with keeping them harmonious. Schwartz (1973) proposes the concept "paranoid ethos" to describe the pervasive suspicion that I refer to as the dark side of the personalistic view. He argues that in Melanesia this "psychocultural" orientation owes much to "the uncertainty of life," not only in the natural world but also in the social world (1973:155–156). The negative dimension of personalism in Kragur undoubtedly has roots in the very real dangers of the human environment villagers faced in the past. Prior to the colonial suppression of indigenous violence there was reason to fear not only the silent danger of sorcery or hidden anger, but also the thrust of a spear in a dawn raid or a quarrel with a fellow villager. While anything more violent than a shouted argument is rare in village life today, there are still sources of chronic social tension that arouse concern about village cohesion and often cause people to look askance at others' motives.

Intervillage Conflict

While there were alliances among Kairiru villages in the precolonial era, there was no centralized political authority to mediate intervillage disputes, and these sometimes ended in shocking violence. The raid on Chem that the fathers of older Kragur men took part in as youths provides a good example of the uncertainty of intervillage relations in the past. While all villagers have heard tales of the raid from their elders, many have only vague ideas of the events leading up to it. According to details pieced together from several sources, it seems that a woman from Kragur ran away to join a man in Chem, which then stood about two-thirds of the way down the opposite side of the mountain. When Kragur men went to bring her back, the Chem people threatened them and drove them away. While that grievance still stood unresolved, two men from Reo—a site on the northeast side of Kairiru from which the ancestors of several Kragur koyeng had originally come —were ambushed and killed by men from Chem while fishing in the channel between Kairiru and Mushu (for reasons none of the Kragur storytellers could recall). Men from Reo then sought allies, asking other villages, including Kragur, to join with them to take revenge on Chem. When they came to Kragur, bearing a large bunch of betel nuts as a gift, at first the Kragur men declined the invitation; but the visitors ridiculed them, telling them they were only young boys and not men enough to fight. Stung by this and smarting from their own grievance against Chem, they finally threw in their lot with Reo. On the appointed day, the men of Reo, Kragur, and their allies met before dawn at the place near the top of the mountain today called *Iupulpul* ("place of the gathering of spears") in the Kairiru language and proceeded to Chem. Creeping into the village at dawn, having used war magic to render the Chem people unwary, they set fire to the houses and, as men, women, and children rushed out in panic, set about slaughtering them.

The people of Chem may well tell the story differently, but there is no doubt about the end result of the raid. After Father van den Hemel had visited the people of Chem, now living on the south coast of the island, in 1907 or 1908, he wrote:

> At first view I notice that I am amidst dejected people. The houses are badly built, low and without care. Big stones lie between the houses, grass growing on the place, which usually is well kept, well swept and clean. . . . The very young coconut trees are an indication that the place is only recently inhabited. That is so. The people of [Chem] have been through a great deal this time. About one and one half or two years ago they were attacked by the Reo people; many had been killed, their houses higher on the mountain destroyed. To have some rest and a bit of protection they have come down the mountain and built themselves emergency huts. . . .[8]

It must be remembered that all the events surrounding the Chem raid took place within a rather small geographical space. Today a healthy young villager can easily travel from Kragur to the old mountainside site of Chem in less than an hour and a half. The trails have been greatly improved since the beginning of the century, but even then it cannot have taken a young warrior long to cross the island. In the past, villages lived at close quarters with their enemies.

Village Instability

Violence was also a possibility within villages, as illustrated by the story of the founding of Kragur itself, as told to me by Suairu of koyeng Nalwun. The principal figure in the story, Mren, was the great-grandfather of the senior generation, in 1976, of koyeng Kragur. He lived at Piu, a site on the mountainside southeast of where Kragur village stands today, part of the larger area known as Reo. One day a man named Saurum was burning felled trees and brush to make a new garden bordering an area that Mren was still clearing. The fire went out of control and spread into the bush where Mren was working. Mren lost his temper, grabbed his spear, ran to find Saurum, and killed him. Fearing revenge, Mren ran away to the coast and hid at the place called Bungeru, on top of the cliff overlooking the beach. (Bungeru is just a short distance northwest along the coastal trail from where the houses of koyeng Kragur stand today. In 1976 one the village's two copra drying sheds was located there.) Fearing that Mren might be killed by people from Shagur village further northwest along the coast, Salmung (Mren's sister's son), Talmiyai (Salmung's half-brother), and Babung (whose relationship to the others I am unsure of) came looking for him. They found Mren and decided to settle there on the coast rather than return to live in Piu.

The principal figures in this story are the predecessors of three of the present koyeng: Mren of koyeng Kragur, Salmung and Babung of koyeng Nalwun, and Talmiyai of koyeng Shewaratin. Later, settlers came one by one to found the other koyeng. Like Mren, some came to Kragur after disputes (though not necessarily homicides) in other villages, for example, Kalem, the founder of koyeng Bomasek. The motives of others are lost to memory. Tracing the genealogies of most, although not all, of the present koyeng, one can find kinship ties between their founders that help to account for their migration to Kragur. With few exceptions, most koyeng oral histories lead back to ancestral sites in the same northeastern quadrant of the island, although the ancestors' paths to Kragur were often circuitous, some having migrated as far as Mushu island and the mainland during a famine several generations back before coming to Kragur. Villagers often make much of stories of common origin; and whatever their koyeng origins, since coming to Kragur denser social ties have been formed through marriages, the village-wide men's cult, and a host of other traditional and contemporary institutions. It remains true, however, that Kragur formed as a result of the fissioning of other communities. Taking the long view, Kairiru villages in general are probably nodes in a constant process of gradual aggregation and disaggregation. In the normal course of events, the splits that formed Kragur will not be the end of it, and Kragur may be expected to make its own contributions to the growth of other villages. Historically, Kairiru villages do not appear to be stable entities.

Social tensions are usually the immediate cause of village fission. Today, of course, the discontented or the ostracized can remove themselves permanently to an urban area as well as another village. Some villagers claim that sorcery is the most common cause of the breakup of villages. At least one of the many families that have migrated to one town or another has not returned and may never do so, according to some villagers, because they were driven out of Kragur by allegations of sorcery. Sorcery allegations have also strained relations between a large part of the village and a substantial segment of one of the koyeng.[9]

Koyeng Rivalry

Rivalry among koyeng is another source of intravillage tension. Even koyeng with clear historical links often vie for precedence. We can turn again to the story of Kragur's founding for an example. I once mentioned to one of Salmung's descendants that Mren's descendants, of koyeng Kragur, had told me the story of how their ancestor founded the village. Salmung's descendant, of koyeng Nalwun, met the koyeng Kragur assertion with scorn. Mren, he said, did not found the village. Mren was "a wild man," hiding in the bush without fire. It was Salmung and the others who were the real founders, he asserted, because they had started clearing the bush and building houses.

Villagers themselves decry koyeng rivalry, but there are few who will pass up the opportunity to make a claim for their own koyeng's superiority in some respect. The claim of being directly descended from the first settlers in Kragur, even though it is disputed, brings prestige to a koyeng. The most important source of koyeng prestige and influence, however, is the rights to magical knowledge held by the kastom or ramat walap of a koyeng. Some koyeng presently have no members of true kastom status. On the other hand, two koyeng have a near monopoly on primary rights to gardening and fishing magic and enjoy significant influence on that account. Even koyeng members with no magical rights of their own find the importance of their kastom a source of invidious distinction from members of other koyeng. "We're the bosses," one such villager told me, although he himself bosses little.

Leaders and Followers

While kastom are strongly identified with particular koyeng, rank-and-file villagers sometimes view the kastom in general as quick to anger, quite capable of using their knowledge for selfish ends, and moved by motives different from those of ordinary people. Discussing the alleged role of the kastom in despoiling the taro, one village man, himself a member of a koyeng known for its prominent kastom, comments, "That's what the kastom, the big men, are like. They have their own ideas." The case of the taro also clearly illustrates that the kastom and their constituents may not agree on just what their respective responsibilities are.

Many kastom clearly enunciate public-spirited ideals of using their knowledge to ensure the village's well-being; but, like elites everywhere, their motives are not always identical with those of people with less power and influence. Customary leadership is as much a matter of private pride as public trust. Many kastom speak of their superior knowledge with imperious self-satisfaction. Some are quick, in private, to point out that they fulfill their public roles better than other kastom, or that their knowledge is broader or has been held longer by their patrilineal lines than that of other kastom. Less influential villagers often suspect the kastom, especially those of other koyeng, of being more interested in "making their names"—that is, increasing their own reputations outside as well as within the village—than in looking after the general welfare. The kastom might protest that it benefits everyone if Kragur's leaders are widely respected, and many villagers would agree. Yet suspicion lingers that the kastom "have their own ideas."

A Delicate Balance

There are many concrete reasons for Kragur people to have found the human environment threatening in the past. Cultural memory is long and still colors villagers' attitudes. Longstanding features of the social structure—in particular, rivalry among koyeng and real and perceived disparities of interest between kastom and the rank and file—continue to interact with a personalistic bent to sow suspicion of others and make harmonious relations problematic.

Obviously, however, there must be countervailing factors; for despite suspicion, disputes, factions, and attrition, there is still a village. There are ties that bind as well as factors that breed tension and rivalry. For example, villagers marry outside their patrilineally defined koyeng, creating a web of cross-cutting kinship ties.[10] Also, in relations with external entities—for example, government agencies or other villages—identification with the community as a whole often submerges narrower koyeng loyalties and tensions between leaders and followers. Hence, Mowush, a young man in his thirties, warns against criticizing the village's kastom in public: "If we speak against them, the big men of some other village may use sorcery against them. They'll think 'The young men [of Kragur] want to replace their leaders, so we'll do away with them [i.e., the leaders].' " Even beliefs and practices springing from the dark side of the prevailing personalism provide some balance for the suspicion they generate. For example, failure to cure an illness thought to be caused by hidden anger can lead to further accusations and suspicions; but the curing process provides a means of airing disputes and resolving grievances, and the explanatory theory itself may act as a check on the escalation of minor disputes. The picture that emerges, then, is not one of a social world being blown apart by discord but of a delicate balance, albeit a balance in which the benign nature of human relationships never can be taken for granted.

Why Good Social Relations Are Important

Kragur people live in a densely packed and intimate social world in which controlling conflict is a chronic problem. They live at close quarters with the natural environment and with little technological defense against its dangers. These circumstances nurture a personalistic worldview with a dark side that, in turn, colors perceptions of the social and natural worlds, often in somber hues. In such a world, to maintain material well-being—good health, good crops, good hunting and fishing—one has to keep social relations running smoothly, with minimum cause for anger and conflict. That would be reason enough to be concerned about the quality of social relations. But there is another important side to Kragur people's concern: villagers also value good social relations for themselves, not simply as the precondition of health and prosperity. Sometimes, in fact, they speak as though they value health and prosperity primarily because they make good social relations possible. One young married man, complaining of what he sees as the current spate of malign magic ruining crops and causing illness and death, suggests that this has been brought about by a decline in village prosperity, which, he implies, has made tempers short. A middle-aged woman says the village would be a better place to live if there were more communal activities, like the feasting, dancing, and men's-cult festivities she says were frequent in the past. In those days, she says, "The men and women were happy, they sang and danced; the village prospered." Asked why this is no longer so, she replies, "We don't have all the good things we had before that made us happy, that made us want to join together." Another man complains of the use of malign magic to ruin the fishing and the gardens, and regrets not only the diminished food supply. "If they would fix things," he says, "if there were plenty of food, everyone would always be happy, everyone would work hard. [Now] people aren't happy, they don't take pleasure in their work, in singing and dancing together." Says still another:

> If everything were going well, if there were plenty of food, everyone would be happy and behave well. They would cooperate and listen to their leaders. But now this isn't the case because the big men are doing wrong. Before, if we organized a singsing all the old men and women would come and have a good time. But not now. They don't feel like it, they don't want to come. That's a sign that the village is in trouble. Before, if there were a singsing or a meeting or whatever, everyone would be there.

Given the prevailing mode of explaining misfortune, poor crops and unsuccessful hunting and fishing are very likely to cast a pall of suspicion over social relations, take a toll on enthusiasm for collective activities, and—as villagers may see it—arouse anger that could exacerbate existing material difficulties. There is no way to escape the circularity of such a system. Any attempt to judge which side of the equation—good social relations or prosperity— is a more fundamental concern would have to be loaded down with qualifications. They are highly interdependent and each catches the luster of the other. Just as the effort to maintain good social relations is part of the quest for prosperity, so the quest for prosperity is also an effort to create good social relations.[11]

FOUR

The Supernatural: Old and New

ONE CANNOT UNDERSTAND questions of social relations in Kragur without taking into account the supernatural dimension of the social world. It is impossible to give a full account of the supernatural world as Kragur people saw it before the arrival of Catholic missionaries, as most contemporary villagers were born after that significant event: even the oldest villagers in 1975–1976 had only been youths at the time. Early missionaries sought not simply to introduce Catholicism but to displace existing beliefs and practices. Although their success was limited, some aspects of indigenous religious life now exist only in old people's memories. Much also remains, but the line between indigenous religion and Catholicism often blurs. Villagers have found many ways of accommodating the two, both interpreting indigenous beliefs in Catholic terms and giving Catholicism a Melanesian flavor. They also find precursors of Catholicism in their own past. Catholicism's identification with European wealth and power certainly contributed to its initial acceptance; but Kragur's distinctively close association with Catholicism also owes much to the village's relative isolation from opportunities to participate in the mainstream of political and economic change.

Kragur's embrace of Catholicism has wrought some changes in villagers' views of the supernatural dimension of social life and given some new twists to ideas about the social basis of material well-being. Catholicism has done nothing, however, to diminish villagers' tendency to merge social and material issues. If anything,

70

its own emphasis on social relations and its apparent importance in the materially impressive European society have heightened Kragur people's concern with the intertwining of the social and material dimensions.

Who Is Wankau?

According to Moke: "When the missionaries came, they talked about God. Our ancestors spoke of Wankau." Moke is only one of several villagers who speak of Wankau as though he were the Kairiru equivalent of the Catholic figure God. Some, for example, say that Wankau created the first human being. Others say that Wankau created the first land masses and provided humankind with vital knowledge of how to build canoes, grow crops, and so on. Some also speak of Wankau as still active in human affairs, saying that he can be magically invoked to inspire men carving the prow of a canoe or a log drum.

When described in these ways, Wankau is indeed similar to the Catholics' God. Several mature village men, however, told me versions of the following myth about Wankau and his brother Yabok that indicates Wankau is distinctly different from God in some significant ways. The myth also illustrates an important constant in Kragur views of the supernatural—namely, the very human qualities of supernatural beings.

Wankau and his younger brother, Yabok, decided to make canoes and sail to Wogeo. Wankau used the proper kind of bush-materials binding to build his canoe but hid it beneath a layer of an inferior kind to deceive Yabok. Yabok, thinking that he was following Wankau's example, used the inferior binding. They made the sails for their canoes from the bast tissue of the coconut palm and decorated them with the figures of two children, one above the other, like a child and its mirror image. Around the edge of the sails twined the figure of a snake. Their canoes finally ready, they set out for Wogeo; but they soon encountered bad weather. The bindings of Yabok's canoe broke and it capsized, but Wankau's canoe was unharmed and he continued on to Wogeo. Yabok, angered by what he now saw was Wankau's deception, slowly swam and drifted his way back to Kairiru, clinging to a piece of

the wrecked canoe, all the while thinking of a way to avenge himself on his brother.

A day or two later, Wankau's wife, Moger, was sitting on the
beach where one of Kairiru's streams runs into the sea, looking out
to Wogeo in the distance, thinking of those who had set sail and
worrying about their safety. Yabok saw her sitting there alone
from a point farther upstream. He then carved a fine design on the
hard, round seedpod of a tree and floated it down the stream to
Moger. She retrieved it and admired the fine design, wondering
who had made it and wishing her own skin was decorated so
nicely. She looked around, but she saw no one and went back to
staring out to sea and worrying about her husband, Wankau.
Soon Yabok himself followed the stream down to its mouth and
came upon Moger. When she heard someone approaching she was
afraid, but then she saw that it was only Yabok. Yabok asked her
what she was doing. When she said that she had seen the storm the
canoes had encountered and now she was worried about Wankau,
Yabok replied: "Why should you worry? He's there and you're
here, you shouldn't think about him too much."

Yabok made light of her worry until she began to forget her husband and her attention strayed to the carved seedpod, which she
still held. "Did you carve these designs?" she asked him. "Me? No,
not me," he replied. But Moger insisted that he had. "Oh, you
really like the design, do you?" Yabok finally replied. "Oh, yes,"
she said. "I really do. This design would be so attractive on my
own skin." So Yabok enticed Moger back into the bush with him,
where he attempted to have sexual intercourse with her. At first
she resisted, saying that even though Wankau was on Wogeo he
would know what she had done, but she finally gave in. When
they had finished, Yabok tattooed the design on her thighs and
pubic area.

Just as Moger had feared, Wankau was aware of what she was
up to. On intuiting Moger's infidelity, he immediately roused his
crew and they set sail. As they neared Kairiru, Wankau told his
crew that when they arrived they should not drag the canoe completely up onto the beach. Instead, when the people on the beach
came to help pull the canoe out of the water, they should let it slide
back, so that those pulling the canoe, Moger among them, would
have to wade into the water up to their waists. Then he would be
able to confirm his suspicions, for if Moger indeed had been tat-

tooed, the seawater on the unhealed wound would cause her to wince with pain. Just as he suspected, as Moger waded out to grab hold of the canoe, she hesitated and then grimaced with pain as the salt water washed up around her. Wankau, however, said nothing and began plotting to kill Yabok.

They had brought many pigs and canarium almonds from Wogeo, so Wankau decided that, as they were well supplied with food, it would be a good time to build a men's cult house. He sent his followers to cut posts and gather other building materials. When everything was ready, he invited people from many villages to come and carve their distinctive designs on the posts and rafters. The design Yabok made was the same as the one he had tattooed on Wankau's wife, Moger. He said nothing, however, except to compliment Yabok on his excellent craftsmanship.

They then began to dig holes in which to set the house posts. Wankau asked Yabok to dig one of the holes and Yabok complied. He dug and dug, going deeper and deeper. Suspecting that Wankau was laying a trap for him, he also dug himself a hiding place off to the side of the main shaft. After a while Wankau called down to him that the hole was deep enough. Yabok came back up and rested awhile, smoking and chewing betel nut with Wankau. Yabok collected his red spittle from chewing betel in a coconut shell. When they began work again and he went back down into the hole to help set the post properly, he took this coconut shell with him. Once Yabok was down in the hole, Wankau and his helpers tried to crush him with the post, but Yabok slipped safely into the hiding place he had made. He placed the coconut shell of red betel juice in the post hole, and when those above plunged the post down, the red juice spattered about like blood and they were sure they had killed Yabok. They filled the hole around the post with dirt, but Yabok was busy tunneling his way to safety. Soon Wankau and his helpers heard the sound of Yabok's slit gong from higher up the mountain as Yabok beat out the message: "You think you've killed me? You're not man enough."

When the men's cult house was completed, Wankau invited people from many villages to a feast. The new house had two levels. When the food was served, Wankau and his followers ate on the first level while Yabok and his followers were served on the level above. While Yabok and his followers still sat eating, Wankau and his followers stealthily set the house on fire, hoping *to burn the others alive. But the smoke from the fire formed a huge black column and Yabok, with the others holding tight to the tail of his bark loincloth, rose along with the smoke, hidden by the dense black cloud. When the fire had cooled, Wankau searched through the ashes for his brother's bones but could not find them. Instead he once more heard Yabok's slit gong taunting him.*

Some narrators add other incidents, some tell more truncated versions. But in all the versions I heard, one of the brothers, after repeatedly besting the other, leaves the island, never to be heard from again. According to one narrator, it is the elder brother who leaves; in another version it is the younger brother who leaves, but Wankau is the younger and Yabok is the elder. There is also some difference of opinion about whether Wankau and Yabok should be called *masalai*. This Pidgin term is usually used, however, for dangerous supernatural beings associated with particular places in the natural environment, such as a tree, rock, or whirlpool. The best-known masalai on the island is the masalai Kairiru, said to inhabit the lake at the top of the mountain and to have the body of a snake and the head of a man.

The story of Wankau and Yabok illustrates two important points about indigenous beliefs about the supernatural in Kragur. First, the variation in the versions of this particular myth is an example of a general lack of systematization or, to put it more positively, a lack of dogma. While villagers clearly regard a few of their fellows as more knowledgeable about the supernatural, there is no single authoritative doctrine to which all villagers feel they must defer. When I asked them about the supernatural, many would refer me to one or another of the older ramat walap. In Kragur, knowledge of many kinds is zealously guarded personal property, and this militates against systematizing beliefs. There are some myths, for example, that almost everyone knows in part. Others are widely known, but only a few people recognized as more knowledgeable feel free to relate them. At the extreme, it is said that there are myths known only to a few, who will not tell them to anyone. The men's cult is gone, of course, and many young men spend years away from the village as wage laborers, while others spend years in elementary and secondary schools. These circumstances undoubtedly have impeded the transmission of knowledge between generations, and this may have contributed to the variety of idiosyncratic viewpoints one now finds in Kragur.

Nevertheless, I suspect that there has always been great variety in the details of supernatural belief in Kragur, and a proclivity for forming one's own opinions.[1]

Nevertheless, there are some important constants in that variety, and the story of Wankau and Yabok illustrates one of the most fundamental of these. One thing that all versions of the story have in common is that they portray Wankau, like the other protagonists, as very much like a human being, albeit one possessing exceptional powers: he has a brother, he marries, he travels by sail canoe, he builds his own men's cult house. Wankau is also a local being, sailing between Wogeo and Kairiru. According to Moke, Wankau's abode on Kairiru itself is, or was, on an elevation just above Iupulpul, where the warriors gathered before the raid on Chem. It begins to sound as though the equation of Wankau with God, the first being and creator of all things, is somewhat overdrawn, and perhaps stimulated by a desire to find indigenous parallels for the new teachings. It is even possible that early missionaries, eager to translate Catholicism into local terms, may have suggested it.[2]

The point, however, is not just that Kragur people may be trying to fit Wankau into the mold of God, but that they also are fitting God into a more familiar way of thinking of the supernatural. The supernatural world seen from Kragur is very immediate and down-to-earth. Lawrence and Meggit (1972:9; cf. Herdt 1989: 18–20) have written, of Melanesia in general, that: "the realm of the non-empirical is always closely associated with, in most cases part of, the ordinary physical world. It is supernatural only in a limited sense. Its most important representatives . . . are generally said to live on the earth, often near human settlements. Although more powerful than men, they are frequently thought to be able to assume corporeal form. . . . Occult forces are conceived . . . as purely terrestrial." This sounds a great deal like Kragur. The "nonempirical" beings who share the world with Kragur men and women may be petitioned, coerced, and even held in awe and respect. Some enforce norms of behavior. Wankau is said to punish those who break taboos associated with the wood carving he inspires; and the dead punish antisocial behavior in a very partisan way by bringing illness to those who anger their living kin. No indigenous supernaturals, however, appear to represent any principle of supreme morality or abstract good.

The Dead

Wankau, and a number of other mythological figures, performed their major deeds in a vague past era. They play small parts in contemporary human affairs and have human qualities, but their mode of existence in the present is shadowy and ill-defined in comparison with that of the dead. The spirits of the dead—known in the Kairiru language as *ramat shawaung,* shadows or spirits of men—are very immediately and significantly present in the daily world of living men and women. In many Papua New Guinea societies the dead are thought to spend at least part of their time in an afterworld separate but not far distant from the abode of the living. In the Trobriand islands early in the century, for example, the spirits of the dead were said to travel to the small island of Tuma (Malinowski 1954), and on Wogeo island in the 1930s they were said to inhabit an afterworld in the island's central mountains (Hobgin 1970:55). In the Admiralty islands in the 1920s, as described by Fortune, the spirits of the dead remained with the living as guardians and moral watchdogs, until they were dismissed for failure to ward off misfortune. Then, "they were due to haunt the open sea for a while before becoming crabs, sea snakes and the small vermin of the sea" (1965 [1935]:229).

A few Kragur people told me that their ancestors had believed that the spirits of the dead traveled to the same place the sun went when it set in the west. Most admitted no knowledge of an afterworld. A number of villagers, however, told me of their encounters with the dead in the bush or near the village. As Mowush puts it: "There isn't any special place where the dead go, they just wander around. Why is it they just wander around the bush or near the streams? If they have a place to go, then why don't they go there?"[3]

There is no doubt Kragur villagers feel the dead are still with them. I have already described the role they play in illness, curing, and the success of subsistence activities. Villagers assume the presence, involvement, and power of the dead on a wide variety of occasions. The jawbone of a dead person is sometimes used to divine the causes of crop failures or scarcity of fish and game. While accompanying a group of men felling a large tree for a canoe hull I heard them call the names of male and female ancestors, asking them to send a wind from the proper quarter to make the tree fall in the right direction. Out fishing with Brawaung in his small outrigger canoe, I heard him call on his dead mother to ensure our success. Lapim told me of how he repeatedly called on his dead mother for aid when his canoe capsized far from shore and he clung for hours to a buoyant wooden paddle as he swam slowly back to the island. Sakun told me of how, just a few weeks after his father's death, he and his young son went fishing using spear guns homemade from wood, wire, and innertube rubber. His son, he said, was still consumed with sorrow over the loss of his grandfather. He accidentally let fly his wire spear without aiming, and when he retrieved it found it had impaled two fish. The boy's grandfather, Sakun said, must have felt his concern and rewarded him with this good fortune. Sakun also attributes his son's success in school to his dead grandfather's assistance. Once when I lay ill with dengue fever, Taunur came and sat beside me; as I drifted in and out of consciousness, I could hear him calling on his dead mother and father to help me recover.

The dead also play a role in magic. Magic is important in many spheres of life in Kragur. In addition to magic for improving garden crops, hunting, and fishing, there is magic for different stages of long canoe voyages, magic for curing certain kinds of illnesses, love magic to make one irresistible to the object of one's desires, war magic to dull the senses of one's enemy, magic to control the weather, magic to speed the job of roofing a house, magic to ensure that the smoke from the fire in a newly built house will pass out beneath the roof rather than being trapped inside, magic that makes people satisfied with small quantities of food, and a host of other kinds of beneficial magic. There is also malign magic, such as magic to decimate garden crops and magic to cause illness and death—that is, sorcery. To some extent, magic probably is thought to act directly on whatever the practitioner wants to influence. As Malinowski puts it, "between the object and its magic there exists an essential nexus" (1954:75). This is most clearly the case in sorcery, where the magician acts on some cast-off substance of the victim's body. Also, however, Kragur magicians call on the aid of various supernatural beings.[4] A number of kinds of magic for improving food crops, hunting, and fishing are associated with the mythological figure Moger, wife of Wankau in the story of Wankau and Yabok. As Taunur explains it, the magic opens Moger's birth canal and pulls out crops, fish, and game. He is speaking metaphorically, for Taunur is fond of such colorful images, but this female supernatural figure is clearly associated with fertility and its magical restoration. Taunur and others also say that magicians sometimes invoke the aid of certain masalai, like the masalai Kairiru, who gave human beings the magical spell for growing taro. Both important magicians and many rank-and-file villagers agree that the dead are also important. At the very least they are believed to facilitate the working of magic. Taunur, for example, says that when he uses magic he appeals to his dead father, a renowned magician in his own day, to aid him with his superior powers. "Suppose I want to use magic for fish, I think of my father. My thoughts go to his face, his mouth, his voice, tears come to my eyes and I ask him for help. My father has strength; me, a child, I don't have strength." Mer, another prominent magician, says that when he practices his magic he appeals to his dead parents: "Mother, father, look at me. I want to work now, you must help me."

The dead, then, play a variety of important roles in daily life in Kragur and are widely believed to remain at close quarters with the living. I cannot claim, however, that every last villager is a firm believer. Here, as in many things, there are a few skeptics. In this case, the most eloquent skeptic is not a young man or woman who has acquired doubts in Western-style schools. Kwan has had little schooling. He has been blind since childhood, but he is intimately familiar with the paths of the village and its environs and walks them confidently by night as well as by day. Says Kwan: "I always walk around in the middle of the night. I never hear a ghost. Nothing makes a noise in the bush or touches me. During the rains when the nights are completely dark everyone says, 'Oh, now is the time the ghosts walk around.' But I always walk around in the middle of the night and I don't meet anything."

Nevertheless, ghosts or spirits of the dead loom large in most villagers' conceptions of the supernatural. Hence, in their efforts to make sense of newly introduced supernatural beings, villagers sometimes liken both God and the Virgin Mary to their deceased mothers and fathers. Mowush says: "Our ancestors said there wasn't any God. Your dead father and your ancestors were God. These were your God, there wasn't any other God." Today Mowush and many others are not sure just what to make of the missionaries' God, and some find the dead a useful explanation.

Taunur says that his father, Yabok, is his God and that the Virgin Mary, to whom villagers refer as Santu Maria or simply Maria, must simply be the Catholic missionaries' way of speaking of everyone's dead mothers. "We didn't understand, what's Maria? So we thought, Maria is just our [deceased] mothers. The missionaries were speaking in parables." Taunur also speculates that there *is* a single, all-powerful God who resides in heaven, but that people do not call directly on that God but only on their individual fathers and mothers who reside in heaven with God. Lapim opts for a similar but simpler formulation: "Every man has his own God. When I die I'll be the God for my son. He'll call on me whenever he wants to do something. My God is my father."

The Men's Cult

Although Kairiru island villagers no longer have men's cults, the men's cult house is still the most striking feature of many Sepik villages. In some parts of the Sepik these are towering structures, with long, curved rooflines that sweep to heights of seventy or eighty feet. The men's cult is gone from neighboring Mushu island as well, but a photograph taken at the turn of the century by the German explorer Parkinson in Sup village, in the Kairiru-speaking sector of Mushu, shows a more modest but still impressive structure. The Mushu cult house is several times larger than an ordinary dwelling, with a bowed roofline that forms steeply looming gables at each end. The lower part of the bark facade is covered with ornate painted designs. Kairiru island cult houses may have resembled those of Sup. Kragur men old enough to remember say that the cult-house timbers sported carvings representing men killed in warfare and the facade was decorated with paintings of fish, pigs, cassowaries, and other animals.

Intact men's cults of the Sepik area differ widely in their details, but they share some common features. Cult activities are devoted to propitiating a tutelary spirit, known in Pidgin as a *tambaran,* and initiating boys and young men into cult membership and knowledge of the cult secrets. There are usually several grades of membership, each associated with a higher level of knowledge of secret cult ritual. The most basic secret is that key parts of cult ritual are deceptions. Women and uninitiated young men are told

that during cult rituals the tutelary tambaran spirit, often described as a kind of monster with a gargantuan appetite, is actually present inside the ceremonial house. They are told that the
noises issuing from the house—in fact made by slit gongs, large
bamboo flutes, and bull roarers—are the sounds of the tambaran
itself; and they are told that the large quantities of food that the
women bring to the cult house during rituals, food that is actually
consumed by the men, is consumed by the insatiable tambaran.
Moke says that in his youth, when a village man died, the initiated
men of the cult would pull down coconut palms in the village during the night and tell the women that this was the work of the tambaran, angry at the loss of one of its acolytes.

Men's cults aid in maintaining the established hierarchy in a
community. Denying women and uninitiated men access to the
secrets of what are held to be essential rituals helps maintain the
dominance of men over women and age over youth (Keesing
1982:25–27; Tuzin 1976:296). Yet, the tambaran often is seen as
a tutelary spirit not simply of the initiated men but of the entire
community. Tuzin, for example, observes that among the Ilahita
Arapesh, a Sepik people of the mainland interior, the ideology of
the tambaran cult "views human survival as dependent on the
Tambaran spirits," and the perpetuation of the cult is aided by the
belief that the tambaran spirits "must be propitiated if they are to
continue their favors" (1976:279). Further, the success of the ritual depends on community harmony and when achieved "is exhil-
arating because it implies that the ideal of community unity has
been achieved and that the harsher realities of everyday existence
can be faced with renewed confidence" (1990:367–368).

Several Kragur men who were in their fifties and sixties in 1976
were among the last group of youths to be initiated into the men's
cult in Kragur, and some remember helping to build a cult house
when they were boys. Apparently, however, the cult was abandoned before they could pass beyond the first initiatory level and
gain full knowledge of the cult ritual. The break in the oral and
ceremonial tradition has left little to say about the particulars of
the men's cult in Kragur (cf. Tuzin 1980:126–127). I was told that
there were actually three cult houses in the village. One, called
Manburi, was a village-wide cult, closely articulated with the dual
division of the village and the system of marriage, as noted in
Chapter 2. Men of koyeng Shewaratin, however, told me that

there were also two cult houses involving only men of the Seksik division, on whose ground they stood. One, called Ranbok, belonged to koyeng Ku, and another, called Belokayo, belonged to koyeng Shewaratin.

However many distinct cult houses there were in Kragur, the men's cult as an institution was abandoned around 1930 at the behest of Brigil, the mission's first emissary to Kragur. Contemporary accounts of who supported Brigil and who resisted him differ. Some who are deeply involved in Catholicism tell the story as though there was little dissension. A number of older men, however, say that their fathers, the higher-level initiates of the cult, spoke against Brigil, but the younger men were indifferent and the cult leaders finally gave in. Given the role the cult undoubtedly played in subordinating younger men, and all women, to the older men, it would not be surprising if the former had been attracted by a less exclusive alternative system of religious practice.[5] The cult houses were not destroyed, but the women and children were shown the sacred flutes and other secret ceremonial objects and were told that it was the men themselves who made the tambaran spirit noises and ate the spirit's food. Villagers say that, before this, initiates were forbidden on pain of death from revealing the secret of the flutes, and a woman unfortunate enough to have seen the flutes inadvertently would have been killed. No one, however, could recall such an incident.

Demystification of men's cults continues in many parts of the Sepik. There are still many communities where the ceremonial paraphernalia remain the secrets of male initiates; but in Wewak one can now buy quick knock-offs of men's cult flutes in curio stores that cater to tourists. Once, while I was visiting Wewak, a man from a mainland village offered to sell me an apparently genuine men's cult flute decorated with a skillful carving of a woman bearing on her back an animal with the head of a pig and the body of a bird. He said he was selling it to raise money to pay his council tax. The Kragur flutes, slit gongs, and other cult objects met their end quite differently. Although the cult rituals were abandoned, the cult houses were left standing; but they and their contents burned to the ground along with the rest of the village when it was set ablaze by Allied bombs during the war.[6]

When they speak of the vanished men's cult, some Kragur men laugh at the deceptions perpetrated on the women and the dire threats made to keep them from learning the cult secrets.[7] For many, it seems that whatever reality the tambaran spirits may have had in the past has faded completely. They speak of the cult only as an occasion for enjoyable music and ceremony and a way of tricking the women into preparing huge feasts. This sounds like Hogbin's description of attitudes toward the tambaran spirits of the men's cult on Wogeo in the 1930s (1970:58): "The men when by themselves deny that such creatures exist . . . they are to be regarded by the initiated as . . . a deliberate invention whose dual purpose is to facilitate the accumulation of food before a feast and to serve as a means of keeping the women in their proper place." But Hogbin also finds that in the midst of the rituals the men seem to take it all very seriously. Tuzin finds a similar quality of belief among the cult leaders of the Ilahita Arapesh (1976:278):

> Though they are aware that the incarnate [tambaran spirit] does not attend their feasts, and that this part of cult ritual is a deception, they are not to be dismissed as cynical agnostics. They genuinely adhere to a belief in the mystic reality of [the tambaran spirit], but consider that the rest of society requires something in the way of tangible "proof." This they contrive through elaborate stage effects used when [the tambaran spirit] is said to be visiting the village.

Some mixture of cynicism and ingenuous belief is probably common in attitudes toward religious practices and institutions in many places. There are occasions on which cynicism is possible and occasions on which, in the midst of enacting the mysteries, belief in the fundamental reality behind the stage effects comes to the fore. In Kragur, however, cynicism toward the men's cult has been reinforced by mission teachings, and the ritual, with its power to compel belief, has been abandoned.

Nevertheless, there are still some who speak of the defunct men's cult without disparagement. Many of the older men wax nostalgic when they recount their memories of the excitement and pageantry of the cult. Their nostalgia is not only for the music, the feasting, and the ceremonial. It is also for what they now see as the power of the cult ritual to bring well-being to the village. Some of the mystique the men's cult holds for those who can remember it is captured in a story Moke tells of a men's cult house built by some of the mythical first human inhabitants of Kairiru.

Moke says that the first human beings on Kairiru lived at Arai, a site on the mountainside not far above the present site of Kragur. There they built a men's cult house called Bakur. Inside Bakur were two slit gongs named Lobai and Saketak. These were not ordinary slit gongs, for it was not necessary for men to play them. When the men of Arai assembled in the house to sing and play their *kundus*—Pidgin for hourglass-shaped hand drums—two bamboo poles would miraculously descend from the ceiling and play the slit gongs without human assistance. The music from Bakur drew fish, pigs, and other game straight to the cult house. Other villages, however, became jealous of the miraculous cult house and the two marvelous slit gongs. When the men of Arai refused to teach them their secrets, the other villages banded together and made war on Arai, eventually destroying Bakur, Lobai, and Saketak. With their loss, the people of Arai also lost the knowledge and power to almost effortlessly ensure material plenty.[8]

Moke says that if the other villages had not made war on Arai, people today would still have that power. He attributes no such miraculous powers to the men's cult of his boyhood, but he speaks with similar regret of the loss of knowledge of the Kragur cult rituals. "We don't know. If our fathers were here they could teach us. But we children don't know. Now, all we know about is the rosary and prayer. We're ignorant of all the things of our ancestors. We could still build [a cult house], but who would do the work inside?"

Kragur Catholicism: Getting Things to Fit

Moke is exaggerating when he says that Kragur people now know nothing but prayer and the rosary. It is true, however, that Catholicism plays a very visible role in daily life in Kragur. My house stood on the edge of the clear space in the center of the village. Almost every evening the primary-school children are gathered here for prayers and hymn singing. The adults follow later, drifting in one by one and sitting about on stones and mats made from the barklike leafstalks of the sago palm until one of the leaders of Catholic religious life calls them to assemble for prayers in front of the small wooden altar to the Virgin Mary. It would be almost impossible to live anywhere in Kragur without coming across visible evidence of Catholicism. Some villagers display pictures of the Virgin or Jesus in their houses. Many pause to cross themselves before eating. Attendance at evening prayers is highly variable, but almost everyone turns out for Sunday morning services, usually led by Ibor, Kragur's strongest proponent of Catholicism. Villagers participate actively in the service. They recite the responsive prayers from memory with vigor, and they sing Pidgin hymns energetically, also from memory. Only a few young people own and use Pidgin hymn and prayer books. The women sit on low log benches left of the aisle, and the men sit on the right. The older women sing the hymns in the style of indigenous vocal music, and their strident, keening voices almost drown out everyone else.

Villagers also celebrate Catholic holidays. Many walk to St. Xavier's for the Christmas Eve mass held there. They stay overnight, camping out in the vacant student dormitories, and walk back to the village on Christmas day. This takes some dedication, because they are accustomed to sleeping in comfort in Kragur, where the precipitous terrain and exposure to the open sea keep the village relatively free of mosquitoes. A night without mosquito nets at St. Xavier's—on the flatter, wetter coast of Kairiru—can be miserable for north-coast islanders. Also, as Christmas falls during the rainy season, the trip back and forth to St. Xavier's can be an uncomfortable exercise in mud and drizzle. Easter in 1976 found almost everyone from Kragur at the primary school in neighboring Bou village, where an American priest from the mainland came to give a mass. For All Souls Day, Kragur villagers decorated their two European-style cemeteries, the larger one at the east end of the village and a smaller one at the west end, with split and feathered palm fronds. Virtually everyone turned out for a procession to the cemeteries, led by a young man holding aloft a crucifix fastened to a pole, where Ibor led them in prayers.

Kragur people often claim to be especially loyal and active Catholics. As Kanau, an older man, puts it, "We're number one in the eyes of the mission." There is some basis for this claim to distinction. Although almost all Kairiru people probably would identify themselves as Catholics, not all villages have their own church buildings as Kragur does. Nor do they all have, like Kragur, active chapters of the Legion of Mary. Kragur's proprietorship of the statue of the Virgin near the top of the mountain is certainly unique. Indigenous priests and brothers or nuns are still novelties in Papua New Guinea, but Kragur has produced one priest—Taunur's adopted son, Yabok, only the second indigenous priest in the Wewak diocese—and a Marist brother—Kanau's son, Pawil. Besides Ibor, three other Kragur men have worked as catechists in mission primary schools in other parts of Papua New Guinea.

Despite all the visible involvement in Catholicism, some aspects of the mission teachings have been more difficult to assimilate than others. Many villagers find the notions of heaven and hell a little perplexing. Ibor speaks with evident conviction about the dangers of hell, sometimes called *bikfaia* (big fire) in Pidgin, and the rewards of heaven. "There's no hard work there," he says of heaven, "you just sit and think about whatever you want and everything you want appears without effort." In contrast, hell is a place where you have to work hard. Others speak of more exotic forms of suffering. Taunur says that the early missionaries told them that hell is a place of eternal fire where there is no water; when the condemned cry out for water, the virtuous urinate on them from somewhere above. Many villagers, however, are skeptical of both the warning and the promise. Some wonder if the foreign priests have ever actually seen heaven. Villagers can repeat what they have heard of heaven and hell, but many admit they are not sure what to think about it. Many would agree with Misiling, a woman of koyeng Ku, who says: "We don't know about these things. That's just what people say." Since there appears to be no indigenous notion of reward or punishment in an afterlife, it is not surprising that villagers are noncommittal about the ideas of heaven and hell.

Some also have problems with the idea of sin, called *pekato* in Pidgin, following the Latin once used by the mission. Ibor frequently speaks about sin in Sunday church services, but some still find the idea inscrutable. Mowush, who himself once worked as a catechist, says he has asked priests to explain sin to him, but they could not. He has decided that sin is just "a word for making people afraid. If they call people for prayers, they speak of sin so that people will be afraid and go. They've given this word power. If I write a letter to someone I can say, 'You've done something wrong to me.' That's the right way to speak. You can't use this word *sin*."

In the indigenous view, plenty of bad things can happen to you if you violate the norms of proper behavior. If you make people

angry, they may use sorcery to retaliate, or, more likely, the ghosts
of their dead kin may make you ill or ruin your hunting, fishing,
and gardening. One also has to be careful in dealing with powerful
supernatural beings. If, for example, a man invokes Wankau to
aid him in carving a garamut, when he finishes he must use the
proper ritual to remove Wankau's power from himself and his
tools. If someone were to use the tools later without such ritual
cleansing, they might be afflicted with severe boils or sores. Also,
like people everywhere, Kragur villagers are concerned with their
reputations. They like others to think of them as good men and
women, quite apart from the need to keep social relations running
smoothly in order to maintain material well-being. Sin, however,
is not just an intended or unintended offense against other men
and women or carelessness in dealing with powerful supernatural
beings. Sin is also an offense against a distant and poorly understood supreme moral arbiter, God.

If one has to understand God to understand sin, it is not surprising that many find sin puzzling. Ibor speaks of God with apparent
confidence and says that in the past when people called on their
dead kin for help it was really God who responded; but he is one
of a very few who seem to find it easy to replace familiar supernaturals with God. Describing how his dead mother sometimes comes
to him at night and tells him where to find game, Mowush says:
"[God] is different, because you can't see God, you can't see his
face. Your mother and father, you've seen their faces. This is what
makes it [God] so hard to understand."

Unless they have decided that God is just a new name for familiar supernaturals, villagers find it hard to imagine a being so distant and relatively abstract taking an interest in their daily conduct, keeping a tally of their offenses, and punishing them
accordingly. When Paypai, an ordinarily robust young man in his
twenties, fell ill, a few suggested that his illness was punishment
for a pekato committed by one of his close female kin. It was
rumored that she had been unfaithful to her husband. Advocates
of the sin hypothesis argued that this was a violation of one of the
Ten Commandments—in Pidgin, the *Tenpela Mandato*—and this
sin or pekato had brought illness on her kinsman Paypai. This was
a novel diagnosis, and in the end it did not sway most of those
involved in the curing meetings. Mansu, the village councillor, and
his wife, Kelmiai, sat with me one night while we waited for eve-

ning prayers to begin and Mansu explained why he found the sin diagnosis implausible. "Dispela sik i luk olosem i no gat papa bilongen," he said in Pidgin. Literally, this means the illness has no father; but what Mansu means is that, according to the sin hypothesis, no one is responsible for this illness. Mansu pointed out that if illness is caused by anger or sorcery, there is a "father," someone responsible. "Illness," he went on, "doesn't happen for no reason. It has to have a father or a mother." In his view, God apparently is too distant and impersonal to be responsible, and sin itself less satisfying an explanation than the anger or ill will of human beings.

Other aspects of Catholicism, however, appear to have been assimilated more easily. While they may have their doubts about God, many villagers seem to have adopted the habit of prayer with relative ease. The communal prayer sessions almost every evening are not entirely voluntary. There is a good deal of social pressure to participate at least occasionally. The councillor lends his influence to that of Ibor and the Legion of Mary. Some grumble about the nightly ringing of the village bell and the occasional shouted admonitions to leave their houses and hurry to the clear space for prayers. Nevertheless, I never heard villagers puzzle over the nature of prayer as some did over the nature of heaven, hell, God, and sin. Ibor himself articulates a view of prayer that, if widely held, would explain this. Ibor once told me that magical spells, or bos in the Kairiru tongue, were "like the prayer of New Guineans." He continued: "What is prayer? It's just speaking. We speak and something results. It [bos] is just like prayer." This appears to be a variation on the common view that human physical efforts alone are not enough to accomplish material goals; supernatural power is also necessary, and human beings bring this to bear on their endeavors through speaking magical spells. "Samting i kamap long maus bilong man tasol," as it is phrased in Pidgin—"Only the speech of men can make things happen."

Ibor presents prayer as a new kind of magic, readily available to all. I have heard villagers pray in their own words, but the most common form of prayer is recitation of the rosary. Ibor preaches that it is important for everyone to be able to repeat the rosary accurately so that, in case of an emergency, such as being adrift at sea, they can call on the Virgin for aid. Much prayer, then, is formulaic, like magical spells; and in magic, reciting the spell and

performing the ritual correctly are more important than understanding exactly how this is translated into effects on one's environment.

Most prayer in Kragur is addressed, not to God, but to the Virgin Mary, a figure whom villagers appear to find more understandable and accessible.[9] The Virgin is by far the most important
of the Christian supernaturals in Kragur, if one judges by how
often people speak of her and how often people appeal to her for
aid. This is probably due in large part to the prominence of the
Legion of Mary in Kragur Catholicism. Most of the foreign mission personnel I spoke with on Kairiru and in Wewak had little
interest in the Legion of Mary. During the 1950s and the 1960s,
however, two foreign priests, absent from the area since the early
1970s, had promoted the Legion throughout the East Sepik Province. The Legion in general is devoted to spiritual improvement
and social service. As its name implies, its organization is based on
the hierarchies of the ancient Roman legions, with appropriate
Latin titles for its levels and functionaries. This aspect is not pronounced at the village level, although some Legion members do
speak of a hierarchy of Legion personnel that leads all the way to
the pope. The Kragur Legion has four or five members, including
Ibor. Their main concern is encouraging devotion to the Virgin
and attendance at Catholic observances. They take a head count
at evening prayers and at Sunday services and report to Ibor at
weekly Legion meetings following the Sunday service. These
attendance records are eventually passed on to the bishop's office
in Wewak, although foreign mission personnel now seem to have
little interest in them. In the village, however, the Legion treats full
and regular attendance at frequent religious observances as the
keynote of Catholicism and a prime imperative of Catholic
morality.

Why has the Virgin Mary caught on so well in Kragur? A
female supernatural well may have especially strong associations
with fertility and material prosperity. Although Kragur society is
strongly patriarchal, villagers recognize the primary role women
play in food production, especially in gardening. When describing
their way of life to me, both men and women often said that
although they had no stores as the whites did, their gardens were
their stores, and the women were the clerks, or *cuscus* in Pidgin.
Forging a broader association, some say in Pidgin that *ologeta*

samting i kamap long meri—that is, "all things come from women." Some villagers evoke this association to explain the prohibitions on sexual intercourse that are part of the magical ritual for increasing the productivity of foodstuffs of all kinds, the fish and game that men contribute as well as garden produce. To have intercourse, says Taunur, blocks the birth canal and "closes the road" of the abundance the magic seeks.

A few villagers draw a parallel between the Virgin Mary and the mythical figure of Moger, who is associated with some kinds of gardening magic. But although Moger appears in mythology as an adultress, the Virgin Mary's sexual purity is a key aspect of her nature in villagers' eyes. In the indigenous view, sexual intercourse not only robs magical ritual of its power, aspects of sexuality pose more direct threats to material well-being. For example, contact—either direct or indirect—with a menstruating woman or a woman who has recently given birth is held to cause such afflictions as shortness of breath and failing eyesight. Similarly, menstruating women are prohibited from going to gardens, because it would cause the plants to become diseased. A number of older men told me that too frequent intercourse and excessive loss of semen caused premature aging, and some added that too early and too frequent sexual intercourse prevented young men from achieving their full adult physical stature.

There are obvious parallels between indigenous notions about the dangers of sexuality and elements of Catholic religious practice. For example, the celibacy of brothers, nuns, and priests is reminiscent of the prohibitions that magical practitioners must observe. Similarly, most of those with whom I discussed the story of Adam and Eve saw intercourse itself as the original sin. As Ibor tells the story, prior to their sin Adam and Eve had only to desire something to obtain it. Even the effort of childbirth was unnecessary, for children arose without human effort as Adam and Eve themselves had. But when Adam and Eve first engaged in intercourse, they lost their power to create things effortlessly, and work and effort became their lot and that of their descendants. So did death, because eternal life was also theirs in their presexual state. Ibor says that human beings lost God's grace in the Garden of Eden, and to lose grace was to lose the power to create abundance effortlessly. "If we had grace, " he says, "we would only have to think of things in order to obtain them." Like magicians, Adam and Eve had the power to bring forth material plenty so long as they suppressed their own fertility.

Other factors, however, may be equally important in Kragur's Mariolatry. For one thing, the Virgin is a supernatural being with very human characteristics. Like deceased mothers and fathers, she has a face that villagers have seen in pictures and, now, on the statue that stands on the trail over the mountain. Following a theme found in Catholicism throughout the world, Ibor preaches that the Virgin acts as an intermediary between human beings and God. However abstract and dimly conceived God may be, the Virgin is a figure cut more to human scale.

Interest in the Virgin was running high during my first visit to Kragur because 1976 was the year of the statue. According to villagers, one of the priests responsible for promoting the Legion had set the statue project in motion before leaving the Sepik area. Other mission personnel with whom I spoke, including the bishop, knew little of the project—where the statue came from, why Kairiru had been chosen to receive it, and who had proposed the project. Whatever the case, the statue arrived on Kairiru, via the *Tau-K,* in a heavy packing crate early in 1976. The original plan was for Kairiru villagers to carry it to all the island's villages for prayer services before erecting it near the top of the mountain; but the crated statue proved too cumbersome. Instead, it was simply slung from a heavy pole and carried to the highest point on the trail across the mountain. The statue, which stands about five feet tall and represents the Virgin praying, was erected on a platform of concrete donated by the mission. The ground around it was cleared and bordered with crotons and other ornamental plants. Kragur people took the lead in erecting the statue and in preparing for the dedication ceremony held in April. They built a long table of bush materials to hold the large quantities of food that people from several villages brought to the ceremony and decorated the table and the area around the statue with split palm fronds and ornamental leaves and fruits. The parish priest came to Kairiru to give a mass in front of the statue on the day of its dedication. I imagine that Kragur people played the major role in all this largely because of Ibor's vocal involvement in affairs of the mission far beyond the village. In any event, since its dedication Kragur people have taken responsibility for caring for the grounds around the statue, and many think of it as theirs.

Making Catholicism Their Own

When I first arrived in Kragur I saw so much evidence of the influence of Catholicism that I could easily have believed it had successfully taken over the village. As I learned more of villagers' beliefs and saw how they had created ways of understanding Catholicism with a distinctively local flavor, it became apparent that in many ways the villagers had taken over Catholicism (cf. Gostin 1986: 107–120). This appropriation of Catholicism goes beyond the reinterpretation I have been discussing. For one thing, many claim that they knew about God long before the first missionaries came to the village. Virtually everyone in Kragur is familiar with the story of how, before the first missionaries came, God spoke to Masos, Taunur's paternal grandfather and Ibor's maternal great-grandfather. Sometime around the turn of the century, Masos was at the place called Sumulau, where one of Kairiru's many streams passes near the village. He was sharpening his stone knife on a large boulder while his small granddaughter, who grew up to be Ibor's mother, played in the water. Suddenly, his hands stuck fast to the rock. He feared this was the work of a masalai, so he sent his granddaughter running back to the village to tell people to bring gifts for the masalai so that it would free him. When she returned—accompanied by men bringing bananas, coconuts, and shell rings—Masos was already free. Masos told them that after the little girl had run away, a voice spoke to him, saying it was the voice of God who lived above in the sky. God then gave him a set of instructions to convey to the other people of the village and told him that he wanted to bless Kragur so it would prosper. God's instructions were that villagers should sweep well inside their houses and burn all their old and decaying bark mats, fiber skirts, bark-cloth loincloths, and string bags, and put on new skirts and loincloths. Some who tell the story, including Ibor, add that God also said they should not steal or fight among themselves, and when strangers came to the village they should not kill them but give them food and shelter and treat them well.

By the time the first mission personnel, indigenous catechists, showed up in Kragur, Masos was dead. But, as a number of villagers told me, Kragur people were able to tell the missionaries that they already knew about God. Some say that not everyone had believed Masos' story, but when the missionaries came and spoke of God, many of the skeptics decided Masos had been telling the truth.[10] This independent relationship to God is important to many Kragur villagers, even those most deeply involved with the external Catholic hierarchy. Ibor, for example, has served the mission as a catechist in other parts of Papua New Guinea and is probably more orthodox in his personal beliefs than most other Kragur people. Yet even he pointed out to me that I should be familiar with the Masos story so I would not think that in his preaching he was just parroting the mission.

Many villagers look even further into the past to establish an independent claim to Catholicism. They do this by claiming a kind of moral superiority for Kragur that is reminiscent of themes in mission teachings, and by maintaining that this superiority has its roots deep in the past, long before Masos. Some clearly imply that God appeared in Kragur and Catholicism took hold there because it was already a morally superior place.

Chapuan, an older Kragur man, voices a common sentiment when he says: "Other villages aren't equal to us, their ways aren't good. We Kragur people have good ways." He goes on to point out that "our ways came from our ancestors, to our fathers, to the present day." When Chapuan and others talk about the village's good ways they have several things in mind. One of these is Kragur's allegedly unique hospitality to all visitors. According to Tarakam, "with us, if people come from far away, we give them food and sit and talk with them. In lots of other villages, a visitor can't expect anything unless he already knows someone in the village." Others say that if a boat arrives and stands offshore waiting for canoes to come out and ferry passengers and cargo to the beach, in Kragur people will hurry to their assistance. In contrast, in many other villages, the boat will be left to wait, sometimes until it gives up and leaves. If someone finally does help the waiting boat, he will probably ask to be paid, while Kragur people ask nothing in return. People usually say all comers can expect hospitality, but many point out that priests, brothers, sisters, and white people are especially fond of Kragur because they are so well received there.

Another of Kragur's good ways is said to be the village's unusual degree of internal harmony. Tarakam says that in some other Kairiru villages with which he is familiar—he names three on the other side of the island—"when they do the council work, or work in some kind of business, they don't work together. Each person works alone; that's hard. But we're different." And Sogum says that when people build houses in other villages, the villagers do not pool their resources to provide the food that custom demands be served to all who help at the end of each day's work. Instead, they wait for the owner of the house to accumulate the necessary food for each stage of building, so it takes forever to finish the job. Half-finished houses in other villages "stand until the timbers start to rot," he says. Sogum concludes: "We're different. All the other villages talk about our good ways." Many villagers also told me, usually while we were drinking beer at some special event, that when people in other villages drink they usually get into fights with each other. They admitted that sometimes one or two Kragur men get belligerent when they drink; but, they said, the others always restrain them. Once when I sat drinking with a group of men late into the night, Sogum explained to me how fortunate I was to be living in Kragur. If I were living in some other villages, he said, naming a near neighbor and a village on the other side of the island, the people not only would fight among themselves when they drank, they probably would beat me up as well. Many villagers also claim that during the Japanese occupation the Japanese executed a number of people in other Kairiru villages because fellow villagers accused them of stealing or other crimes in order to settle old scores. In contrast, no one was executed in Kragur.

Kragur people sometimes sum up some of their alleged special virtues by saying that, to use the Pidgin terms, they *harim tok* and they do not *bikhet*. Narrowly construed, to harim tok is to obey orders or instructions and to bikhet is to ignore orders or instructions. People usually, however, use these terms to refer to larger virtues. More broadly construed, to harim tok is to cooperate not only with authority but with the group as a whole, and to bikhet is to be selfishly individualistic. To cooperate willingly in council work or communal copra production and to appear regularly and punctually at meetings or religious services is to harim tok. Extending hospitality to visitors and going to the aid of arriving boats are also ways to harim tok. Not to cooperate willingly or aid visitors is to bikhet. Practicing sorcery or other forms of malign magic is a more serious way to bikhet. As I will discuss at greater length later on, Kragur villagers have some doubts about how truly cooperative and harmonious they are, that is, about whether

they harim tok enough within the village. There is wide agreement, however, that with respect to outsiders and external institutions they harim tok exceptionally well. Beyond extending hospitality to the rare lone traveler, they point to their loyalty to the
Catholic mission as an example. As old Kanau puts it, "Whatever
they ask of us, we hurry to help them." Kragur people also pride
themselves on their readiness to help the primary school build
classrooms and houses for the teachers and maintain the grounds.
More than this, they are proud of the exceptional success of Kragur young people in school, and many ascribe this to the cooperative attitude of Kragur students. Students from other villages,
some say, do not do as well in school because they do not harim
tok, and they do not harim tok because their parents have set them
bad examples.

All these virtues, many claim, have come down to present-day
villagers from their remote ancestors. Mansu, for example, says of
the people of Arai, where the wondrous men's cult house Bakur is
said to have stood, that "they were good people, they didn't fight."
This and some other claims to moral uniqueness do not square
easily with some of the facts of Kragur's history—for example, the
bloody raid on Chem—or with some contemporary attitudes and
behavior. For one thing, the strong sense of autonomy that in part
motivates Kragur people's claims to moral superiority and a premissionary knowledge of God sometimes makes it hard to harim
tok. For example, Kragur people took an active part in an island-
wide movement in the early 1970s to refuse to pay the yearly
council tax as a protest against the Wewak-But Local Government
Council's alleged neglect of the offshore islands. Those who told
me of this were proud that Kragur saw the tax strike through to its
conclusion whereas some other villages, they said, capitulated at
the first sign of adversity. I have also seen Kragur people become
embroiled in disputes with the local primary-school teachers and
be less than perfectly hospitable to visiting priests.

Villagers themselves sometimes seem to take their claims to
moral uniqueness with a grain of salt. Several men who were visiting on my veranda one evening noted that I often did not lock my
door when I left the house. They suggested I do so because, as one
of them put it, "not everyone here is good." Some villagers can
look at Kragur quite analytically when speaking of its special
qualities. Taunur says that when he visits a certain mainland vil-

lage with which he is familiar, "I tell them: 'Your ways aren't good. You think of nothing but money.' " He reflects, however, that "Kragur people are just the same, only they don't have a way to get to the market. If they did, they'd be just the same." Nevertheless, most villagers, including Taunur, feel that their good ways also reflect something deeper.

There is evidence that Kragur's especially good ways are not all talk. A Department of Agriculture, Stock and Fisheries patrol that visited Kairiru in 1974 reported that they found "the people from southern parts . . . not very willing to cooperate," while those on the northern side of the island, Kragur's side, were "more effective in assisting the patrol," gave the members of the patrol "kindly treatments [sic]," provided them with food, and were attentive to the patrol's educational efforts. Area mission personnel often are not inclined to single out particular villages for either praise or criticism. When I asked one priest who knew the village what he thought of Kragur, he only replied, "Well, they're not saints." Another priest, however, spontaneously spoke of Kragur as "a real stronghold of Catholicism. [There is] something in that place," he went on, "which produces a type of man that is very devout and loyal." A nun from another parish who visited Kragur briefly during my stay was most impressed by what she saw of the Catholic religious life there and went away convinced of villagers' single-minded devotion to the Virgin Mary. The headmaster of St. Xavier's High School, a Marist brother, felt that the people of Kragur had a particularly "good attitude," manifest in their interest in education and the cooperativeness and enthusiasm shown by students from Kragur. From 1963 through 1976 Kragur did send a greater percentage of its male population to school at St. Xavier's than any of the other larger Kairiru villages on which I could obtain information.[11] Since high school education in Papua New Guinea is not free and entry is competitive, the number of young people from a village who attend high school does reflect a community's attitude to some extent. Finally, although I witnessed plenty of disputes and much dissension within Kragur, my own observations of drinking there confirm villagers' claims. With only a few exceptions, Kragur people tend to become more rather than less convivial and hospitable when they drink.

Although Kragur villagers speak of their good ways as rooted deep in the past, many of the special virtues Kragur people claim could be seen as adaptations of the teachings of missionaries and colonial administrators. Certainly the Catholic mission and every secular colonial power have encouraged hospitality to strangers and cooperation with external institutions. Suppressing indigenous warfare and creating a social climate in which both indigenous people and Europeans could travel freely without fear for their lives were major goals of secular colonial administrations. Missionaries also preached the Christian ethics of peace and charity, discouraged hostilities among indigenous communities, and encouraged the hospitable reception of mission personnel and other whites. A pre–World War II manual for those being trained as indigenous catechists at St. Xavier's admonishes them to respect all visiting whites, often referred to in Pidgin as *masta,* greet them cordially, give them directions or any other information they require, and provide food, water, and firewood. The manual also notes that the catechist should not display anger at a white person's bad behavior, but leave correction of abuses in the hands of the mission and the colonial government.

More recent mission literature sounds a similar theme. Several Kragur villagers have copies of the *Buk Bilong Beten end [sic] Sing Sing Bilong Ol Katolik,* the Pidgin version of the *Prayer Book and Hymnal for Catholic Natives of New Guinea,* printed in 1968. The book contains lists of questions one should ask oneself about observing the Ten Commandments in preparing for confession. Concerning the fourth commandment, the commandment to honor one's father and mother, the *Buk Bilong Beten* suggests that one ask if one has disobeyed or been angry with one's father, mother, or "master," an anglicized version of the Pidgin term *masta.* This last term can refer narrowly to one's employer, but villagers use it more often to refer to white people in general. At least some contemporary mission personnel encourage harmony among indigenous people as well as with outsiders in general and whites in particular. On one occasion, for example, an American priest came to the north shore of Kairiru to perform a mass at Bou primary school. As people from several area villages lined up to receive the Sacrament, the priest admonished them, in Pidgin, that when people gathered for worship and approached the altar, they should not harbor anger against anyone.

Many villagers, however, argue that Kragur's special qualities are deeply rooted in the precontact past. They can do so without straining credulity because there are real continuities. Their alleged hospitality is reminiscent of the role of gift-giving in indigenous society. Their claimed internal harmony reflects the indigenous ideal of conflict-free social relations as the foundation of material well-being. The harmony demanded during Catholic ritual is also said to have been a condition for successful performance of men's cult ritual (cf. Brison 1991; Tuzin 1990). Villagers have found enough similarities between indigenous beliefs and practices and the teachings of Catholicism to be able not only to live with the new religion, although it remains puzzling in many respects, but also to embrace it without denying the value of their own traditions or sacrificing their independence.

Catholicism's teachings undoubtedly have colored contemporary interpretations of indigenous values and practices. I doubt that Kragur villagers were as much like good Catholics, as they define this, before European contact as some claim they were. More likely, the kind of Catholicism presented to Kragur villagers has probably intensified concern with some issues of indigenous importance. While pre-mission notions of hospitality and community harmony may not have been exactly like those encouraged by Catholicism, the latter resonate with long-standing concerns about the importance of good social relations to material well-being. I suspect villagers have been strongly influenced by these aspects of Catholicism because of such resonance, and that concern about issues of good social relations not only has taken on a slightly new flavor but has also heightened. It has heightened because the Catholicism they know harps on similar themes, and because this Catholicism has been a major element in Kragur peoples' efforts to find their way in the radically new world of the postcontact era, a world in which villagers' goodness has been called into question.

Embracing Catholicism: Great Hopes, Limited Opportunities

When villagers who were children at the time talk about the Catholic mission's early forays to Kragur, many say that the younger men were more enthusiastic about casting in the village's lot with Catholicism than were their elders. This makes good sense, since

the older men controlled the men's cult and the cult strengthened
their authority over the younger men and the women. Accordingly, the younger men may have seen in Catholicism a way of
diminishing the authority of their elders. Many say the older men
spoke against abandoning the men's cult. The village as a whole,
however, eventually acquiesced to the mission's demands and
plunged into a long and active involvement with Catholicism.

Given the difficulty many villagers still have with some of the
major ideas of Catholicism and the way early missionaries in Kragur attacked such indigenous institutions as the men's cult, this
seems a bit strange at first glance.[12] But it was not just Catholicism
that Kragur people embraced in the early decades of this century.
In those years the Catholic mission was the major representative of
colonial European society on Kairiru and in the surrounding
region. That society displayed material goods of all sorts—sailing
vessels, firearms, new types of food, novel arrays of tools—in
impressive quantities. What Kragur people learned of European
society in the era immediately following first direct contacts they
learned largely through their experiences working on mission
plantations and as crewmen on mission vessels. Many must have
seen Catholicism as virtually identical with European society, its
wealth and power. Given the importance of magical ritual and
knowledge in creating wealth and gaining power in indigenous
Kragur society, in the early years villagers may have seen Catholicism, with its elaborate ritual and new teachings about the supernatural, as the magical basis of the European way of life. To be
Catholic, then, was to possess the generative core of European
wealth and power. Some missionaries may have fostered such an
impression deliberately, but this may not have been necessary.
Today, many villagers still look to the Catholic mission and Catholic schools for guidance in the new world that has engulfed them
since first European contact. These institutions continue to be
among Kragur's most important links to the world beyond the
island.

Involvement with Catholicism is very common in Papua New
Guinea. In 1975–1976, extrapolating from the 1966 national census, Catholicism was the single most popular denomination
among the 90 percent of Papua New Guineans taking part in the
census who identified themselves as Christians (Firth 1975:347),
and some 70 percent of the residents of the East Sepik Province

claimed membership in the Catholic church (Bureau of Statistics 1966, cited in Huber 1988). But Kragur's particularly noticeable involvement with Catholicism merits explanation. Taunur is probably right when he speculates that Kragur's isolation has allowed one of its good ways, the people's noncommercial attitude, to flourish. That isolation also helps to account for Kragur's intense involvement with Catholicism. The obstacles separating Kragur from urban and commercial centers from the beginning of the colonial era have limited villagers' opportunities to participate in the larger social, political, and economic life of colonial and postcolonial Papua New Guinea. A 1974 government study of economic growth in the East Sepik District, as it was then called, speaks of all the islands lying offshore from Wewak as "disadvantaged," for they do not possess "some of the social and economic benefits which are currently enjoyed by larger numbers of people on the mainland" (Philpott et al.:54). Lying on the seaward coast of Kairiru, Kragur and neighboring villages are particularly disadvantaged, because transportation to and from the mainland is even more infrequent here than on the southern coast. As noted earlier, Kairiru's rugged terrain, especially on the north coast, has severly limited islanders' opportunities in commercial agriculture.

Other villages on the precipitous seaward side of Kairiru, however, suffer from similar handicaps, and one well might wonder why Kragur has developed its association with Catholicism more than they have. This makes sense if we assume that Kragur's degree of self-conscious involvement with Catholicism is a way of distinguishing itself from other villages, as well as an effort to gain access to the advantages of the world beyond the village and the island. Schwartz (1976:112) notes that in Melanesia in general, when one group seizes on a cultural innovation—a new ritual, for example—as a symbol of distinction, rival groups are likely to avoid imitating it for fear of appearing to be mere followers. There is certainly enough rivalry between Kragur and at least some of its neighbors to discourage the latter from making Catholicism too prominent a part of their village identities. Similarly, this may have something to do with prevailing ideas about property rights, including rights to intangible property—that is, the idea of tiptip. Although virtually every Kairiru islander is at least nominally Catholic, if Kragur somehow managed to stake an early claim to exemplary leadership in Catholicism, the village as a whole may have acquired a kind of unspoken tiptip for this role, thus discouraging others from claiming Catholic leadership.

No attempt to explain Kragur's involvement with Catholicism would be complete without mentioning the efforts of the present leader of village Catholic life, Ibor. His life has been one of extraordinary devotion to the cause of spreading Catholicism. It is difficult to imagine what Kragur would be like today had he not worked so diligently to establish Catholicism and to promote schooling, which for many years was available only through the mission. It is just as difficult, however, to imagine Ibor's career outside the context of Kragur's particular historical and geographical circumstances.

Whatever mechanisms have come into play, and whatever particular individuals have contributed, the end result is that Kragur people are deeply enmeshed in Catholicism. Their Catholicism, however, is highly colored by indigenous views of the nature of the supernatural that are rooted in a more general view of the world in which material well-being is intimately intertwined with the state of social relations among human beings and between human beings and humanlike entities. Catholicism's own emphasis on matters of social relations—to some extent inherent in Catholicism and in some ways, such as the concern with a cooperative attitude toward whites, a product of the colonial context—has made it easier to assimilate. In turn, involvement with Catholicism probably has reinforced villagers' ever-present concern with issues of social relations, heightening their significance both in attempts to deal with everyday problems and in efforts to meet the new challenges of the postcolonial epoch.

FIVE

The Case of the Konan

I WAS UNAVOIDABLY DETAINED in Wewak in April 1976, when Kragur villagers and other islanders were celebrating the dedication of the statue of the Virgin. I later had the good fortune, however, to observe a series of events that probably revealed more about religious life and prevailing views of the world in Kragur. June through September is the heart of the season of the southeast trade winds, the season of calm seas and good fishing. During these months in 1976, many villagers were preoccupied with fishing and rituals to secure supernatural support for their efforts. The events of this time tell a great deal about the deep interpenetration of the human and the nonhuman worlds many villagers see, the intimate connections they find between social relations and material well-being, the difficulties of controlling supernatural powers through harmonizing social relations, and the ways in which Kragur people blend Catholicism with indigenous beliefs and practices in pursuit of material well-being and social harmony. The connections between some of the events that make up the case of the *konan* are obvious and straightforward; but prevailing Kragur views of the relationship between the natural and the supernatural and between social relations and material endeavors led villagers to find crucial connections between events that appear quite unrelated to an outside observer, and to find hidden significance in seemingly mundane incidents.

Kragur villagers spend much less time fishing and hunting than working in their gardens or processing sago, but this probably is not a good index of the importance of these activities in village life. Fish and game provide only a small part of the calories that villagers consume, but they are highly valued foods. An ordinary meal sometimes includes no fish or meat; but it is almost a requirement that a generous portion of fish or game top the large plates of taro, yams, sweet potatoes, or sago contributed to the feasts marking the completion of a new house, a funerary observance, or other special events. While everyone who helps build a house contributes to the communal meals that end each day's work and the more elaborate meal that marks its completion, the owner of the house is expected to make the major contribution. Ideally, he should provide generous quantities of fish and game. The owner of a new house sometimes will delay completing it until he and his close kin can amass sufficient smoked fish and game—but mostly fish—to make a good showing. Canned mackerel may be substituted; but even if its cost were not an obstacle to many, it would be a second choice.

Kragur people use a number of fishing techniques. Deep-sea fishing with hook and line from canoes is almost exclusively the province of men. Women also fish with hook and line, but usually from the rocks along the shore. Men and boys sometimes use homemade spear guns, but there are few good places for spearfishing along Kairiru's north coast, where the water is often rough and turbid.

The events described in this chapter concern only a particular kind of fish, known in the Kairiru language as *konan,* and in Pidgin as *talai,* a term used for several similar fish. The konan is probably a type of long tom *(Tylorus sp.)* that inhabits Sepik coastal waters. Konan are approximately eight to twelve inches long, narrow-bodied, with long, pointed mouths. They appear off the north coast of Kairiru during the season of the southeast trade winds. Large schools often come close to shore to spawn, particularly in more sheltered areas. When spawning, they turn tail-down at the surface of the water and cause patches of the sea to erupt in violent silver agitation as they struggle to deposit their eggs. This is the favored moment for catching them, by scooping up the momentarily helpless masses of fish in large, long-handled, triangular nets wielded from the prows of encircling canoes.

Men of koyeng Shewaratin own primary rights to the magic for ensuring that abundant konan will come close to Kragur's shores to spawn. According to Taunur, the leading konan magician, the konan come originally from a place deep in the interior of the mainland. Tarakam, another senior Shewaratin man, says that there was once an old woman on the mainland who had a hollow bamboo container from which she could produce konan at will. She kept it a secret, even from her two sons, hiding the bones of the fish she had eaten so she would not arouse suspicion. One day, however, one of her sons found some fish bones, and, searching further, the two brothers finally found her miraculous bamboo container. When they unplugged the end, all the konan escaped and swam down to the sea. That is why, says Tarakam, when people today want to eat konan, they have to use magic to bring them close.

In the past, performing the konan magic would have involved both solitary and collective ritual. According to present accounts, the magician would have displayed in his house the carved wooden figures, known as *kaikrauap,* that were once part of the paraphernalia of many kinds of magic. These stylized human figures were believed to have magical potency in themselves, but like other traditional ritual objects, say villagers, they were destroyed at the behest of the missionaries in the first flush of Catholic conversion. The magician's house would have been decorated inside with palm fronds and gifts of betel nut, coconuts, and cooked food. At one point in the proceedings, male villagers would have gathered near the magician's house, drumming and singing until dawn. The konan magician still performs some parts of the indigenous ritual. Although I have not seen it myself, I am told that as he recites the magical spells he casts into the sea scales scraped from a konan kept in a sealed bamboo tube. As in other magic, the magician also must observe a number of ritual prohibitions, called *tambu* in Pidgin. He and his close patrilineal kin must not engage in sexual intercourse and he must not eat certain foods, particularly food cooked in water. Like sexual intercourse, this is said to render the magic "cold." Taro, yams, or sweet potatoes, for example, must be baked in the coals of the fire, rather than boiled, and eaten dry.

Not everyone agrees on just how the magic works. One middle-aged man explained to me that the konan were in an enclosure, but they were aware of the rituals performed by human beings and responded by coming out into the open sea. "These are smart fish," he said. "They aren't like fish, they're like people. They have

eyes to see and ears to hear." Two other men sitting with us nodded their agreement. I later asked Taunur if the konan were in an
enclosure from which the magic released them. He replied that
magic to spoil the fishing drives the fish into an enclosure and
magic to spoil the hunting drives pigs into enclosures in the trunks
of trees. "It's true, it's not a lie," he concluded. "But its like an
'example.' [Here he used the English word.] Don't think that pigs
really go inside trees."

In 1976, petitioning the Virgin was a major part of the public
ritual for controlling the konan, and the village Catholic leader
played a major role. I was told that adding such a heavy dose of
Catholicism to the konan ritual was something new. To my
knowledge, however, there had been no moves to supplement
other indigenous subsistence magic with Catholic elements, and
the leading konan magician was still active and respected. What
accounted for this new departure?

There is ample biblical precedent for applying Christian religious practices to fishing. Many villagers know the story of how
Jesus provided a bountiful catch to fishermen on the Sea of Gali-
lee. On the wall of his house Ibor displays a vividly colored picture
of a scene from that story, in which the fishermen are hauling in
nets so overladen that their small craft threatens to capsize. Ibor is
also fond of telling how he, members of his family, and other
members of the Legion once prayed for four straight hours petitioning the Virgin for fish, and how their prayers were rewarded
by the appearance of large numbers of tuna, kingfish, and mackerel in the sheltered bay below the cliffs.

There were also other factors at work in 1976. Taunur, the
chief konan magician, had apparently already tried using his
magic unaided by Catholic practices, but to no avail. He told me
himself that his efforts to control the fish the previous year had not
been very successful because people had not cooperated with him.
The charge of noncooperation can cover a broad range. In this
chapter I shall describe a series of assemblies of the village men to
deal with the konan situation. Simply failing to attend such an
assembly can be a serious, if not necessarily deliberate, act of noncooperation. The assemblies are not just organizational meetings
for discussing issues and reaching decisions: they are also ritual
acts by which Kragur people demonstrate and express the village's
harmony and unity of purpose to each other and to any attending

supernatural power (cf. Tuzin 1990). Noncooperation also can go far beyond neglect of one's responsibility to take part in collective ritual. A few villagers suggested that the previous year someone had used magic to undermine Taunur's own magical effort.

Many villagers, however, felt that there was a deeper problem, that is, that today's magicians simply do not have as much power as their forebears. Some suggested that this was because those with primary rights to magic had given secondary rights to so many others; that is, nobody's magic worked right because too many people were using the magic at once. Many also said that most of today's magicians had spent so much time away from the village as migrant workers when they were young that they had not learned their craft thoroughly from their elders. A few spoke of the mission's past suppression of indigenous magic.

Concern about Taunur's and other magicians' loss of power is, I think, one aspect of a larger, vaguer feeling that changing times call for new measures. The obvious material wealth of the Europeans certainly recommends Catholicism as a superior solution to problems of material well-being. This may have been particularly so in 1976, the year of the statue. In the eyes of many villagers, erecting the statue created a more concrete bond between the village and the Virgin, and initiated what they hoped would be a new era of favor in her eyes. According to Mowur, a man in his thirties, speakers at the dedication of the statue said, "We're going to erect this statue of Maria; now if we want something we must ask her for it."

A few villagers spoke to me of the statue as though placing it on the mountain marked a radical turning away from indigenous beliefs and practices, especially in the matter of the konan; and a few criticized the mixing of Catholic and indigenous practices in the konan ritual. On the whole, however, there was little sign of wholesale rejection of indigenous practices in favor of Santu Maria. Rather, villagers found many ways to accommodate Catholic and indigenous practices; and, as in any complex social event, different actors often had different views of what was really going on. Whether they emphasized the role of Catholicism or that of indigenous magic in the konan rituals, most villagers were struggling to bring about material plenty by harmonizing social relations—relations with powerful, humanlike supernatural beings and relations among living men and women.

The First Fish Assembly: June 14

For several days prior to Monday, June 14, schools of konan had
been visible some distance from shore. At a brief meeting after
church on Sunday it had been announced that it was now forbidden to fish with hook and line from the shore or to swim in the
sea, in order to avoid interfering with the ritual efforts that were to
begin the following day to draw large schools of fish close to shore
to spawn. Monday was a council workday and Councillor Mansu
rang the village bell for assembly early, as usual. Most adults had
gathered in the center of the village by eight o'clock. Mansu first
announced that there was no primary school that day because it
was the queen's birthday (Papua New Guinea is a British Commonwealth country); then he assigned a few adolescent men to go
to the top of the mountain to remove the decorations left in place
after the statue's dedication. Finally, he reminded the men that,
rather than the usual council work, the konan assembly would
take place that day; and he told the women to prepare food to distribute that evening to complete the konan ritual and mark the
removal of the statue's decorations.

By one o'clock most of the men had gathered for the konan
assembly, not in the center of the village, but in and around a clear
space at the eastern edge of the village on koyeng Shewaratin
ground. They seated themselves, as usual, in scattered groups,
some on the verandas of adjacent houses, some cross-legged on
pieces of bark laid on the ground, all smoking hand-rolled cigarettes or chewing betel nut taken from the small baskets or string
bags that men habitually carry. I sat near Taunur, and before the
formal proceedings began he leaned over to explain to me what
was going on: "It's like I told the people yesterday, if one sits in one
place and another sits in another place, and another in another,
the konan will be scattered around too. But if we gather in one
place, the konan will too. The dead ancestors will see us and
think, 'Oh, this is good, they're sitting together, eating together.' "

Despite the concern of some with pleasing the ancestors and the
fact that, in deference to Shewaratin's primary rights to konan
magic, the meeting was taking place on Shewaratin ground, the
first speaker, a Shewaratin elder and customary leader, called for
emphasizing the Catholic aspects of the event. Munuo rose to
speak and began by calling for everyone to come and sit closer

together in a single group, because this was "Maria's meeting" and not a meeting of the past. Only a handful of men, however, moved. Ibor then took the floor and spoke briefly of how this was a time of many changes and it was appropriate that they try new ways. Munuo spoke again, saying, "We customary leaders must think hard and try to help, see if this new way goes well, try following a new way, help the Legion [of Mary]." Mansu then spoke of how the mission and the customary leaders should work together and not compete. A few other men made short speeches to similar effect.

While others spoke, Ibor, Taunur, and Brawaung, a stalwart of the Legion, were busy splitting palm fronds and separating the leaves into fine streamers. When the meeting broke up, they took these to Taunur's nearby house, where they used them to decorate a small, rough table above which hung a picture of Jesus. The three then went to the bush, returning later with red and green leaves of the victory leaf plant (known as *tanget* in Pidgin), other decorative leaves, and bunches of betel pepper (which is chewed with betel nut), all of which they placed on the table in Taunur's house, the leaves in jars of water serving as vases. While they arranged these items, Taunur remarked that as they were returning from their errand they had seen large schools of fish offshore, much larger than those visible the day before. I later asked each of the three men separately exactly what they had done when they went to the bush, for they had been gone for some time. Each explained that the group had stopped at the church to pray, using the Pidgin term for prayer, *beten.* Brawaung, however, said that the three had prayed to their dead fathers as well as to the Virgin.

That evening there was a special prayer service in the center of the village. Afterward, large wooden plates of food were distributed to mark both the removal of the statue's decorations and the day's fish ritual. As Brawaung explained it to me, "they're parts of the same work." Sharing food is a customary gesture of closure for communal events of all kinds and, like gathering together to participate in the morning's assembly, signifies harmony and unity of purpose.

Several men took the opportunity to deliver speeches to those assembled that evening. The common theme was the compatibility of Mariolatry with indigenous practices. Here, for example, is some of what Ibor had to say:

> Maria is like our mother. She gives us everything we need to be well
> and prosperous. Maria likes a good way; if you follow a way that is
> not good she will not like it; [but] if you follow a straight [i.e., a
> good] way and you ask Maria for something, right away she will
> help us, give it to us. [Before we had kaikrauap], now we have stat-
> ues [of Maria]. The two practices are basically the same. We deco-
> rate [Maria's altar], we pray. It's just like bos [indigenous beneficial
> magic]. The way of the two is the same.

Ibor expanded on this theme for me at a later date, saying that the
two practices are similar because they both require prohibitions
against fishing with hook and line and against anger—as one says
in Pidgin, "man meri i no ken kros." He elaborated on this latter
theme, saying:

> Before, they worshiped the jawbone of a [deceased] man or the skull
> of a [deceased] man.[1] When they wanted konan or whatever, they
> decorated these wooden figures [kaikrauap]. Now we've changed,
> we can't take the bone of a man and honor it. We honor only Maria.
> Before they honored kaikrauap, now we honor the statue [of
> Maria]. I speak of the similar way; people must think and behave
> well, they cannot fight, they cannot strike their children, they can-
> not be angry. When we gather together you see that the konan also
> gather together. Fish do just as we men do. If we sit amicably
> together the fish also gather together.

Others that evening echoed Ibor's general theme. As one eminent
garden magician, Mer, put it: "Don't think that before there was
one road and now there is another road. No! There is only one
road!"

The next day most of the men stayed in the village to build new
houses for Aram, Munuo, and Tarakam. A large school of konan
was spotted offshore in the late afternoon. By the time the fish
entered the bay to spawn, fourteen canoes had gathered, some
from Bou and Shagur as well as Kragur. The canoes encircled the
spawning konan and the men standing in the prows swept up load
after load of fish with their long-handled nets. A few canoes stayed
on the water until long after dark, men spearing by torchlight the
large fish drawn by the spawning konan. That night and the next
day the air hung heavy with the smell of cooking and smoking
fish. Konan are long and narrow, and cooking them sometimes

involves no more than throwing them whole on the coals, where they quickly cook through.

In the days that followed, villagers continued their usual varied rounds of activities; but those in the village or in gardens with a view of the sea frequently turned from what they were doing to look for signs of more konan, and one could sense the mood of anticipation. Occasionally someone would spot what they thought was a large school of konan drawing close to shore, and men at work on the new houses or in gardens on the mountainside would send up a chorus of whoops and yawps. One very old and pious man seemed to spend most of his time praying for more fish. Even as he passed slowly through the village with the aid of a walking stick, on his way to and from the stream to bathe in the heat of the day, he could be heard entreating God and Santu Maria: "We want to eat fish, plenty of fish. Give us much grace, you mother Maria, you father God, have pity on us!"

For almost two weeks there were no more good opportunities to fish for konan. One small school came into the bay to spawn, and a few men hurried to the beach and launched their canoes, but a rising wind made it difficult to use the nets effectively.

The Second Fish Assembly: June 27

A second meeting was held on Sunday, June 27. This meeting lasted from about noon until about six P.M., some two hours longer than the first, and the tone was more serious and critical. People had expected more for their efforts at the first assembly, and now they were looking in familiar places for explanations of the unsatisfactory results. As Councillor Mansu put it, "The wind isn't enough to ruin things; somebody is angry"—and not simply angry, but hiding his or her anger. This assembly was thus an attempt to discover and repair the breaches in social harmony that appeared to be rendering impotent the villagers' attempts to ritually influence the konan. The approach was much like that of assemblies to cure the sick, and some even spoke of it that way. Mansu, opening the proceedings, declared, "We have to get rid of this illness so that things will work right!" Some orators also used the idiom of Catholicism, urging those who had hidden grievances to confess, for to hide one's anger was a *bikpela pekato*—that is, a great sin. Ibor strongly implied that they had to turn to Catholicism in this matter, because here as elsewhere they no longer had the magical knowledge and power of their forebears. Ibor said that Taunur's father "had a lot of power. But we today don't have his knowledge. There's no more magic." But while Ibor seemed to feel that it was God or Maria who was offended by the village's lack of harmony, Moke, an old customary leader of koyeng Kragur, felt free publicly to define the situation without reference to Catholicism. "There is anger here," he said. "So the ancestors are angry and the konan have disappeared." Moke and others who eschewed the Catholic interpretation implied that this was a case of suak, subsistence failure brought on by the ghosts of angry living men and women.

However individual participants in the assembly chose to construe the details, no one questioned that the immediate challenge was to restore social harmony, and all set to work to root out the hidden anger. Although the speeches and discussion went on for almost six hours, the conclusions of the assembly can be summarized briefly. It was decided that a number of people were probably disgruntled because they felt they had not received fair shares of the fish caught after the first assembly. Also, some of the canoe owners who took part in the fishing had not shared their catch with those who had helped them build their canoes. It was discovered, for example, that Aram had shared none of his catch with Fanauk, even though Fanauk had helped Aram build his canoe. Finally, there were a number of men in the village who had the rights to own and use canoes and the triangular konan nets, but they did not at that time have their own nets and canoes. Their equipment had worn out and they did not have the skills to produce these items themselves. There are only a few skilled canoe builders in Kragur, and building a large canoe is generally a collective undertaking, one of the more skilled men supervising others and performing key tasks himself. Making nets, too, takes many hands. The village men thought that some of those with rights but no equipment were probably angry that others had not helped them prepare to take advantage of the hoped-for konan harvest.

Most everyone seemed to feel that all such grievances were justified; only concealing them was wrong. On the other hand, a number of those who were named as aggrieved parties denied that they were concerned with these matters. Nevertheless, the consensus

remained that the assembly's analysis was valid, perhaps because
it only takes a little ill humor to activate the very partisan dead,
and the scale of the dead's reactions often bears little relation to
the strength of the feelings of the living.

It was very clear in this assembly, however, that not everyone's
grievances were considered equally important. One of those with
rights to a canoe, but no canoe, was Chapuan, an older man of
koyeng Shewaratin. Given Shewaratin's importance in the konan
undertaking, the assembled men deemed Chapuan's cause for discontent of great importance. They also deprecated the grievances
of less important men. Just after Fanauk's suggested anger at not
receiving a share of Aram's catch was mentioned, Karum of koyeng Ku dismissed it, saying: "We have to reveal all of the sins.
Fanauk is one issue, but let's leave it. That isn't enough. There's
something more. Some big man has a grievance. Never mind this
problem of Fanauk's, it's not important, it's nothing."

The actions prescribed to settle the matters brought to light in
the assembly did take account, however, of the grievances of the
humble as well as the mighty. Ibor announced that anyone with
any kind of grievance should bring cooked food and ten toea, the
equivalent of twelve or thirteen U.S. cents, to Taunur's house as a
token of goodwill and solidarity with the village's collective
efforts. To forestall further grievances, all were urged to give more
attention to distributing their catch fairly. In addition, the men
began making plans for a communal effort to provide canoes and
nets for everyone who had rights to them. A few began immediately, going to Chapuan's house, which stands on the edge of the
Shewaratin meeting ground, and dragging from beneath it a canoe
hull that had long been awaiting completion. In the two following
weeks, two or three of the most skilled canoe builders spent many
hours building canoes for others. Many people started devoting
evenings and odd moments during the day to making nets. Women
turned bundles of plant fiber into cord by rolling it inches at a time
on their bare thighs. Both men and women used this cord to knot
sections of net. Not everyone knows how to turn cord into nets,
and a few who are expert at this went about teaching anyone who
was interested in learning; one does not have to have rights to own
a net to know how to make one.

Villagers also did some fishing. A few attempts produced modest results, and the smell of smoking fish filled the village on sev-

eral mornings when men slept late after nights on the water. But the konan still were not as plentiful as people thought they should be. Two weeks after the second assembly, a third was called.

The Third Fish Assembly: July 11

Again, from soon after the end of Sunday church service around midday until almost dark, the men gathered on the Shewaratin grounds to try to discover the social causes of the poor fishing. Once more there was some talk of people who might be upset because they had not been given fair shares of fish, but these instances were ultimately dismissed as insignificant. Old Kanau stood up to say that after the previous assembly some of those with grievances had failed to bring offerings of food and money to Taunur's house. During his brief speech, someone spotted a school of konan not too far offshore, and shouted, "Kanau's got it!" There was a momentary burst of enthusiasm for Kanau's analysis, but the school of fish came no closer and Kanau's explanation was passed over rather quickly. Other, weightier men had their own ideas about what was at the bottom of things. In the end, there was wide agreement that a big man of koyeng Kragur, Moke, had a serious grievance that was probably the cause of the most recent poor fishing.

One has to go back several years to explain Moke's alleged grievance. Examining it illustrates the way an event can suck others into its vortex as villagers seek explanations for misfortune in breaches of proper social relations. In the prevailing view, the effects of human actions can spread via the reactions of other human beings and the intervention of the watchful dead until they reach the material bases of life. The spreading interrelations weave a web inextricably linking words, deeds, and natural events that appear distinct on the surface of daily life.

Some ten years before, one of Moke's patrilineal kin, Musaro, had been living in Kreer, a village just off the main road east of Wewak. Musaro fell ill while visiting Kragur and some Kragur men set out to take him home, but he died on the way and the Kragur men helped to bury him. The death and burial of a person of importance is often followed by ceremonial exchanges of goods between the kinsman of the deceased and mourners from other locales. In this case, sometime after the burial, Moke and other Kragur men went to Kreer and presented gifts of sago, taro, and tobacco to Musaro's friends there. One of these, a man of some importance in Kreer, reciprocated with pigs, sago, taro, tobacco, and cases of beer. Apparently, however, the Kreer people felt that the exchange had been imbalanced, that Moke had given too little; and they demanded further gifts. A gift of pigs left them still unsatisfied and in 1976 they demanded gifts again. Moke told me that he found these demands unreasonable, for he had never asked for their original lavish gifts of beer and pigs. He felt constrained, however, to meet these demands—in part, no doubt, out of concern for his reputation, but also, he said, because he feared his disgruntled exchange partners might use sorcery against him if he spurned them.

As in any large gift exchange, Moke needed the help of his fellow villagers, both close kin and others, to amass the large quantity of taro he had been asked to bring to Kreer. There was some grumbling about this among the rank and file, who also felt they had already done enough; but in the end virtually all who were able contributed large string bags of taro for the event. Moke and a few others pooled their money to charter St. Xavier's boat, the *Tau-K*, to come to Kragur to collect the many bags of taro and about thirty men, women, and children and take them to Kreer on June 30.

Although thirty people went to Kreer with Moke, only a very few were vigorous young men who easily could load and unload the heavy bags of taro. Most of the men were, as one villager put it in Pidgin, just *skin man*—that is, men shrunken with age. So unloading at the wharf at one end of Wewak's main street had been difficult. Several bags had been scraped on the rough cement and broken, and one had fallen into the water. Mangoi, a respected older leader who helped unload the taro, had later suffered severe chest pains and had been taken to the hospital, where he remained at the time of the third fish assembly.

Moke himself was visiting kin on the other side of the island when the July 11 assembly took place. Much of the meeting was taken up with angry discussion of just whose fault it was that the Kreer excursion had been beset with problems. Nevertheless, there was general agreement that Moke had a serious and legitimate grievance against those who had not assisted him. Like Moke, other villagers had also complained that the Kreer demand for more gifts was unreasonable, and a few mentioned this in the course of the discussion. Yet, in the eyes of others, especially important leaders, there was no excuse for foot dragging when a big man mounted a gift exchange. As Ibor put it, berating the assembly in general: "You are all in the wrong! When one of our big men does something, you all must help him!"

Despite general agreement that Moke's grievance was legitimate, few had much sympathy for him. The public rhetoric in the assembly implied that his anger had been translated into subsistence failure by the intervention of the dead and/or the Catholic supernatural beings. In private, however, a number of villagers suggested that in this case the aggrieved party had taken action himself. Moke is a magician of considerable reputation and some suspected that he had used malign magic to spoil the fishing. A few cited an incident that had taken place after Moke's return from Kreer as evidence of his guilt. While walking up the main trail toward the top of the mountain, Moke had met a group of women from Bou village. Allegedly, he had told them that there were many konan drawing near shore and they should hurry home and prepare food for their husbands so they would be ready to go fishing that evening. But, said Moke's accusers, no one had seen any konan that day. Hence, they said, Moke had been engaging in what is known in Pidgin as *tok parabel,* speech in parables, or he was speaking circularly, known in Pidgin as to *raunim tok.* He knew there would be no fish, they charged, and was indulging in veiled allusion and heavy irony.

The third assembly did not forget Catholicism. The decorative foliage adorning the table in Taunur's house had become old and bedraggled, and after the meeting a small delegation replaced it with fresh leaves. A few villagers spotted distant schools of konan the next day and ascribed their appearance to the Virgin's pleasure at this renewed attention; but Moke's alleged anger was foremost in people's minds and they could do little to deal with that until he returned to Kragur.

Although attendance at the assemblies had not fallen off and villagers were still busily engaged in canoe building and net making, by this time I was beginning to notice signs of disenchantment with the whole konan enterprise. It is not surprising that I first noticed these signs among women. The men held center stage in this endeavor and had become immersed in the details of the relationships, rights, disputes, and theological points it brought to the fore. On assembly days, while the men debated and declaimed, women trekked to their gardens to get taro and other produce and spent the afternoon preparing the plates of food served at the end of each meeting. Following the third assembly, I sat by Brawaung's fire while he answered my questions about the konan affair, fervently setting forth his views of the matter and speaking of how much effort it took to set matters straight. Finally, Misiling, Brawaung's wife, interjected: "I'm tired of this. Sometimes, just leave it be. Forget it." Brawaung and others, however, did not forget it, and three days later they assembled once again.

The Fourth Fish Assembly: July 14

The fourth assembly began in mid-morning, convening in the breezy shade of a new Shewaratin house still in need of walls, and lasted until nearly dusk. While early arrivals waited for Moke and others, Ibor took the opportunity to address a straightforward question of fishing methods. He said the men were waiting until almost dark to go fishing, which was all right for catching flying fish, but to catch konan you had to be out much earlier. But when Moke arrived the talk immediately shifted to questions of hidden anger and social friction.

Despite widespread suspicion that Moke had been using his magical skills malevolently, all present greeted him cordially and he returned their greetings warmly. After Ibor delivered a summary of the events leading to the decision that Moke's grievance was responsible for the konan failure, Moke himself addressed the assembly. He denied that he was nursing any anger over the Kreer affair and suggested they all look elsewhere for the root of the fish problem. He had heard what people were saying about his remarks to the Bou women along the trail; but he said the women were *longlong*—Pidgin for stupid, crazy, or just confused—and had reported the incident inaccurately. Ibor responded that he himself certainly was upset by the Kreer affair, even if Moke was not. Moke replied that he was, of course, very concerned about Mangoi, who had injured himself unloading the bags of taro. Ibor then commented in Pidgin for all to hear, "Ating em i parabel lik

lik"—that is, "I think he's speaking in parables a little." Ibor meant that this was Moke's elaborately indirect way of expressing his lingering concern over the entire affair, but Moke protested that there was no hidden meaning in his words.

Before the end of the assembly the men had discussed a host of other grievances that might have been affecting the konan. Tarakam suggested that Chapuan was angry because while at the Kreer event a young man had berated him for not handling the event properly; but Chapuan denied any concern with this because the young man had been drunk. Benau, a young unmarried Shewaratin man, openly expressed his anger at Brawaung and Munuo who, he said, had borrowed his net and not returned it promptly. Someone also noted that Chapuan's wife, Kinkin, had sent a package of smoked fish to her son attending the University of Papua New Guinea in Port Moresby in care of another young man returning from his leave in the village. The speaker speculated that when other Kragur young people in Moresby heard of this and received no fish themselves they might have been angry. Another man suggested that according to custom both Moke and Chapuan should be acting as Taunur's assistants, for they also had rights to certain fishing magic, but they had both been preoccupied with the Kreer event: "Chapuan and Moke have been running around all over and now everything is a mess." Old issues, too, came up again. Speakers berated those aggrieved parties who still had not made their offerings of food and money to Taunur and emphasized the need to be sure that all those entitled had canoes and nets and that whatever fish were caught were fairly distributed.

Amid the welter of admitted and suspected causes of disharmony and anger, suspicion of Moke persisted. A significant portion of the fourth assembly was devoted to discussing a dream reported by a man from Shagur. In the dream, two men, one identified as a "man of the sea" and the other as a "man of the bush," walk from the far western end of the village, where Moke lives, to the cliff tops just down the slope from the houses of koyeng Shewaratin at the eastern end of the village. There they produce shovels and begin throwing dirt into the sea below. The "man of the sea" was assumed to represent Moke, who holds rights to various fishing and canoe magic, and the "man of the bush" was taken to represent Mer, who holds rights to important gardening magic. Apparently, Mer had been Moke's ally in the Kreer endeavor, assisting in organizing it and perhaps lending his magical knowledge to the task of raising taro for it. Many thought the dream meant that Moke and his allies had magically despoiled the sea and the fishing.

No one, however, stated the dream's meaning so bluntly in the assembly, and I received such a plain account only after the fact. News of the dream undoubtedly had circulated prior to the meeting and its symbolism is not complicated, so further public discussion would have added little. In addition, while villagers commonly discuss in public such delicate matters as accusations of the use of malign magic or the practice of sorcery, they seldom refer directly to the foul deeds in question. By the time a public meeting is held everyone is already familiar with the accusations. It appears that people take care to preserve at least the appearance of amity, in part to avoid further angering a dangerous magician and in part to retain some small claim to the goodwill of supernatural beings who take offense at human social conflict.

The Shagur man's dream had a second episode as well, and this was said to exonerate the people of Shewaratin from any responsibility for the failure of the konan endeavor. In the second episode of the dream, four Shewaratin men—Taunur, Chapuan, Munuo, and Tarakam—greet visitors from another village who have come for a performance of song and dance. The Shewaratin men then show the visitors the appropriate place to defecate, a pit toilet on Shewaratin ground at the edge of the cliff overlooking the sea. This was said to symbolize both the goodwill of Shewaratin people toward all others and the sincerity of their efforts to ritually ensure plenty of spawning konan. In Pidgin, villagers use the term for defecation to describe the konan depositing their eggs; they say that the fish *pekpek*. Hence, the four Shewaratin men were not just being good hosts by showing their guests the nearest toilet, they were also showing them where they fully expected the konan to appear.

No new action was taken as a result of the fourth assembly. There were admonitions to be fair and generous in distributing any fish caught, and efforts to provide canoes and nets to all who had rights to them were to continue apace. Much of the meeting had been devoted to Moke's alleged grievance, and no doubt some hoped that this attention would sooth his anger and cause him to call back the malign magic he was suspected of using.

After the assembly some villagers continued to try to work out the key to the konan situation on their own. Brawaung, a man known for his prowess as a fisherman as well as his devotion to the Virgin, told me one evening two days after the fourth meeting that he was sure the problem was that people had begun to neglect the Virgin. The fish had been plentiful initially, he said, because of the attention lavished on the Virgin's newly erected statue: "These fish come straight from this woman who stands on the mountain." Brawaung had gone after konan the night of June 15 but they had eluded him by spawning far out to sea. The next day he found that in the night Misiling, his wife, had dreamt that Ulasau—a man several years deceased and, like Moke, a member of koyeng Kragur—was lying beside the Virgin's statue, either asleep or dead. Ulasau then arose and said, "The statue is angry at all of you." Brawaung took the dream to mean that the Virgin was upset because Kragur people were no longer looking after her, coming to clean the grounds around her and praying to her. Brawaung said he had gone to see Ibor to tell him that they had become too absorbed in their meetings and had forgotten Santu Maria.

Despite the contribution Misiling made to the konan discussion through her dream, while awake her patience was wearing thin. After Brawaung told me of her dream, Misiling recounted with a laugh how earlier in the day she had lost her temper at her husband and admonished him: "The fish come and go as they please! You men just stay in the village and hold meetings; when are you going to do some work? All you do is build canoes!" Her daughter Bashi, recently graduated from the Catholic high school for girls on the mainland, sat with us that evening and added that she did not "believe in any of that"—namely, the meetings and prayers and accusations. Mer's adult daughter Nikir was also there, and she responded, "Me too," to Bashi's pronouncement. I suspect that others were beginning to weary of the affair as well, although they did not necessarily share these women's skepticism about the assumptions underlying the fish assemblies.

The Fifth Fish Assembly: July 25

Despite skeptical rumblings, the issue was still far from dead, and on Sunday, July 25, still another assembly was called. Again, the men discussed a number of incidents that might have led to hidden anger, discarding most of them as probably insignificant. For instance, Karum of koyeng Ku had had a fiery argument with one of his matrilateral kin the previous Sunday, but the following day a school of konan had spawned near shore, so it was generally agreed that this argument had not affected the fish. One man suggested that there had been no dangerous hidden anger left because the parties to the argument had expressed themselves freely and openly and their anger had dissipated. The men agreed that there were now enough nets and canoes to go around, for net making and canoe building had been proceeding at a remarkable pace. The men also agreed that the grievance of two elderly widows had probably affected the fish. These two had made most of the cord for the net of a young Shewaratin man, but he had given them only a very small share of his catch of the past week or so. The young man was cautioned to distribute his catch more fairly in the future and the widows were told to bring cooked food to Taunur's house as a gesture of goodwill and termination of their anger.

For good measure, as I learned later, the evening after the meeting Taunur and Mangoi employed an indigenous means of divination to determine if any others were harboring grievances not yet revealed. I was told that in such divination the diviners suggest names to the jawbone of a dead magician and the jawbone reacts with a slight motion if the person named is nursing a grievance. Taunur had once possessed the jawbone of a dead fishing magician, but this had been lost; so they had used Mangoi's jawbone of a dead tobacco magician. The jawbone indicated that at least two men had significant grievances that had not been aired at the assembly, and Taunur and Mangoi approached the two in private.

An issue deeper than any particular grievance was also raised at the fifth meeting—an issue apparently born of frustration with the limited success of the diligent efforts of the past weeks. This was the issue of the compatibility of Catholic practices—often referred to in Pidgin as *bilip,* belief—and indigenous practices—referred to in Pidgin as *kastom,* custom (cf. Tonkinson 1982). Although only one man publicly voiced concern about this, it is of interest in itself and because of the vehemence with which others argued that the two were perfectly compatible.

At one point in the discussion, Tarakam—a customary leader of Shewaratin, second only to Taunur in importance—rose and suggested in Pidgin that if by the following morning there were no signs of konan, they should "traim wanpela rul bilong kastom," that is, try following simply the indigenous or customary way. "If we want to follow bilip," he said, "we can't [also] follow kastom." No one spoke in support of this suggestion, in fact several men in succession spoke against it. All stated, in one way or another, that there was no contradiction between bilip and kastom, and all focused on the similarity between indigenous magical incantations, bos, and Catholic prayer. Ibor's point of view, which he explained to me in more detail after the meeting, was representative. I asked him to whom men appealed when they used bos, and he answered "the ancestors, their fathers." But he also insisted that bos were "the prayers of the New Guineans" because people caused things to happen by speaking. Tarakam, however, was unmoved by the arguments against his contention that they should stop mixing Catholic and indigenous practices. I spoke with him after the meeting and he expanded on his argument. "It's like a ship," he said. "If we choose one course, then we can't have second thoughts. You can't go halfway then change your course; that's wrong. Ideas are the same. One is enough."

No one spoke of Moke's grievance at the fifth assembly, but it had not been forgotten. In private conversations in the following days, many people spoke of their suspicions that a powerful person was magically foiling all their efforts. Taunur, for one, insisted that such persisting problems with the konan could not be the result of the small grievances of unimportant people; some person of importance must be very angry about something and using magic to show his anger. "People talk about suak, but I don't see any suak," he said. What Taunur saw was what he called in Pidgin *maus nogud*. Literally this means "evil mouth"—that is, speaking malicious magical spells.

The Sixth Fish Assembly: August 8

On Sunday, August 8, the men met once more at Shewaratin. There was little trace of the buoyant expectation that had marked the first assembly almost two months before. Weeks of disappointment had cast a pall over the entire endeavor and the failure to eradicate hidden anger and achieve social harmony itself had stretched tempers thin. The men again had gathered in the open, unfinished house. Moke had arrived early and placed several flowers in a bottle of water in the center of the floor and gone about greeting each of those present by shaking his hand and murmuring, "God bless." The first burst of dissension came from another quarter. Tarakam had seated himself at a conspicuous distance from the rest, on the veranda of a neighboring Shewaratin house. As Moke was still making his own show of conspicuous harmony, Tarakam shouted his discontent to the closely packed group in the new house. "All the time meetings, meetings, meetings! One gathering, that's enough! [But instead] they go on and on!" This instantly angered Taunur, who shouted in reply: "This is my work and you're supposed to follow me! You're trying to ruin my work! You come and sit down!" Tarakam fell silent, but he did not move from where he was sitting.

That disturbance over but not forgotten, Ibor began the meeting with a prayer. He invoked the names not only of God and Maria but also of a deceased leader of village Catholicism, Viro, who was now in heaven with God and also could offer his help.

Moke then took the floor. He began by vehemently denying that he was angry over the Kreer affair and then launched into a discourse on the question of the use of both Catholic and indigenous methods for controlling the konan. In his hand he held a feather, which he used as a symbol of indigenous practices. This association may reflect the fact that a type of fish hawk is mentioned in certain magical spells, cast as a swift messenger bringing whatever is desired from distant places. The flowers in the center of the floor stood for Catholicism. Moke did not say bluntly that the two were incompatible, but he did declare that not everyone in the village believed in the latter. Pointing to the flowers with one hand and holding up the feather in the other, he asked if people wanted to follow the way of the flower or the way of the feather and said that in the past the way of the feather had ruled, but today the way of the flower had to take precedence.[2] It seems unlikely that Moke was primarily interested in this theological point. His speech is probably best understood as an attempt either to shift the focus of the debate, or to show his solidarity with this collective endeavor, or both.

Whatever Moke's motives in raising this issue, his remarks were received with predictable protestations that the flower and the feather were completely at ease with each other. In addition, Ibor suggested that the failure of their attempts to solicit the assistance of God and the Virgin did not stem from mixing Catholicism with indigenous practices. His voice filled with feeling, he said that the way of Catholicism was not working for them because they were not behaving like good Catholics. Not only did some continue to steal from other's gardens and to yield to other temptations, the village people were not truly committed to a common goal. Whereas in English one speaks of the heart as the seat of the emotions, in Pidgin it is the stomach. Hence, Ibor lamented that Kragur people did not "stap bel wankain"—that is, their stomachs or feelings were not united and harmonious. This is as much a virtue in contemporary interpretations of indigenous morality as it is a Catholic virtue. At times Ibor is prone to stress the similarity. In this case he seemed to identify Catholicism with a higher order of unity and harmony, a higher moral ideal that villagers had to achieve if they were to flourish in the new era. Anger and frustration in his voice, Ibor concluded: "I'm worried that we can't accomplish anything, that everything is hopeless! Everything is changing; if we go back to the past, things will go wrong!"

The men left many of the konan assemblies with diverse views of what had been concluded and decided, but the outcome of this assembly was conspicuously eclectic. A few men paid Moke small sums of money to "finish his anger" and symbolically mend the rent in social relations among them. No one, however, spoke openly of the suspicion that Moke had intentionally ruined the fishing. This, I was told, was for fear that open accusations would anger him further and, according to one man, so that Moke would feel free to restore the fish to Kragur waters without seeming to do so in direct, guilty response to public demands. Although Tarakam was among those who made conciliatory payments to Moke, he remained disgruntled with the whole affair. After the meeting he repeated to me in private his contention that the meetings had become a waste of time and that, contrary to what some said, this was not like curing an illness. Weeks ago, he said, they should have left it solely in the hands of the leaders who could reach a decision and inform the others, the way it was done in "big companies," that is, the mines and plantations where Tarakam had worked in his youth. Brawaung told me that the upshot of the meeting was that now the customary leaders were going to assume control of things; hence, when asked by a few other men to replace the wilted flowers on the altar to Maria in Taunur's house, Brawaung had declined. I had not noticed that the meeting had reached any such consensus, and it could not have been a strong one.

For his part, the chief customary leader in this matter, Taunur, was not at all happy with the state of things. He was still upset with Tarakam for disrupting the meeting, for Tarakam had remained apart and continued to punctuate it with occasional shouted remarks on what a waste of time it was. This was not only a personal affront, it was also an affront to Sherwaratin's reputation—"He wants to put out Shewaratin's fire!" Taunur complained. It was in itself enough to ruin the fishing, according to him. Further, Taunur suggested that Moke was likely to take this discord as evidence that the people of Kragur did not really care about the konan, and he would thus be disinclined to rectify any damage he had intentionally done (cf. Brison 1991:334–335).

Throughout the konan affair Taunur emphasized good relations among villagers to please the ancestors, responsible use of magical power, and deference to traditional authority. Ibor emphasized harmony as the hallmark of Catholicism, loyalty to the Virgin, and commitment to Catholicism as vital to coping with the new epoch. Like most other villagers, both complained that the fundamental problem was a lack of unity. "Plenti het moa!" Taunur grumbled in Pidgin—too many heads, too many different ideas and interests.

Floods and Fish Hawks

There was only one more major public discussion of the konan that year and it took place on August 23. Most of the men had spent the day building a new house. Following the communal meal ending the day's work, the men gradually gathered in the center of the village; some sat on the rough bench along one side and others were scattered about, seated on large rocks or bark mats. Most of the women had gone off to the stream to wash dishes, but as they returned many stopped and lingered on the periphery of the male group. The assembled men spoke about a number of issues before getting down to the fish question. Ibor, for example, had recently dreamt that Kragur people had stolen a chicken from Bou village. After some discussion it was determined that the dream referred to the fact that a young Kragur man, Mowush, had married a Bou woman, Malangis, several years before, but his kin in Kragur had yet to provide a wife in exchange to her kin in Bou. The men agreed that steps should be taken either to match a marriageable Bou man with a young Kragur woman or, if no woman was available, to make a cash payment to Malangis's kin in Bou to lay the outstanding obligation to rest. The men addressed a few other questions in a desultory way; but not long after the meeting began, Samof, like Moke an important elder of koyeng Kragur, rose to raise a question that quickly led back to the konan.

In the days just preceding this meeting there had been heavy rain in the higher reaches of the island. As a result, the stream on which both the men's and the women's bathing places are located had temporarily become a surging torrent, brown with mud, overflowing its banks, and shifting and toppling the large boulders that surround the bathing pools. Samof said that the stream had often flooded before, but he had never known it to toss the boulders around like this. In his view, a spate of this magnitude could not be taken as an isolated and meaningless event. Someone, he said, must be responsible. As I confirmed later, he clearly was implying that someone must have used malign magic to bring about the flood. Although a close patrilineal kinsman of Moke, Samof had not been his ally during the past weeks of debate and accusation. Indeed, Samof seemed publicly to distance himself from Moke. Now, when he spoke of a human agent behind the violent flooding of the stream, he accused Moke's cosuspect in the konan affair, Mer. His accusation was unusually open and direct, but Mer's reply was soft-spoken. As might have been expected, he denied not only his culpability in this instance but also any knowledge of the magic for controlling such events.

Discussion of this accusation had not proceeded far when Sakun, a young householder of koyeng Shewaratin, suggested that they were looking for an explanation in the wrong quarter and brought the debate back to the question of the fish. He argued that the flood was a punishment from the Virgin for the villagers' lack of proper devotion to her and her laws, a failure made manifest in their failure to achieve the harmony and solidarity needed to control the konan. "The fish came as a test!" he said. "When the fish left, the flood came!" He spoke in particular of the lack of unity among village leaders, clearly implying that some had used their magical power against the work of others for selfish ends. Now, he warned, "Maria is angry! It won't be long until there is an earthquake!" Ibor also spoke in this vein, allowing that it was possible the flood was indeed a sign or a punishment from the Virgin. He pointed out that when they had erected the statue they had committed themselves to abandoning all the evil ways of the past and he drew a connection between this commitment to the Virgin and the coming of national independence only six months before they had raised the statue.

More specific alleged failures of devotion to the Virgin occupied the meeting briefly. Someone charged that two Kragur men, while processing sago near the top of the mountain, had stayed for several nights in a small shelter that stands near the statue, but they had not prayed regularly at the statue. Thus, the speaker argued, they had angered the Virgin and perhaps precipitated the flood. The accused hotly denied the charge.

The flood itself eventually relinquished its hold on the meeting and the men returned to the issue that preoccupied them all, the fish. There was still no dearth of new explanations for the futility of their weeks of effort. Mer suggested that the people of Sup village, on Mushu island, also had been trying to magically lure the konan and that this might have counteracted Kragur people's efforts. He also suggested that a konan magician in a nearby Kairiru village might have dispersed the fish from the north coast waters because of a grievance of his own bearing no relation to events in Kragur. Although suspicion of foul play within Kragur itself had not dissipated, the men debated these hypotheses with some interest. No one, however, proposed any specific actions and the gathering ended without plans for pursuing the issue further. A number of speakers seemed decidedly discouraged and resigned. Tarakam voiced his disgust plainly, saying that he was through with attempts to control the konan because others continued to ruin the work of his Shewaratin koyeng and to bring shame on them all.

There was some successful konan fishing in the weeks to come, but not enough to satisfy the hopes with which people had begun the konan season. Although the flood meeting marked the end of public discussion of the issue, many villagers continued to talk about it in private, and preoccupation with the issue colored perceptions of many events. The day after the flood meeting a few people saw two fish hawks emerge from the canopy of the forest higher up the mountain and fly straight down toward the beach below Kragur. They circled over the beach briefly then flew directly back whence they had come, crying loudly all the way. This was not as striking a natural phenomenon as the flood, but in the charged atmosphere of the village it also took on special significance, and I heard much speculation on its meaning as small groups of men gathered to talk, smoke, and chew betel. Some dismissed the event as meaningless, but others pointed out that the fish hawk is not an ordinary bird. It is not only skilled at fishing, it is also mentioned in magical spells. One man suggested that the birds' message was that Kragur's failure with the konan was the result of mixing indigenous practices, represented by the birds, with those of Catholicism. The birds' message, he said, was "if you want to follow our way, then follow our way only." If not, the fish would come and go as rapidly as the birds themselves. The meanings most others suggested for this event were less specific and straightforward, but they were all in some way reminders of or rebukes for the village's failure.

Failure and discouragement notwithstanding, villagers remained alert for signs of konan. Nearly a month after the flood meeting, a large school of konan did come into the bay to spawn and villagers made a substantial catch. I did not take a wide sample of opinions on why the konan had appeared in abundance one last time, but the opinions that Brawaung and Taunur volunteered are worthy of record.

The decorations on the altar to the Virgin in Taunur's house had been left intact after the last konan assembly, but just a few days before the final spawning in the bay, Taunur, Ibor, and Brawaung had ceremonially removed them and disposed of them in the sea. Brawaung told me that he thought this had somehow brought the fish back for one last fling. These last konan, he said, were of a larger variety that comes down from the lake at the top of the mountain, not from the mainland.[3] Just before the decorations had been removed from the altar, one of Taunur's sons, a student at St. Xavier's, had come home to visit, bringing a friend from school, and they had paid a visit to the lake. On their return the boys had brought with them some foliage picked near the lake that, unbeknownst to them, was a kind used in the magical procedure for controlling the konan. When Taunur saw this he placed the foliage on the altar. Taunur speculated that this might account for the sudden appearance of what he said was a lake variety of konan, although once the fish had reached the sea they stayed only momentarily because the sea still suffered the ill effects of whatever had rendered previous attempts to control the fish worthless.

Soon thereafter, the question of the fish again came to public attention by an oblique route. A young unmarried Shewaratin man had been seriously ill for several days, and successive curing efforts had failed. His was the case presented in Chapter 3 to illustrate ideas about the causes of illness. It may be remembered that the final verdict on the cause of his illness was that some harbored grievances against him because he had violated the prohibition on sexual activity for close kinsmen of the leader of magical efforts to improve the fishing. The young man's father paid compensation to Taunur for the damage allegedly done to Taunur's undertaking by the young man's actions, although it was not suggested that Taunur's grievance alone was at the root of the illness.

This, of course, introduced another possible explanation for the failure of the community's efforts to control the konan. This possibility drew even more attention when, after the young man began to recover, his younger brother became ill with the same symptoms. Again the cause of the illness was sought in public assembly, and the conclusion reached was that some still harbored grievances against the elder brother. In this second instance, the boy's father paid compensation to Moke and Mer, who had been suspected of using malign magic to spoil the fishing. The curing assembly concluded that these two had a special grievance, for they had been held responsible for the failure of the past month's endeavors when those endeavors had been undermined, at least in part, by this failure to observe ritual prohibitions.

These events were the konan issue's last public gasp that year, for the konan season was rapidly drawing to a close. It almost looked as though the villagers had achieved a final resolution of the konan quandary and had exonerated those suspected of malign magic. Some men and women, perhaps more eager than others to see the incident closed, did speak as though this were the case.

The issue, however, was not so easily resolved. I suggested to

one man that the compensation paid to Moke and Mer represented public recognition of their innocence of malign magic, and
he replied simply that such an idea was "bullshit." Many still suspected Moke and Mer of using malign magic to vent their anger at
other villagers for not cooperating with them in the Kreer episode.
There was also the implication that Moke's and Mer's alleged
anger, no matter how just its origins, deterred the favor of the
ancestors and / or the Catholic supernaturals.

The suspicion that these two were using malign magic, however, had roots many years in the past. Villagers suspected and
feared Moke and Mer, not just because they were believed to have
the motive and the power to scatter the fish, but also because of a
long history of disputes and factionalism involving these two. Yet,
although suspicions continued to simmer, the issue received no
more public attention.

Collective Identification and Collective Failure

During the months that the question of the konan occupied center
stage in Kragur, villagers offered a plethora of explanations for the
failure of all efforts to control the fish. Almost all of these focused
on acts or conditions that thwarted the quest for social harmony
and unity of purpose. Whether villagers preferred the idiom of
Catholicism or that of the indigenous belief system, they tended to
see lack of harmony and unity as the reason for their failure to
secure the aid of supernatural forces.

The issue of the impropriety of mixing Catholic and indigenous
practices was clearly secondary, but the charge that Kragur people
had simply not shown enough commitment to Catholicism also
displays a concern with social harmony in the shape of unity of
purpose. Some seemed to think that lack of common commitment
to Catholicism was enough to lose supernatural favor.

While villagers singled out particular individuals for blame,
there was also a sense of collective failure. Although, as in any
community, there are factions and divisions in Kragur, people do
identify themselves with the village as a whole and feel they share
in its reputation and its fate, its successes and failures. As I have
pointed out, a few were skeptical about the dependence of good
konan fishing on perfecting social relations in the village. The pre-

vailing view of things in this episode, however, was that collective identification was not just a matter of sentiment, it was also a fact of material life. Village prosperity depended on village unity and harmony.

Kragur people wanted lots of fish in 1976, but there was more at stake than fish. Granted, many villagers were preoccupied throughout with how to end specific disputes and grievances so they could fill the smoking racks above their fires with fish for the next few days and weeks. But, given the prevailing view, failure in collective material endeavors always reflects on the village's moral stature. As I will discuss at greater length in later chapters, in these times of rapid and perplexing change, many villagers feel that failure in such endeavors reflects on Kragur's moral capacity to cope with the new era.[4] This theme was not central in the konan affair. It did come to the fore at times, nevertheless, as in the assemblies some spoke of the declining power of indigenous magic, the need to adopt new methods for these new times, the challenge posed by their new commitment to the Virgin, and the association of this new commitment with the challenge of independence. In the chapters that follow, I will explore some of the ways in which the familiar association between the quality of social relations and material prosperity is affecting villagers' approaches to distinctively contemporary problems.

The deputy *kaunsil*, or *komiti*, gives assignments to women assembled for a day of communal work.

Kragur men launch a canoe from the village's rocky beach.

A *ramat walap* of *koyeng* Shewaratin makes a speech at a gift exchange honoring the dead. He holds a bundle of tobacco, a common gift on important occasions.

A group of women from Kragur stop to rest and pose by the statue of the Virgin Mary at the top of the main trail across Kairiru.

A woman of *koyeng* Ku prepares sago for the evening meal by stirring it with hot water.

A man of *koyeng* Ku, an expert wood carver, puts the finishing touches on the decorated handle of a taro pounder.

The principal exponent of Catholicism in Kragur leads a prayer in the center of the village.

A *ramat walap* of *koyeng* Kragur addresses a meeting held to discuss the flooding of the stream that feeds the men's and women's bathing places.

SIX

Understanding Poverty: The Mundane, the Extraordinary, and the Moral Preoccupation

PERHAPS THE SINGLE MOST overwhelming problem Kragur people see facing them, the problem that constantly lurks in the background when it is not pushed in their faces, is their poverty. Villagers have never had much material wealth by the standards of economically more developed societies. Today they have many things they did not have in the past—metal tools and cookware, nails, flashlights, ready-made fishing line, and a host of other items that would have aroused their grandparents' acute envy. Villagers regard many of these new possessions as invaluable improvements over the past. Yet now they also compare themselves with the whites in Papua New Guinea and the small, emerging indigenous elite, and this makes them feel poor in a new and deeply troubling way.

Villagers have done most of the things suggested to them as ways of prospering in the new world and working their way up from the bottom of the heap: they have sent their children to school, gone to church, planted coconuts, and joined the Local Government Council. A few individuals have succeeded in the educational system and gone off to join the small, largely urban Papua New Guinean middle class; but the village and those who remain there are stuck on the far edge of the new society with its new forms of material prosperity and political power. In explaining this, and so many other things, villagers tend to focus on moral and social issues; that is, they assume that goodness has a lot to do with the new prosperity and they tend to define goodness in terms of the quality of social relations. Villagers also offer other types of explanations, both more mundane and impersonal and seemingly more fantastic. The mundane, however, frequently take second place, and the extraordinary—that is, ideas about the roots of wealth and poverty associated with cargo cults—also betray a moral preoccupation.

A New Kind of Poverty

In precolonial times there were differences in wealth and power among villagers. Possession of immaterial property—rights to magic or to possession and use of particular kinds of material goods—was undoubtedly a major source of distinction among individuals and koyeng, as it is today. Those with rights to magic for producing crops, hunting, or fishing had more power to control and amass material wealth, but what they accumulated or helped an ally to accumulate was generally distributed to others. This increased the prestige and influence of the giver but tended to level the material standard of living. Men of influence may have had the opportunity to accumulate shell valuables, dogs' teeth, or other items of wealth more easily hoarded than food. I suspect, however, that in precolonial times it would have been difficult to tell a ramat walap from any other villager by his clothing, his house, or what he ate for dinner. This is certainly the case today.

Neither is it easy to tell important people from others by what they do. In the past, men of influence would have devoted some of their time to applying their esoteric magical knowledge and would have spent more of their time than others on trading expeditions, discussing village problems, or traveling to other villages to deal with such matters as sorcery accusations, marriage exchanges, or war alliances. Today some villagers spend more time than others in ritual, administrative, or political activities; but everyone also works in his or her own garden, fishes, processes sago, joins in to build houses, and performs a multitude of daily household and subsistence tasks.

Just as distinctions among Kragur villagers are not conspicuous, neither are there conspicuous distinctions among Kairiru villages. Some are larger than others, some have more convenient or more picturesque sites than others, but at first glance they are very similar in the quality of the houses and the health and vigor of the peo-

ple. At one time or another, particular villages may suffer short-
ages of taro, sago, or other staples, and some may profit more
than others from their copra or the remittances they receive from
migrants. Many such distinctions, however, are temporary, and
few are glaringly obvious.

The distinctions between Europeans and the emerging indigenous elite, on one hand, and villagers, on the other, are of a different order. Villagers now must compare their material way of life
with that of people who live in houses built of milled lumber,
cement, glass, and metal, with many rooms, modern plumbing,
refrigerators, electric lights, and telephones. These people also
own multiple suits of clothes, move around town in cars and
trucks, and travel to Port Moresby, Australia, and beyond by
plane. Further, they perform very little hard physical labor. I could
not count the number of times Kragur people pointed out to me
that whites carry everything in trucks and lift things with winches,
while they have to carry heavy loads on their backs over steep and
slippery bush trails. Kragur life is filled with heavy lifting—house
and canoe timbers with the girth of small telephone poles, net bags
brimming with taro or coconuts, loads of firewood—and, from
experience as migrant workers, many villagers know that when
there is heavy lifting to be done in the white world, most whites
prefer to have someone else do it. From observation, hearsay, and
their own experiences working as "houseboys" for Europeans, villagers also know that many whites do not do their own domestic
labor either.

Europeans and the indigenous elite also have money in comparatively abundant supply, and villagers know that, at least at one
level, this is what gives them access to all the other goods and privileges of the postcontact world. Paypai points out that whites can
travel easily because they have money to pay for food and lodging
and thus do not have to carry food with them or rely on the hospitality of relatives or friends. They also have money to buy airplane
tickets. "You can't take a bag of food and buy a ticket for Australia, or America, or Moresby," he observes. To many, the opportunities money brings in the present social world have deep significance. Money can buy not only convenience and mobility but also
full participation and a sense of worth in the new, larger society.
As Kanim observes, in these times "money makes you a man."

The material gap goes hand-in-hand with a great disparity in political power. In the colonial period the Europeans simply appropriated supreme power to themselves. National independence did not return Kragur people to their precolonial state of autonomy. They are well aware that major decisions affecting their lives are still made by elites in the towns who care nothing for the authority of a barefoot ramat walap from an obscure corner of the province.

The differences in power and wealth among villagers and whites and indigenous elites are starker and more extreme than the differences among villagers themselves. In their harsh light, distinctions among villagers do not entirely disappear, but they do pale. Villagers find themselves pondering their position as a group, the big men and their followers alike rendered small in comparison with new kinds and degrees of wealth and power.

I have already described the geographical factors that make success in cash cropping difficult for Kragur people—the steep, rocky terrain, the village's distance from mainland markets, and the lack of regular and economical transport. Villagers are well aware that these conditions place them at a disadvantage. Kragur, they say in Pidgin, is a *ples ston,* a hard and rocky place, and a *lus ples,* a lost or far away place. They are also well aware that migration has cost them many men and women in their prime working years. On top of all that, in 1976 the price for their major crop, copra, had been falling. Some found this puzzling. One man, for example, could only complain that the same thing had happened years ago when the government had urged them to plant peanuts: at first prices were good, but then they plummeted and villagers were advised not to plant any more. Others, however, had heard that there was too much copra on the world market, so prices had fallen. "Don't think only New Guinea has copra," explained Tarakam. "Lots of countries have copra and sell it. If some of these countries didn't have it, they'd raise the price a little."

Cargo Cults in Kragur

Despite their recognition of such factors as lack of transportation and the state of the world market, many Kragur villagers have

been drawn to cargo cults. These typically promise sudden attain-
ment of social and material equality with Europeans, usually
through intervention of dead ancestors whose aid is sought
through collective ritual. A thorough examination of anthropological thinking on cargo cults would lead us from a consideration
of millenarian movements around the world (Burridge 1969)
through nationalist politics (Worsley 1968) and Melanesian cultural psychology (Schwartz 1968; 1973). My focus here, however,
is on the continuity in Kragur of cult belief and lore with common
cultural features, including a tendency to link moral and material
issues.

Some Kragur people are aware of two of the most widespread
and enduring cargo cults in Papua New Guinea, the Yali movement (Lawrence 1964) and the Peli Association (May 1982), the
latter of which is centered in the East Sepik Province. Neither of
these, however, ever gained a foothold in Kragur to my knowledge. I know of only two instances of overt Kragur involvement in
cargo cults. The earliest of these took place just prior to World
War II, when a number of young men from Kragur are said to
have taken part in a cult based in another north coast Kairiru village. The cult ritual consisted mainly of marching and drilling, on
the pattern of European soldiers. Participants hoped that this
would bring about the return of the dead ancestors in ships filled
with material wealth of all kinds. Allegedly hopes ran high, but
the sudden advent of the war brought the cult to an end. One current detractor jokes that the cultists did finally see ships on the
horizon, but they turned out to be full of Japanese soldiers.[1]

The only postwar cult activity I know of peaked in the early
1970s. The principal cult ritual was communal prayer in the village cemetery, including both saying the rosary and petitioning
deceased kin. By all accounts, almost all of those who took an
active part in the cult were members of only one of the village's
divisions. An outbreak of illness hastened the demise of the cult.
Many villagers apparently feared that the cult activity had somehow precipitated the illness, perhaps because, while villagers
turned to the dead for assistance in the cult, as they often do in
everyday life, they knew the dead could also be dangerous. In
addition, a few of the more active cult participants had occasionally been accused of practicing sorcery, and many villagers simply
did not trust them.

Cults and Cultural Precedent

Cargo cults hold out the hope of access to contemporary forms of wealth if one possesses some secret, although simple, knowledge and performs the proper ritual. While cults appear extraordinary on the surface, they are in many ways variations on familiar cultural themes. For example, although Kragur people know well that they cannot produce food without hard physical labor, most also feel that one must have good relations with the supernatural and/or perform proper magical procedures to produce abundant and high-quality crops and to hunt and fish successfully. Some older villagers are also quite convinced that the same must apply in the white world. One man, the heir to rights to important subsistence crop magic, once asked me if there were a singsing or magical spell for producing rice, which he and many others think of as a quintessential European food. I told him that there was not; he insisted, however, that there must be, but I just did not know about it.

The idea of easy access to contemporary forms of wealth may have some roots in a misunderstanding of how whites marshal material goods with relatively little observable physical labor. When telling me of the men's cult house at Arai that produced wealth miraculously, Lapim explained parenthetically that what Papua New Guineans called a men's cult house, the whites called an office (in Pidgin, "waitman ol i kolim opis"). In both, he said, "You sit and talk and everything appears without effort." A similar theme, however, appears to predate European contact and is common in indigenous mythology. The story of the Arai men's cult house would be a good example, except that this may be a relatively recent creation, for some say that Lapim learned it in a dream; but there are other examples. The story of the origins of the konan tells of a time when the fish simply could be extracted from a bamboo tube. Taunur tells of a masalai named Nufaung who could produce completely processed sago starch simply by kicking the sago palm. Taunur also tells of an old woman who lived at a place called Abilingingi, in the general vicinity of Reo. Once, while looking after her grandchild, she went to wash. When she did so, she simply removed her old skin, revealing a new white skin underneath. When she returned wearing her new skin, her grandchild was afraid and cried. So she went back to where she had hung her old skin on a tree and put it on again. These are, in a sense, stories of a lost golden age. The konan were inadvertently released from the bamboo tube; the masalai Nufaung neglected to tell his children how to produce sago the easy way so they had to labor all day, just as villagers now do; and, after the old woman of Abilingingi put her discarded skin back on, knowledge of how to renew one's skin vanished.[2]

The notion that the world can be transformed suddenly and dramatically is central to cargo-cult beliefs and consistent with characteristic features of the view of history in Kragur—that is, a tendency to see the past as shallow and past events as noncumulative. The longest list of consecutive patrilineal forebears I collected, for example, extends only nine generations back. Genealogical depth, of course, does not necessarily indicate the limit of the conception of the past, but it is suggestive. Also, some genealogies I collected, although rather short, reach back to the era of mythological events that created features of the present world.

There is a tendency to see the past of the outside world as well as the local past as shallow and relatively immediate. For example, in discussing Catholicism with them, I asked a number of villagers when Jesus had lived. They usually placed his life within the span of local historical/mythical events, frequently within the last five generations, or even during their grandparents' time. One could see this shallow view of the past as another aspect of the small-world perspective, a vision of the world as limited in time as well as in space. Like the limited geographic perspective, this, too, is wearing away among younger people under the influence of wider experience and Western education. But the long-standing compressed view of time still asserts itself in the face of new kinds of knowledge. Paypai, for example, is in his late twenties, has a sixth-grade education, and is competent with English numbers— for instance, when dealing with money. Once, while discussing Papua New Guinea's recent independence, he speculated that the United States had only gained its independence two or three years before. When I told him that it actually had been exactly two hundred years since U.S. independence, he asked if I had already grown to adulthood then or had still been a child. Paypai can count out two hundred kina or two hundred taro or stones or pigs or bottles of beer. In this case, however, and in similar cases I could recount, I believe the idea of two hundred years as a large quantity relative to the length of a human life was less compelling than a deeply ingrained tendency to see the past as shallow.

The past is not only shallow, it is also rather hazy. While villagers often speak of events that took place before the era of their parents and grandparents, they do not agree on the sequence in which they took place and generally seem unconcerned with chronology.[3] Many villagers recognize the dearth of systematized knowledge of the past and express regret that their parents and grandparents did not recount it to them more thoroughly, although I suspect that previous generations had their own near thresholds of clarity as well. The problem, however, is not inadequate record keeping but a lack of interest in chronology. This suggests a view of historical time that is not linear, cumulative, and directional, like that familiar in the developed Western world. Past events are important in themselves, but not as cumulative steps toward the present (cf. Schieffelin 1976:141). This is highly compatible with and perhaps an integral dimension of a view of the past as shallow, for without depth there is little need to stack events in neat consecutive order, and vice versa.

To bring the discussion back to cargo cults, there is little room in such a shallow past for the gradual evolution of technology or cumulative change in the material standard of living. If it does not in itself decree that even massive change must be swift, even apocalyptic, it certainly does not encourage a view of change as a more gradual process. McDowell (1988) points out that in a number of Melanesian societies historical change is commonly seen as abrupt and discontinuous. People expect dramatic transformations, like those wrought in the past by ancestors and culture heroes, and they often seek to control or facilitate them. Cargo cults thus can be seen as the application of an old idea to new circumstances in which dramatic change seems possible and desirable.[4]

There is, then, much indigenous precedent in Kragur for the kind of reaction to European colonial domination seen in cargo cults.[5] As noted earlier, however, even though all villagers to some extent share the views and orientations that underlie some key aspects of cults, only a part of Kragur village became actively involved in recent cult activity. Individual experience and psychology may have played a role here, but it appears that existing social divisions and rivalries were the major factors determining participation.[6]

Cults, Catholicism, and the Moral Dimension

The emphasis on moral themes in Kragur cults also links them to broader cultural phenomena. Many villagers are reluctant to speak about past cargo-cult activities in Kragur, but a few who had been deeply involved still think they may have been on to something and were glad to discuss their ideas with me. They also told me stories, which they claimed to have learned from returned migrants or in dreams, that supposedly validated their hopes for transforming their world through cult ritual. Some of these are largely concerned with secret wealth-producing knowledge and have little or no obvious moral content. There are, for example, apocryphal tales of whites with knowledge of how to secure material goods magically who simply refuse to share that knowledge. Some tell of a white priest on Karesau island who knew how to petition dead Papua New Guineans for money, which he kept for himself rather than giving it to their descendants, to whom it rightfully belonged. Says Taunur, after recounting this tale: "We know this story so we keep an eye on [the priests] now. People say that if you see them come to steal [from our dead] to drive them away. [Some] have seen them and now we know." Another villager tells of a deceased Kragur man who served with the Australian colonial police force and claimed that a friendly Australian patrol officer had taught him how to obtain money from the dead. The Australian allegedly told him not to tell anyone else, and the Kragur man told other villagers that the government had forbidden anyone to reveal the secret.

Cargo cults, however, involved collective ritual, petitioning both Catholic and indigenous supernaturals. Social harmony and unity of purpose were probably as important here as they are in such other collective rituals as that for controlling the konan. Similarly, a moral theme predominates in some cult lore. Here, for example, is a story associated with the cult of the 1970s, allegedly divulged to a cult leader by his dead father in a dream.

Wankau created the first man, Tau, at a place near the top of the mountain not far from where the statue of the Virgin now stands. Tau, whose skin was white, eventually created his own son, named Lapim, just as Wankau had created him, without the aid of a woman. Lapim's skin was also white. Both Tau and Lapim could create anything they wanted just by wishing for it, so they did not have to work. Tau instructed Lapim, just as he had been instructed by Wankau, that he must never have sexual relations with a woman. Wankau, however, decided to test Lapim by giving him a woman. When he saw the woman, Lapim immediately forgot his father's instructions and had sex with her. She subsequently bore two children, Manwau and Mari, but their skins were black and neither had the extraordinary powers of Tau or Lapim. Mari, however, remained unmarried and thus had much greater knowledge and power than his brother. Manwau married and thus became ignorant and without power. Because Lapim disobeyed Wankau, all his descendants have black skins and none have knowledge or power like that of the whites.

Another story told by some who had taken part in the 1970s cult emphasizes the same general theme, only the authority figure here is not Wankau but the Catholic bishop, and the events recounted allegedly took place in the recent past. According to one story-teller, his father and others who worked for the Catholic mission on Tumleo island said that the European priests there taught the local people how to "pray" to their dead ancestors and solicit material wealth from them; but the islanders disobeyed the mission's teachings and even told the missionaries to leave. With that, the bishop deprived them of their power to petition the dead.

Catholicism obviously has helped to shape cult ideologies and practices in Kragur (cf. Huber 1987:120), although it may not have been necessary to their development (cf. Schwartz 1968:45). One of its chief contributions probably has been to reinforce the moral dimension. Cargo-cult lore echoes the indigenous tales of a lost golden age, but some, like the story of Tau and Lapim, also appears to echo the Christian theme of sin and the fall from grace with which villagers are familiar from the story of Adam and Eve.[7] Ibor's interpretation of Adam and Eve makes it quite clear that he sees the fall from grace and the possibility of the restoration of grace through Christianity as central to the problem of poverty and prosperity. "Adam and Eve didn't follow God's laws," he says, "[so God] closed the door to heaven, and did away with their grace. [If] we had grace we would only have to think to create everything." He goes on to say that Jesus came to open the door to heaven again. As noted in Chapter 5, many villagers find both heaven and hell puzzling ideas; but in his Sunday sermons Ibor presents heaven, the restoration of Adam and Eve's state of grace, as a place where hard work is no longer necessary. "When you die," he says, "it's like a contract laborer finishing his time. This world is a place of work, [but] when you finish you can rest."[8]

The line between cargo cult and Catholicism is, in fact, rather blurred in places. Not only do their practices and ideologies interpenetrate, they probably have served as functional alternatives. It has often been observed that failure to achieve their stated goals does not necessarily lead to the demise of cargo cults.[9] In Kragur, faction and fear of illness and sorcery appear to have been largely responsible for the most recent cult's loss of public acceptability. There is little doubt that some cargo-cult activists subsequently found an alternative vehicle for their hopes and energies in Catholicism. The practice of what appears to be orthodox Catholic ritual in Kragur at times takes on a cultlike intensity, and some of those reputed to have been among the most active in the last cult were among the most vigorous proponents of regular Catholic ritual a few years later. This is not to reduce Kragur enthusiasm for Catholicism to a desire for material wealth. Cargo cults themselves are not so simple. Burridge (1969:141; 1960:247) sees "moral regeneration" as the main theme in cargo cults, and cults in Kragur certainly appear to have linked moral and material accomplishment. The functional equivalence or continuity between Catholicism and cargo cults lies not only in the hopes for material transformation they carry; both also offer the chance to correct a perceived moral deficit and to demonstrate moral worth in the form of collective harmony in their respective, but very similar, rituals.[10]

The Moral Preoccupation and the "Good Way"

Outside the context of cargo-cult lore and practice villagers emphasize the moral theme even more in explaining persistent relative poverty. I was struck by how often villagers criticized their own moral fiber when discussing their failure to make good in the new economy, despite their acute awareness of the concrete obstacles to more successful participation in modern markets. This is merely one dimension of a moral preoccupation that colors all aspects of Kragur people's views of the nature and problems of the current age.

The claim to moral uniqueness on which villagers build their self-image as Catholics is a good place to start an examination of this moral preoccupation. As discussed in Chapter 4, Kragur people were fond of explaining to me how this long-standing moral uniqueness suited them to become especially good Catholics and made them different from the people of other villages. They are, they would say, uniquely hospitable to visitors and unusually harmonious and cooperative among themselves. Villagers pointed this out to me so often and spoke so often of Kragur's *gudpela fasin*—good fashion or good ways—that I came to think of this bundle of claimed special qualities as simply the "Good Way." I do not think the villagers themselves regard it as such a well-defined entity, but it has the feeling of a shared ideology, like the "work ethic" or "American know-how" or "soul."

Some Kragur people assert their village's special virtues with such persistence and give so much weight to acting out the precepts of the Good Way that it takes on the quality of a ritual performance. Like full participation in a fishing assembly or faithful prayer to the Virgin, it appears to be a demonstration of moral worth to whatever powers may be attending, whether they be priests, government officers, dead ancestors, or God and Maria. However, the people enacting the ritual are also part of the audience. As an expression of moral worth, the Good Way may be, for villagers, as much a matter of reassuring themselves as impressing others. Such reassurance is needed because, as I have already proposed, the colonial and postcolonial devaluation of indigenous forms of material wealth, political power, and social standing calls villagers' moral worth into question.[11]

To speak of the Good Way as such a ritual expression of moral worth makes it sound a great deal like a cargo cult. Belief that collective moral improvement is essential to overcoming contemporary relative poverty is quite compatible with cargo-cult ideology that promises sudden supernaturally mediated material fulfillment. It is also compatible, however, with the desire to generate "ritual heat" through collective action (Brison 1991:341) in order to empower more limited pragmatic goals, or with a Western-style interest in gradually increasing technical productive efficiency through better cooperation and coordination of efforts. Its compatibility with diverse perspectives on the problem of poverty helps make the Good Way widely acceptable and available to all as a means of moral reassurance.

The resonance of Catholicism's moral emphasis with currents in the indigenous culture provides the groundwork for constructing Kragur villagers' contemporary identity. To the extent that the Good Way prescribes noncommercial behavior—that is, generosity and unstinting hospitality—it has flourished in part for one of the same reasons Catholicism has: lack of opportunity to find a secure place and identity in the postcontact world through participation in the commercial economy.

The Good Way also seems to have a momentum of its own, as villagers' self-image and behavior and outsiders' expectations reinforce each other. Hospitality extended to one mission representative may have brought others in his wake; the success of a few Kragur students in school probably led teachers to receive others with high expectations, which contributed to their success; the success of those who became catechists, brothers, and priests undoubtedly increased mission esteem for the village and the village's friendliness toward the mission. It is impossible to say how such a spiral might have started. Perhaps God's visit to Kragur, or whatever event came to be so interpreted, gave a special quality to the later meetings of villagers and missionaries, beginning a process of village self-presentation, external recognition, and reinforcement of village self-image.

My own choice of Kragur as a field site was in part the result of this process. When I first went out to Kairiru I had already visited some other mainland and island Sepik villages, a number of which would have been perfectly acceptable as field sites, but I decided to go on to Kairiru out of curiosity. I came from Wewak on a boat from St. John's seminary and stayed the night there. The next day I walked to St. Xavier's, where I met the school's headmaster, a Marist brother who had lived on Kairiru for several years. He suggested that I visit Kragur before I chose a field site because, through his dealings with Kragur students and their parents, he had formed an especially good opinion of the village. That same day I went over the mountain to Kragur, guided by one of Ibor's sons, then a student at St. Xavier's. On that first visit, the village's striking setting and the abundant cold water that filled the bathing pools probably impressed me as much as the warmth of my reception by the people; but the whole package was very attractive, and I decided to ask the villagers' permission to live among them and observe and write about their lives. At the time I was not aware of Kragur's history of involvement with the Catholic mission and Catholic schools and the ideology of the Good Way. It eventually became clear to me that all this was behind the headmaster's suggestion, my friendly reception in Kragur, and the villagers' acquiesence to my request to live among them.

My first visit to Kragur and my request to stay and work there, then, were in a sense the result of God's alleged visit to Kragur decades before. My desire to stay and work in their village probably further confirmed and strengthened the Kragur people's Good Way self-image. I also propagated that image beyond the village as I spread my favorable impressions on occasional travels to other villages, St. Xavier's, St. John's, and Wewak. Certainly my presence in Kragur added to its distinction in the eyes of some other Kairiru islanders, for when I visited other villages older people would sometimes ask me to have my superiors in America send someone to do whatever it was I did in their villages too. There were those in Kragur who noticed such signs of envy with pleasure and probably took them as further confirmation of their village's special worth.[12]

External recognition of Kragur's good relations with missionaries, anthropologists, and other outsiders has not only confirmed villagers' self-image; it may also have discouraged other villages from pursuing a similar path to distinction. That is, following a pattern found elsewhere in Melanesia (Schwartz 1976:112), other villages may not have wanted to appear to be imitating Kragur. I did find that Kairiru islanders from other villages sometimes said all Kairiru people were especially hospitable and especially good Catholics. The events that guided me to Kragur, however, and the perceptions of it I found among the staff at St. Xavier's and the mission personnel on the mainland suggest that Kragur in fact has developed this public image and self-image to an unusually high degree.

Moral Comparison and Moral Self-Doubt

While the Good Way has its own momentum, moral self-doubt also helps to sustain its brand of moral assertion. This becomes

clearer if we look at how villagers see themselves in comparison
with others. They often speak of how present Kragur people differ
morally from those of the past and how their village differs morally from other villages.

Their own past provides villagers with one standard of comparison. Looking back, the past they see is not bathed uniformly in
nostalgia. Many speak of technological changes that have made
their lives easier: for example, nylon fishing line, steel tools, and
the pieces of lead pipe that have replaced the bamboo once used to
tip sago-pounding tools. Women note with approval the relaxa-
tion of restrictions on their conduct during menstruation or
widowhood. Although some villagers tell tales of past warfare and
violence with relish, most see the end of intervillage raiding and
violent settlement of disputes within the village as welcome
improvements in the quality of life. Despite all this, there is a
strong tendency to focus on what are seen as the superior features
of the past.

Many villagers say that their forebears had more magical
knowledge, were bigger and healthier, and had more and better
food. Health and food, of course, are intimately related to the
moral condition of the community, and more often than not villagers speak explicitly of the moral superiority of their predecessors. In the past, many say, both leaders and the rank and file were
more cooperative, villagers were more responsive to their leaders,
disputes were settled with less rancor, and people took more pleasure in communal activities. Although one might expect older villagers to speak more wistfully than younger ones of the days gone
by, I found no clear distinction. Here are the words of a migrant in
his late twenties: "The time of our fathers and grandfathers was
good, a good time. They had plenty of garden produce and fish.
Now, times are hard. Before, they had one leader, they cooperated. Now, one man knows a little magic and he wants to use it
just for himself. One man is a leader over here, another is a leader
over there—they don't work together."

Similarly, a village resident in his sixties describes the moral
decline he has witnessed: "Now, in these times, people are rough.
They don't treat each other right. Before, in our fathers' time, it
wasn't like that, they were good people. If you were angry with me
you'd come quietly to my house, [you wouldn't just shout and lose
your temper]. We've departed from the ways of our fathers and
grandfathers."

Such characterizations of the past are probably highly romanticized, and villagers' own accounts of specific events in the past sometimes contradict them. It would be surprising, however, if the great changes that have occurred in the world around Kragur in recent decades had not had some effect on the kind and quality of social relations in the village. A few villagers do speak of the effects of externally instigated changes. Says one young man: "I think the customs of the past were all right. People lived in a good way. When the mission came and taught about God, things went wrong. Now we have many different ideas about things; before they had one idea." Nevertheless, when most villagers speak of moral decline in terms of diminished harmony and cooperation, they are more likely to blame themselves than their circumstances.

Nostalgia for the past is not unusual. In Kragur, as I have already discussed, it includes images of a lost golden age of comparative ease, power, and plenty. The self-critical context of much of the talk of the past in Kragur, however, suggests that such nostalgic images are a way of expressing feelings about the present and are not the primary source of those feelings.

On a number of occasions I heard Kragur men compare their own village unfavorably with others in public orations. In the New Year meeting, for example, one man spoke of Kragur's economic stagnation and asked angrily: "Why isn't our village in good shape? Why are all the other villages doing well?" Still, villagers seldom draw critical conclusions about their moral stature from comparisons with the pace of progress in other villages. They are more likely to explain such differences by reference to Kragur's harsher geographical circumstances. Indeed, there is wide agreement that when it comes to internal harmony and solidarity and to hospitality and generosity toward outsiders Kragur is superior to most other villages—or at the very least no worse.

The sense of moral inadequacy that currently troubles villagers and informs visions of the past is, I believe, largely a product of the contrast they see between themselves as Papua New Guineans and white or European society as they know it. Kragur people compare their way of life with that of the whites in many ways. They often speak of specific practices—different ways of treating illness, cooking food, building houses, or getting married—without labeling the practices of one society as better or worse than those of the other. More often, however, they draw more general and evaluative comparisons. They speak of the obvious disparity

in wealth; the comparative luxury in which all whites known to
them live; the heavy burdens villagers are obliged to carry, while
whites carry everything in cars and trucks; the way in which
whites travel freely back and forth to Australia, Germany,
America, and other places, while only a very few Papua New
Guineans can afford to do so. A few Kragur men recognize that
not all whites have good jobs, money, or advanced knowledge,
and that some whites are *rabis*—that is, rubbish—as one says in
Pidgin. Nevertheless, most villagers consider white society vastly
superior in its wealth, comfort, technological accomplishments,
power, and mobility.

Just as some know that not all whites are wealthy, many villagers know from experience that not all whites are good. Despite
this, comparison with whites often goes beyond material contrasts
to moral ones presented as the root of the material gap. One can
still hear white residents in Papua New Guinea explaining that the
"natives" remain poor because they are lazy. Kragur people do not
feel that their moral weakness lies here. They do, however, draw
more subtle moral contrasts, most of which concern the quality of
social relationships.

The least subtle of such contrasts is between what Kragur people see as their own violent and warlike disposition and the peace-
fulness of the whites. White colonial control suppressed intervillage warfare, homicide, and violent settlement of disputes, so
villagers associate the present era of relative freedom from violence with the white way of life. Similarly, villagers often speak of
how whites deal with their anger in a superior way. Papua New
Guineans, they say, hide their anger rather than bringing it out
into the open so that it can be resolved, and, if confronted, they
will deny that they are angry with someone. Whites, it is sometimes said, honestly admit their anger and freely air their grievances. Since most villagers believe that hiding anger leads to covert
retaliation through sorcery or illness mediated by ancestral ghosts,
it is a moral failure with serious consequences. Whites are sometimes said to enjoy better health as a direct result of their openness
and honesty in dealing with anger and grievances. According to
Taunur: "You whites don't have sorcery. When you have a dispute, right away you shake hands, sit down together, eat together;
it's over. In Papua New Guinea, no way. I'll go off somewhere and
you'll go off somewhere else and we'll both brood about it until
one of us gets sick."

Some villagers also say that whites are not prone, as they are, to disputes over women inspired by jealousy and suspicion. As the village councillor explains, "We [Papua New Guineans] are the birthplace of jealousy." Aram, a middle-aged man, explains further: "If I go around anywhere with another man's wife and we talk and laugh [or we walk together to the bush], later that man will worry. [He'll think,] 'He's trying to seduce my wife.' " Tarakam contrasts such a tendency with white customs: "Among you whites, young women can dance with young men, and married men too. Among us, if my wife dances with another man I think, 'She might go with this man now,' and I'll be angry and I'll fight with the man."

By far the most common moral contrast villagers see is that between the supposed unity, cooperation, and responsiveness to leadership of the whites and the alleged lack of such qualities among Papua New Guineans. Sakun is worth quoting for his description of this contrast:

> At a meeting or whatever kind of social event all the men and women must be happy and celebrate together. When the children in school have a special event, right away all the parents must be there. We don't do things that way. One person thinks they're most important, another thinks he's most important; everyone keeps to himself. When the bell rings people stay in their houses. It's making the village go downhill. If you just keep to yourself in your house it doesn't make the village joyful, it doesn't make the village happy. You whites, if there's a special event anywhere, everyone will be there, celebrate, make everyone happy. That makes the country grow and prosper.

Some villagers fear for the future of their country because of what they see as the selfishness and lack of disinterested public spirit among Papua New Guineans in positions of relative power and influence. For example, one older man says he does not trust Papua New Guinean medical personnel or policemen because they will neglect their responsibilities unless closely supervised by their superiors. In contrast, "Whites do things right, like the policemen or the doctors. They take their duties seriously." Similarly, another villager complains of the favoritism shown by airline-ticket clerks and the operators of passenger boats to members of their own language groups—in Pidgin, *wantoks*—and another complains of how it is no longer safe to send money through the mails since Papua New Guineans took over the postal service from Australians.

Certainly there are qualifications to this view of white moral superiority. Ungwang, for example, has worked on the crews of commercial fishing vessels and reports that white crewmen are just as apt to neglect their duties when unsupervised as Papua New Guineans. In larger ways, too, Kragur people see whites as no better or even worse than New Guineans. The issue of money is the clearest illustration. Although many villagers are eager to participate more in the cash economy, they often criticize whites for the extent to which the commercial spirit seems to govern all their social relationships. Also, although villagers often speak of the need to follow what they call in Pidgin the *lo bilong waitman,* the laws or customs of the whites, this remains to some a very vague prescription. Women tend to be less specific in their discourses on the moral contrasts between whites and Papua New Guineans, doubtless in large part because of their relative lack of direct experience with white institutions. As Ranuk, a middle-aged woman, says: "All the time the men admonish us, 'You must be good, correct your ways, follow the customs of the whites. How else will we get money and business?' I don't understand this speech they're always giving us." And another, older woman concludes: "We think, 'You [men] have been to the whites and seen. You follow their customs and we'll follow you. You find the way and show it to us.' "

Nevertheless, from young and old, men and women, one frequently hears more or less elaborate versions of the sentiment "Yuropean i gudpela lo"—that is, "The Europeans [or whites] have good customs." Numbushel, a young migrant, seems to see the United States as the epitome of the enviable white way of life. "America," he says, "is a good place. Life is happy there." Other predominantly white societies also receive praise. Says Brawaung: "You people of America, Australia, all those places, follow God's laws so you don't get sick, you don't have problems. You follow the ways of God, you can't be angry with others, fight with others. You follow a good way and so you aren't troubled with illness and pain."

Brawaung appears to be speaking of supernaturally mediated illness, but villagers seldom state explicitly just how the kinds of moral superiority they attribute to whites give rise to a better material way of life. Some may see harmonious cooperation simply as the prerequisite for the technically efficient way whites work together to produce their amazing material abundance. Yet, given prevailing views of the tie between good social relationships and material well-being when fish, taro, illness, and other familiar things are at issue, it seems likely that many villagers assume that here, too, the good quality of human relations enlists the support of the nonhuman world for worldly human efforts.

Several factors, each reinforcing the others, probably account for the tendency to see whites as more harmonious, cooperative, self-controlled, and so on. Although secular colonial authorities did not shrink from using force to impose their will, their suppression of indigenous violence greatly impressed Kragur people, and most feel it improved their lives.[13] Colonial pacification, however, might not have contributed as much to the elaborate image of white goodness one finds in Kragur or have taken on the aspect of a moral event had the Catholic mission not been the predominant feature of the white world on Kairiru during the colonial epoch. For years, Kragur people's experience of the white world was dominated by an institution preoccupied with moral issues—the confession of wrongdoing, maintaining good relations with supernatural beings, and suppressing anger and vengeance in interpersonal relations. The predominance of Catholicism may have led villagers to perceive secular colonial institutions and their campaign against indigenous violence as having similar moral aims and concerns.[14]

Villagers have also observed the external order of white life—the regular, coordinated activities and compliance with authority of white people in schools, plantations, the mission, and other white institutions. They do not necessarily speak of such external aspects of a supposedly deeper harmony as peculiarly Catholic. Catholicism, however, does have its own characteristic forms of external order: the weekly worship services that shape the temporal world of the whites as well as the order of the collective ritual, with the participants neatly arranged in parallel rows as they recite the litany. Some villagers clearly do see such external order as an attribute of Catholicism. When gathering at Shewaratin for one of the fishing assemblies, for example, the men settled themselves in scattered groups in the shade of trees, houses, and verandas, as

they do for curing sessions or other events; but one of their number called out for them all to come sit together in a single place,
because this was "Maria's meeting."

There is evidence that early Society of the Divine Word missionaries in the Sepik saw indigenous life as disorderly (Wiltgen 1969:
337), but I do not know to what extent mission and colonial
administration rhetoric contributed to Kragur villagers' negative
assessment of their own capacity for cooperation. Brison (n.d.)
argues that the picture of indigenous disorder painted by the South
Sea Evangelical Mission elsewhere in Papua New Guinea probably
contributed to villagers' images of their own anarchic nature.
Lindstrom (1992) argues that the "alien discourses" of "development, Christianity, and a popularized version of social evolution"
have fostered the spread of an image of indigenous disorder
among urban Papua New Guineans. Nevertheless, if the white
world were not a world of great material abundance and apparent
physical well-being, Kragur villagers might not have considered all
of these factors—colonial pacification, Catholic preaching, the
obvious external order of both secular and religious white institutions—evidence of white moral worth. The crucial impetus to perceptions of white moral stature is the whites' striking material
accomplishment. Kragur people tend to see this in the light of
indigenous belief in the interdependence of moral and material
accomplishment, a belief given new and heightened significance by
the importance of the Catholic mission and its moral concerns in
villagers' encounter with the white world.

"Wild" Villagers, Business, and the Romance
of Community Cooperation

Kragur people generally do find themselves morally superior to
whites in their generosity and hospitality, and this is an important
component of their distinctive Good Way. Harmony and cooperation, however, are another story. Although they often claim to be
more harmonious and cooperative among themselves than the
people of other villages, Kragur people feel they suffer in comparison with their forebears and, in particular, with contemporary
white society. It is the latter comparison that they feel most deeply,
that they speak of most, and that suggests to them most pointedly
that they might not be up to coping with the challenges of the

larger contemporary world. Villagers' vigorous assertion of their moral uniqueness is, at least in part, a reaction to and a defense against the sense of inadequacy aroused by their perceptions of white moral superiority. These perceptions not only help account for their preoccupation with their own moral stature; they are also critical to understanding villagers' explanations of their difficulty in mastering the quintessential white institution, business.

Over the years there has been a trickle of experimentation with small business in Kragur. It was one of several Kairiru villages that, in the early 1960s, banded together to invest in a boat to carry cargo and passengers between the islands and the mainland; but the venture failed. There have been several trade stores, but when I first arrived in late 1975 there was only one. Two more opened during the following year; but by 1981 they had both closed. The owner of one store had died and the other store had gone bankrupt. In 1976 a fraternal segment of one koyeng was planning a piggery, to be financed by a migrant brother, although by 1981 little had been accomplished. In 1981 a household in another koyeng had begun selling kerosene in a venture owned and financed by a migrant kinsman. A few men were also talking about getting a license for a village beer club.

In the years since my first arrival in Kragur I have seen the beginning, the decline, and the fall of two attempts at village-wide cooperation in business. In 1976 villagers began a Village Development Fund or Village Account and succeeded in collecting several hundred kina from residents and migrants for the purchase of another cargo and passenger boat. In the late 1970s they also initiated what was called the Community Development Youth Club, which drew its membership from throughout the village. The club engaged in a number of moneymaking projects, including making market gardens and buying and reselling garden produce, and purchased a small aluminum boat with an outboard motor, paid for by a government grant, to carry produce to boarding schools and the hospital on the mainland.

In 1981 the club still existed, but it had been inactive for several months. The Development Fund was still in the bank, and its organizers were still meeting and contemplating their next move. I am not certain that the club is now completely defunct, but at the very least it has lost its village-wide membership and support. In 1983 I received a letter from Shim, who had been chairman of the club in 1981. He reported that he had given up that position because there was too much dissatisfaction: "Ol man i complain nambaut," he wrote in a mixture of English and Pidgin. His letter, and another that came at the same time, also described a new business venture on which some villagers had embarked, buying green copra from other island villages to dry and market. They had spent considerable money to build a modern copra dryer and were trying to raise more—through government loans, grants, and the contributions of migrants and recently returned migrants—to buy a boat to serve this venture. The list of participants included a number from various koyeng who had been active in and enthusiastic about the club in 1981, suggesting that they had begun to put their efforts into this new venture. I also learned from Shim that the Village Development Fund had been dissolved and redistributed to the contributors because, as he wrote in Pidgin, "em ol man long Kragur . . . i krai nambaut"—that is, everyone was complaining.

What went wrong with these latter two ventures? Although some villagers were enthusiastic about the club and the fund in 1981, there was also a great deal of grumbling, including talk that the leaders were only interested in self-aggrandizement and accusations that they were misappropriating money. I sat in on a few meetings of the leaders of the development fund, and although they took their responsibilities seriously, there was a tendency to conduct the affairs of the fund in a closed and autocratic way, a style undoubtedly borrowed from traditional village leaders, the ramat walap. To some extent, disaffection with these efforts may have been in part the result of lack of cooperation, which took the form of lack of unity between leaders and rank and file. Disunity, however, was far from the only problem.

In considering obstacles to business success in Kragur, one must first ask if villagers' goals themselves present an obstacle to success as an outside observer might define it. Consider, for example, Schwimmer's (1979:308–309) discussion of the striking rate of failure of small businesses among the Orokaiva of Papua New Guinea's Northern Province. He concludes: "it is only the White observers and social scientists who see anything tragic in these failures. If the Orokaiva thought them tragic, they would stop setting them up again and again. . . . You gain status even by, and especially by failing. Your business dies, its limbs and assets are spread among the multitude and increase exceedingly. It is a religious practice."

The point is that it is not safe to assume that when people appear to be doing business, they are doing what we might at first suppose. Kragur villagers *are* interested in making money, and this interest is increasing, but that is not all they are interested in. I think that, like the Manus villagers whom Schwartz (1982) describes, Kragur villagers take pleasure simply in participating in some of the trappings of European wealth and power—boats and outboard motors, stores, and "*bisnis* groups," to use an increasingly common English-Pidgin phrase. Simply having something that others do not—a speed boat, a youth club, a new copra dryer —is surely a source of invidious satisfaction in an atmosphere of competitive political relations. Such motives account in part for the poor quality of financial management, for they can be indulged in the absence of financial success, and they thus do little to encourage the acquisition of greater business expertise (cf. Guilford 1982).[15]

Villagers, however, also want to see cash, both for what it will buy and for its confirmation of their moral adequacy. Even when they manage to attain a satisfying level of material well-being by indigenous standards, the comparatively enormous wealth and power of the Europeans remains an inescapable suggestion that villagers are somehow morally deficient. This contributes to their desire for success in the cash economy, and the strength of their desire for money for whatever reasons is likely to contribute to an increasing propensity to engage in business on something like its own terms.

I say "something like" its own terms because many villagers do not understand the nature of money or the mechanisms by which it increases in the same way white business people do. Some villagers definitely see knowledge of business as akin to indigenous esoteric magical knowledge and to the knowledge of effortlessly producing wealth they say was lost when Adam and Eve were expelled from paradise. Also, I think that, for some, taking part in the outward forms of business activity has much the same expressive ritual significance as daily prayer to the Virgin or the marching and praying of past cargo cults. Like the members of the Kaun cargo movement in the Duke of York islands, some Kragur villagers may see business, not only as producing immediate material benefit, but also as a demonstration that they "are capable of the same kind of disciplined, orderly control that is implicit in European business and life" (Errington 1974:263; cf. Allen 1976:251–252, cited in Huber 1988:150).

However, even those who grasp more firmly the prosaic actualities of white business are hampered by a lack of basic business skills and experience. The club appeared to suffer from poor financial management; the accounts were haphazard, and the club easily could have been operating at a loss without knowing it. Some of the leaders of the Development Fund were educated migrants and competent in their own fields of endeavor, but they had little experience in planning business ventures. They did not have well-worked-out plans, and they let the fund languish between sporadic bouts of activity. Many resident villagers have only limited competence with either the indigenous numerical system or Pidgin and English numbers (Smith 1978:115–117). Those who handle numbers with relative ease are unfamiliar with the conventions of bookkeeping and lack the kind of experience that would facilitate recognition of new market opportunities (cf. Epstein 1970; Jackman 1977).

It is easy, then, for an outside observer to find reasons for Kragur people's difficulties in the world of business; but how do villagers themselves explain their problems? One hears a lot of public oratory in Kragur about the village's alleged general failure to improve, and much of this focuses on the lack of cooperation and unity. I also heard the same theme mentioned frequently in private conversations. To confirm my impression that this was the predominant theme in Kragur people's analyses of alleged village stagnation, I made a point of raising this issue in conversations with about a quarter of the adult population, both men and women. I asked each of them what was needed if Kragur was to become a better place in which to live. A summary of their responses, arranged in general categories (see Table 1), illustrates the private concern with the issue of unity, cooperation, and harmony that also dominates public debate. This emphasis appears even more pronounced if we also regard opinions that recognize the importance of cooperation among leaders and better relations between leaders and other villagers as referring to aspects of unity, cooperation, and harmony.

When Kragur people speak specifically of business failures, the

Table 1
What Is Needed for Village Progress or Improvement?

NEEDS	NUMBER OF TIMES MENTIONED*	PERCENTAGE OF TOTAL
Unity, Cooperation, and Harmony (a more communal approach to work, more communal social gatherings, less gossip and jealousy, etc.)	21	31
Leadership	25	37
Better leaders	2	3
Less dispersion of authority, less factionalism, more cooperation between elected/customary leaders and among all leaders	9	13
Willingness to follow village leaders	6	9
No more use of sorcery and malign magic by customary leaders	6	9
Leaders who support cash production more vigorously and who won't stand in the way of innovation by the younger generation	2	3
Economic Change	11	17
More cash production	5	7
Reduction of traditional exchange, gift-giving, and obligation to kin	4	6
Other (a village guest-house run on a cash basis, moving the village to better land)	2	3
More Personal Freedom	7	10
More freedom of choice for women in marriage and other aspects of life	3	4
More freedom for young people in social activities	2	3
Less compulsory work (e.g., council work) and more freedom to work independently on business ventures	2	3
Miscellaneous	4	6
Total	**68**	**100**

*Some informants gave more than one response, and I made no distinction by order of response.

theme of unity, cooperation, and harmony also takes center stage. Of course, they know that copra prices are chronically unstable. Some blame this on the ineffectiveness of the managers of the Cooperative Society or the Copra Marketing Board, or on the failure of copra producers themselves to demand better prices. Some have no opinions. A good number of village men are able, however, to relate falling copra prices to a glutted world market. Similarly, when villagers compare Kragur to other villages in terms of success in the cash economy, they tend to point to factors out of their control rather than to the quality of village social relations. For example, they say that the people of south coast Kairiru villages have more money because they are closer to mainland markets and have more flat land suitable for growing coconuts. Villagers appear to be less concerned, however, with such uncontrollable obstacles than with the question of why they do not do better with what they have, for they frequently ignore other issues and focus on the question of unity, cooperation, and harmony. Manup, an educated young migrant home in Kragur for a brief visit, echoed the opinions of many residents when he spoke, in English, of the village's difficulties. In Kragur, he observed: "It's a bit hard to start up business, because people are still wild. If you ring the bell, you can't expect anybody to attend. They will find silly excuses. If everybody would agree and attend the meeting, it would be very good. Things would run smoothly."

In 1976 Lapim had this to say about plans to buy a boat for commercial use: "Now we'd like to buy a boat. But the way the New Guineans are, one village wants to work alone, another village wants to work alone. They don't think of working together to start a business with a boat or something. The whites don't have that kind of idea."

When I returned to Kragur in 1981 there was still much talk about investing in a commercial vessel, although Kragur was then planning to go it alone. Explanations for the slow progress of this plan sounded familiar. As one young man put it: "We're thinking of buying a boat, but we don't have good cooperation." Referring to the slow pace of commercial and other material progress in Kragur, Numbushel, a young man recently returned from several years as a wage laborer in an urban area, offered this opinion. "If we worked hard, the village would really amount to something, but we aren't unified yet."

In 1981 some were concerned that koyeng sectarianism stood in the way of better cooperation. Ibor complained that too many people were trying to start business enterprises including only members of their own koyeng. This, he said, was wrong and could not lead to success, because Kragur is really "one family." Similarly, when proposing the establishment of the Village Development Fund to a group of resident villagers, one of the young migrants who put forth the idea declared, "Forget about koyeng, all of us together!"

Villagers have some reason to worry that prior internal divisions of the community may impede the development of village-wide unity in business ventures. As noted in Chapter 2, the dual Seksik/Lupelap division appears to determine membership in copra marketing groups and the pattern of investment in trade stores. Some of the business ventures recently begun in 1981 included only segments of single koyeng.

The contemporary concern with village-wide unity and cooperation as the key to business success, however, must be understood in the light of villagers' perceptions of white unity and cooperation and their own failings in this regard (cf. Brison 1991; Errington 1974). Some villagers' opinions make it explicit that perceived white superiority in this area is the standard of comparison. While Papua New Guineans are inclined to fragment in business ventures, as Lapim said, "Whites don't have that idea." Manup said it is hard to start a business in Kragur because people are "still wild." This judgment can only mean that villagers are not yet accustomed to white or European ways, for Manup illustrated his point by noting their indifference to the authority of the village bell and their lack of interest in assembling for meetings. Unfortunately, the many obstacles to business success besides poor cooperation make business failures likely, and these failures only confirm villagers' suspicions of their own inadequacy (cf. Smith 1990:218–220; Brison 1991:341–347).

When younger villagers speak of the need for more unity, cooperation, and harmony, some may mean that this would help bring about more Western-style technical efficiency in Kragur. It is unlikely, however, that even such relatively well-educated migrants as Manup are completely uninfluenced by the need for moral reassurance fostered by the current epoch and by the idea that morally correct social relations place human efforts in tune with nonhuman powers. Indigenous conceptions of the social and moral dimension of all material endeavors certainly influence middle-aged and older villagers. They seek unity, cooperation, and harmony in business for much the same reason they seek it in hunting, fishing, or gardening; and they are stung to heightened concern by their belief that white mastery of business and the wealth it brings are, in part, demonstrations of the superior quality of white social relations.

SEVEN

Redefining Good Social Relations: Reciprocity vs the Commercial Spirit

THERE IS WIDE AGREEMENT IN KRAGUR on some features of good social relations. Most villagers agree that being cooperative and harmonious inside the village includes not hiding anger and not practicing sorcery, and that being hospitable to outsiders includes helping visitors to beach their boats or unload their cargos. In areas where the practices of white society now provide contrasts with long-established ways of doing things, however, uncertainty is creeping in and familiar notions of good social relations are being opened to question. One of these areas is the manner of organizing and conducting work and other activities, which I address in the next chapter. Another is the way in which goods and labor are distributed and exchanged.

My own experience learning to organize giving and receiving with Kragur people was instructive. The villagers and I had to find a way to integrate me, a novel kind of outsider, into the flow of goods and services in the community. This task made us all self-conscious, and the way in which villagers chose to present themselves to me revealed much about Kragur thought on the nature of good social relations. I eventually learned, however, that not all villagers agreed about how I should be treated, and that the face Kragur first showed me represented only one school of thought, albeit the dominant one at the time.

I also found that I had walked into the midst of an ongoing debate about how to handle the distribution of goods and services in more common situations. Villagers were thinking and arguing about how much generosity was good and about the proper role of

163

commercial exchange, some advocating a much wider role for buying and selling in both intra- and extravillage relations. An examination of the strains in the indigenous system of reciprocity reveals a number of reasons why Kragur people may be open to alternatives; but one cannot fully understand why and how this realm is problematic without examining the complexities that flow from the prevailing fusion of moral and material issues. While European wealth suggests to villagers the moral superiority of European social relations, in the realm of economic practice the Europeans present them with more than one model. Mission precepts, and to some extent observed mission practice, contrast with the model presented by secular European institutions. This complicates the problem of weighing different forms of economic practice and grappling with their moral implications. The discussion in Kragur over the relative merits of thrift versus generosity in the use of alcohol, described later in this chapter, illustrates how the contemporary problem of defining goodness in distributing and exchanging material goods enters daily life.

It is easy to find evidence of calculation behind villagers' often militant generosity and rejection of monetary relations. The public concern with moral issues, however, cannot be reduced to a strategy for pursuing material well-being, because moral and material aims are so tightly interwoven. Yet there are signs that Kragur people are starting to redefine good social relations in the economic sphere in a way more compatible with the surrounding capitalist economy in which commodity exchange predominates, pulling goods and labor loose from identification with people and enduring social relations.

I Meet the Economic Good Way

When I first arrived in Kragur it was a new situation for everyone involved, and villagers and I had no ready-made rules to guide us in our relations and transactions. I was the first white person to stay for such an extended period in the village, I was not connected with either the mission or the government, and I was not engaged in business. I had spent three months in Papua New Guinea's Manus Province two years before, with a research team from the University of California, San Diego, but my experience there turned out to be a poor guide to handling transactions in goods and services in Kragur.[1] In Manus we spent much of our time in Pere village, a community whose experience with visiting anthropologists dates back to the residence there of Margaret Mead and Reo Fortune in 1928. In Pere we purchased the local produce offered us with sticks of trade tobacco or Australian currency—for in 1973 Papua New Guinea had not yet achieved independence—and villagers assumed that we would pay wages for the services of a cook and housekeeper, which we did. I had planned on doing my own cooking and housekeeping in Kragur, but I expected to supplement the supplies I brought from Wewak by buying local produce. This would have been a comfortably simple arrangement for someone born and bred in a commercial economy; but it was not to be.

When I first took up residence in Kragur, I stayed in the Shewaratin men's house, or *haus boi* as it is called in Pidgin. This is a small house built for the use of Shewaratin young men when they return home on holiday from schools or jobs. Resident Shewaratin men also gather there to talk or sleep on the long narrow veranda. During my early days in the village many people, some of whom I already knew and some who were still strangers to me, came to the haus boi to give me fresh produce from their gardens, fish, bananas, papayas, pineapples, and plates of taro and sweet potatoes boiled in seawater and grated coconut. Making my own distinction between the raw and the cooked, I asked people if I could pay them money for the fresh food and I offered them sticks of tobacco or cigarettes when they brought me cooked food.[2] A few would accept tobacco, but most refused either money or tobacco, often with apparent embarrassment. Some paused to explain to me that it was not their custom to buy and sell things among themselves, and if I were going to live among them it would not be right to sell things to me either. Women sometimes stopped by the haus boi on their way to the stream to wash dishes and clothes and asked if I had anything that needed washing. When they brought back my clean dishes or my laundry, many would accept cigarettes or tobacco, but their embarrassed refusals soon discouraged me from offering coins. Toward the end of my first month in the village, Kirar, a young migrant worker home on Christmas holiday, explained to me that if I were a government officer or a businessman they would charge me for things, but they did not because I had come from a great distance to stay and I had no garden here to feed myself.

The flow of giving, however, did not move in only one direction. It was not long before women and children began coming to the haus boi, often after dark or when no one else was around, to ask quietly if I could give them a little rice or a can of mackerel. Their behavior when making such requests—embarrassed, occasionally furtive—sometimes suggested uncertainty about the etiquette of the situation, my reaction, and that of their fellow villagers. Others, however, saw the situation as a simple question of reciprocity. During my first month in Kragur, Kanau told me that when they asked me for things "some women and children are ashamed; but I tell them 'Don't be. We've given lots of things to him.'"

Many who asked me for things had previously brought me gifts of food and I was happy to have the chance to reciprocate; others had not, but I gave to them as well. A few also offered to buy things from me, in particular, kerosene, batteries, rice, and canned mackerel. The small village stores rapidly run out of these items, and everyone knew that I had brought a supply around from St. Xavier's by boat, including a large bag of rice and a five-gallon can of kerosene. At first I simply gave people what they offered to buy and, like them, refused payment. I explained that I had not come to Kragur to set up a store and, having observed that they did not buy and sell things among themselves, wanted to follow the same custom.

I began to worry, however, that this policy might soon leave me without some essentials, such as kerosene for my lanterns, that were very hard to come by on the north side of the island. So I began to refuse requests for some items, saying that I had only enough for myself, except in the cases of two or three families that had been particularly generous. Eventually, my entire pattern of giving and receiving narrowed. Although I continued to engage in some reciprocal giving with people throughout Kragur, I also began to establish closer ties with some households than with others. As the flow of gifts and assistance with these households increased, villagers seemed to recognize that my links with them would shape my reciprocal giving in much the same way that kinship links and friendships shaped theirs. As I settled into this more predictable and manageable pattern, I worried less about providing for my material needs. I found that I could safely give away most of my rice and canned fish and count on gifts of garden produce, sago, fruit, fish, and game to replenish my larder. I still, of course, could not exercise the same control over the flow of material goods that one can in commercial relations. I took what I could get when I could get it, cleaning fish delivered at dawn for breakfast or trying to do justice to a stalk of one hundred and fifty ripe bananas. Perishable gifts too large to consume went out again as gifts in a different direction.

I was also sucked into the gift economy when I set out to build a house. The haus boi was cramped and Kragur had no rest house built for the use of government patrols where I might have lived, so I made it known that I wanted to build a new house. I told village leaders that I wanted to pay for the necessary labor and materials. I had already heard villagers' complaints about the difficulty of earning money in their isolated location. Given that, and the magnitude of what I was asking, I expected that my offer would be accepted. However, the councillor—at that time, Lapim—and several customary leaders informed me that it had been decided that my house should be built according to local custom, in other words, I was not to pay them money. I protested that some people would be glad for an opportunity to earn some money and that it was a lot of work to add to their usual tasks. Nevertheless they insisted. Doing things according to local custom meant that I was to provide most of the food for a meal at the end of each day's work and also for a feast to mark the house's completion. I was also to contribute the few building materials that had to be purchased, which only amounted to padlocks for the doors and a couple of pounds of nails. Villagers provided all the other materials—timbers, poles, sago-palm-leaf thatch, hand-hewn planks for doors, sago-palm-leaf ribs for the walls, and betel-palm bark for the floor.

Work on the house proceeded in fits and starts, but it was completed in only a little over two months. The bulk of the construction was done on council workdays, and virtually all the able-bodied men and women took part, as they did when building houses for each other. I distributed rice and canned mackerel each workday, but villagers, as was customary, supplemented this with their own contributions of sago, garden produce, fish, and game. In the late afternoon of each workday, plates of prepared food

were assembled at someone's house (when building a house for
another villager, the prepared food is usually brought to the owner's existing house), the men ate there, and plates of food were sent
to the women and children.[3] The event to mark the house's completion was more elaborate; food was more plentiful, I provided
beer, as villagers often do on such occasions, the drums came out,
and there was music and dancing far into the night.

I spent far less on building the house than I would have had I
purchased all the materials and paid the rural minimum wage, as I
had first intended. In addition, I contributed food and token labor
to the construction of other people's houses for only a little more
than a year, not for the life of the house. All told, the reciprocity
was, in my view, rather out of balance. At least some villagers,
however, did not see such imbalance. Sogum even thought that I
was spending too much money and getting the bad end of the deal.
Sogum had worked for the mission as a carpenter and pointed out
that, when he built a house for wages in those days, he worked on
it every day until it was finished, whereas here in Kragur they were
only working on my house sporadically. He implied that the latter
kind of work was not worth a lot of money. He was also concerned that I was not going to stay in Kragur long enough to get
full value from my investment. "It's not like you're going to stay
here ten years or something," he said. "You'll spend your money
and then go back to America. Who will give you your money
back?"

Those who made the decision to organize the construction of
my house in this way, however, were undoubtedly much less concerned with whether I fulfilled the requirements of reciprocity than
with whether they were living up to a particular ideal of good
social relations. Many villagers took pains to point out that their
treatment of me was simply an example of a long-standing principle of behavior in Kragur. Brawaung proudly told me, "We don't
sell things for money; we just try to help people." To give things
away is known in Pidgin as to *givim fri* or *givim nating*. Sawot, a
woman in her thirties, explained to me that the custom of givim fri
had deep roots in Kragur; it was "the law of our ancestors, and up
to today we follow it." Musuau, a young migrant who worked for
the Department of Public Health in Wewak, agreed that "We've
been like this a long time." He explained: "If we want to sell something, we take it to the market. [But if] someone from another vil-

lage comes to our village, we give him things. I think you'll find that the young people from Kragur who live in town are the same." Many also alleged that this generosity and lack of concern with money was something found in few other places. Said Taunur: "Other villages, if a European comes they'll just ask him to pay, pay, pay. Other places, if you ask for something, they'll just say 'you pay.' "

I was to find, however, that while Kragur people were in fact extremely generous to me and continued to keep commercial principles out of our relations, this behavior and statements of principle like those just noted did not tell the whole story. There was a broader range of opinion in the village on how I should be treated than was easily visible, and division of opinion on this question was a manifestation of disagreement and uncertainty about the roles and norms of gift-giving and commercial relations that obviously predated my arrival.

To Give or Not to Give

Disagreement about the limits to generosity and the respective roles of commercial and noncommercial relations arose in a number of contexts during my stay in Kragur. For one thing, as I have already mentioned, there was dissent from the "official" policy of cleaving to noncommercial relations with me, a policy I myself had encouraged by refusing to accept payment for items from my stock of supplies. For the most part this dissent was quite subdued. A few villagers did request payment for the goods they offered me, but only two or three, and on fewer than a half-dozen occasions. They did so somewhat clandestinely, which suggested that there was social pressure not to enter into monetary relations with me. Also, other forms of dissent had been suppressed. Not long before I left Kragur late in 1976, an unmarried man in his early twenties confided to me that he and some other young men had wanted to accept my offer of wages for building my house, but the older men had forbidden it. He seemed, however, to harbor no hard feelings about this, and in the event he had worked energetically with the others.

Not all dissent was so benign. During my fourth month in Kragur, just as my house was being completed, I received a letter from a group of young Kragur men in Port Moresby, some of whom were working there and others attending the university. The letter asked me to explain who had approved my plan to conduct research in Kragur, asserted that I was engaged in an enterprise that would bring me considerable financial gain in which Kragur people would not share, and demanded that I make a substantial contribution to a fund for the economic development of the village. A few of those who signed the letter had been in Kragur for the Christmas holiday when I first arrived and knew that I was not paying for anything. This probably contributed to the impression that I was exploiting the village, an impression undoubtedly also shaped by general anticolonial feelings. I wrote back to these young men, answering their questions as best I could, explaining the process of applying to Papua New Guinea government agencies for a research permit, telling of the discussions I had had with village leaders, and informing them of the generally nonlucrative nature of a career in academic anthropology and my meager research budget. When I met a number of them later that year and in 1981, we were able to reach cordial mutual understandings.[4]

Better educated, more politically sophisticated migrants, however, were not the only ones in Kragur to take exception to the practice of unquestioning generosity toward agents and emissaries of the postcontact social world. Taunur felt it was right that villagers not ask me to pay for things. "You're living right in the middle of us; they'd be ashamed," he said. Yet, he also said that while they had once regularly given free food to the teachers at Bou primary school, Papua New Guineans from other parts of the country, villagers now sold it to them because they needed the money. Similarly, not all villagers agreed on how much generosity visiting mission personnel should expect. On one occasion a visiting American priest was sitting on Ibor's veranda with a group of men when one of them spied Siragum passing by with several green coconuts he had just retrieved from the top of a palm. One of the men called out to Siragum that the priest was thirsty and would like to drink a coconut, but Siragum walked on, calling back that he only had enough for himself and his friends. Later Siragum told me that priests talked a lot about generosity but did not practice what they preached. "Fuck him!" he concluded.

Forms of giving that predate European contact are also subject to criticism. A few villagers, for example, say they are ready to give up the practice of building each other's houses with unpaid collective labor. "Now a good custom has arrived," says Fanauk, "I have to work for money. That's a good way." Some also advocate establishing a market in the village where Kragur people with momentary surpluses of tobacco, betel nut, or garden produce could sell it to other Kragur people. Many attack the giving of warap as wasteful.

Similarly, the practice of giving gifts of taro and tobacco to visitors from other villages draws fire. In part, what is at issue is the continuation in a very attenuated form of the trading relationships that once linked Kragur to Wogeo island, Murik Lakes, and other locales. Many villagers still value what is left of these ties. In 1981, I traveled down the coast from Wewak with Brawaung's son, Moraf, to a village in the Murik Lakes region to visit friends doing research there.[5] On our return to Wewak we met Brawaung, and he berated us for not taking a bundle of tobacco from Kragur with us. In fact, men in the village we visited asked if we had brought Kairiru tobacco with us and had been pleased to accept the handful of leaves that Moraf was carrying for his own use. Some villagers, however, speak against this traditional form of noncommercial exchange. "All these [customs] of the past are over; we're after money now," says Taunur. "All this 'free' stuff is over. If people from Wogeo come and want tobacco, I'll say I have tobacco but you have to buy it. If I go ask them for a pig, they'll say they have a pig but I have to buy it."

Taunur himself became the object of criticism on a similar score on one occasion. A man from another Sepik island, with whom Taunur had become friends when they were both migrant laborers, visited Taunur for several days and was preparing to leave one morning on a boat chartered to take Kragur's copra to Wewak. Taunur had given him a small basket of taro as a parting gift. Sometime before the boat left, Kragur's representative to the Cooperative Society rang the bell and assembled most of the village for an announcement about copra sales. The cooperative representative is sometimes called in Pidgin the *bisnis komiti*—that is, the business committeeman. On this day the representative was taking his responsibility for business very seriously and took advantage of the gathering for his copra announcement to criticize

Taunur sharply for giving away taro. He inveighed against such gift-giving in general and said that if Taunur would not ask his visitor to pay for the taro, he himself would do so.

In the end, no one asked the visitor to pay for the taro. A number of villagers with whom I spoke later that day thought the cooperative representative had been wrong and what Taunur did with his taro was his own business. Yet, while the cooperative representative's approach was extreme, the general issue was not of his own invention. Earlier that year, in the New Year meeting, Ibor had railed against too much gift-giving to visitors. Part of his speech and Lapim's reply are worth quoting verbatim, because they suggest the ambivalence I think many villagers feel when they contemplate abandoning long-standing customs of reciprocal giving, thus perhaps jeopardizing their self-image as an especially generous, noncommercial community. The discussion had turned to Kragur's lack of money, and Ibor said: "It's a good way, this way is only found in our village, not in other villages, they've all changed completely. But it doesn't work, to give things away, to give to friend after friend after friend. No!" When Ibor had finished speaking, Lapim rose to remind him, somewhat sarcastically, that he was as guilty of this practice as anyone. "You yourself, when people from Walis [island] come, you give them gifts, or when people come from somewhere else you give them gifts. We just follow your example."

Younger villagers tend to be more eager to dive into the cash nexus than their elders; but, as Ibor's exchange with Lapim illustrates, there is not only disagreement among villagers on questions of reciprocal giving versus buying and selling. There is also individual uncertainty and ambivalence about such matters. What is the cause of such tension, uncertainty, and ambivalence?

In the world Kragur people now live in, money has great and obvious attractions, conceivably great enough in themselves to arouse criticism of premonetary customs. Yet, one would not expect villagers to discard long-standing customs easily. They are not only familiar and well understood, they are also deeply enmeshed with ideas about character, status, morality, and the social bases of health and prosperity. The inevitable tension between novel economic practices and economic practices firmly interwoven in the broad social and cultural fabric may be exacerbated in Kragur by a tendency to exaggerate the dominance of commercial relations in white society. For example, as noted in Chapter 2, a few villagers claim to have observed that among whites even brothers and sisters have to pay for food and lodging if they are guests in one's home. Tension between the attraction of money and immersion in a contrasting tradition is not, however, enough to account for the degree of uncertainty and disagreement that surrounds questions of exchange and distribution in Kragur.

Strains in the System of Reciprocity

Morauk says that he, for one, does not care if other people are generous with the fish they catch. "If a man wants to give fish," Morauk says, "he can. If he wants to eat them himself, he can. It doesn't bother me. If I want to eat fish, I'll go catch them myself." Misiling says proudly that her husband, Brawaung, is not concerned when he lends money to people and they fail to repay him. "I ask him to go get our money back, but he says, 'Never mind.' He doesn't worry."

I do not doubt the sincerity of these claims and others like them. Nevertheless, there is also ample evidence that Kragur people sometimes do feel the obligation to give as a burden and suspect that others cannot always be counted on to return their generosity. I observed resistance to the ethic of sharing mostly in small things. Occasionally, for example, if a family invited me to share a meal including a scarce delicacy they would caution me not to mention this to others, who, they feared, might be annoyed because none had been offered to them. Also, villagers are constantly chewing their last betel nut. The demand for betel chronically harries the supply, and people feel free to ask almost anyone seen chewing if they have another nut. More than one villager, however, confided to me that when they do not have very much betel they reply that the one they are chewing is their last. They advised me to do the same if I wanted to keep any of my own supply for myself.[6]

The last-betel-nut stratagem is a way of maintaining some control over one's resources in the face of social pressure to share and indicates that villagers do not always feel they can rely on the generosity of others to make up their losses. Yet, while betel is always in demand, it is not a staple of subsistence. I got the impression that villagers were quite aware that the last-betel-nut ploy was common and did not regard it as a significant breach of norms. The possibility that people might fail to meet their reciprocal obligations to distribute staple goods is taken more seriously, and in at least one case villagers have adopted a collective means of coping with it. From early July to early September 1976, villagers devoted most of their food production efforts to making sago. As the weeks of sago making passed, cylinders of sago powder bound in sago palm leaves accumulated and hung in profusion in the sago groves on the mountain. Sago keeps well and villagers intended to process enough to last for some time, but I finally asked why the completed bundles were not being brought down to the village. I was told that villagers were waiting until there was enough so that each household could get its share at once. Benau, an unmarried man in his twenties recently returned from several years of migrant work, explained that if households brought their shares back to the village one by one, those who did not have theirs yet would borrow from those who did and the sago of a few households would be rapidly consumed. If those who received their shares later could have been counted on to share in turn, this would not have presented a problem. In this particular situation, however, villagers clearly preferred a more sure safeguard of their household resources than the norms of reciprocity.

The desire to control individual resources manifest in the last-betel-nut stratagem and the sago case probably is one source of the attraction of a more commercial system of exchange and distribution. Placing the distribution of goods on a commercial footing means one can refuse to sell, one can discourage buyers by setting a high price, or one can at least receive an immediate and certain return. One older woman once complained to me at length about how she worked hard to grow tobacco, but when people saw it hanging from the rafters of her house they all asked for it and she did not feel free to refuse. She seemed to see putting things on a commercial footing, an innovation she associated with the achievement of national independence early that year, as at least a partial solution to her problem. Berating the alleged stream of villagers come to carry away her tobacco, she pronounced: "We're Papua New Guinea now! You must pay for my tobacco! I worked hard on it!"

There are also features of the system of reciprocity rather darker than loss of control over one's resources that may well contribute to the attraction of commercial relations. I already have discussed the way in which inadequate generosity is believed to lead to individual failure in hunting and fishing and how, in the case of the konan, failure to distribute the catch properly or to reciprocate for the loan of equipment or assistance in making fishing equipment was thought to imperil the entire village's fishing efforts. Similarly, when grievances are aired in curing sessions one often hears references made to quantities of taro, bottles of liquor, or other items given in aid of a commemorative mortuary feast or other event but never adequately repaid. In short, the system of reciprocity is not simply the warm and spontaneous expression of goodwill; it is also a system prickly with sanctions and fraught with opportunities to endanger subsistence and good health.

Excessive accumulation is thought to be a special source of danger. One educated young migrant who holds a salaried position on the mainland is the object of his mother's great concern. As she said to me: "If someone makes too much money, people will do away with him. [They'll think] 'It's no good he makes so much money. It's better we do away with him and then his family will be poor just as we are.' All the time I tell my son, 'You shouldn't drink too much or someone will poison you.' " She used the Pidgin term *kif,* a poison taken internally, rather than *poison,* meaning sorcery, and apparently feared someone could easily administer kif to her successful son while he was drunk. She also could have meant that people might take excessive drinking itself as an offensive display of wealth and be aroused to strike at her son with kif.

Similarly, Manup told me that many villagers still had caches of territorial coin, long since replaced by Australian national currency and Papua New Guinea's own currency. Some had held on to this money until it became nonnegotiable, he said, simply because they were afraid to spend it for fear of arousing envy. Manup is young and critical and may have been exaggerating. Yet many villagers do feel that anything that might be interpreted as invidious display, like excessive wealth, can be cause for envy and retaliation. Not long after the war, for example, Sheltar of Shewaratin died while bombing fish when a homemade dynamite charge went off in his hand. Some of his kin say that this was the result of sorcery performed by someone in another village envious of Sheltar's elaborate trading canoe, *Urim Terakau.*

Fear of envy of, or anger at, having too much, then, is also one of the drawbacks of the system of reciprocity. Bailey has observed a similar phenomenon in European peasant and postpeasant communities. He writes (1971:282) of "the logic that equates superiority with egoism and evil," the logic being that "evil is rewritten as self-interest and this in turn is translated into attempts to upset the existing pattern of equality." Kragur villagers, however, only spoke to me of their concern that others might be envious, not of their own envy. One can infer, however, that many Kragur people may see neglect of the social responsibility to share one's abundance not simply as neutral indifference to others but also as active hostility to collective interests.

Goodness, Prosperity, and Contrasting European Models

The system of reciprocity, then, although an integral part of Kragur society and culture, has a dark side. It poses problems and generates tensions and fears that probably make some features of the commercial alternative attractive in comparison. The debate and speculation in Kragur about issues of exchange and distribution, however, probably owe more of their intensity, perseverance, and special flavor to the entanglement of moral and material issues that has developed out of the confrontation of indigenous precedent and the ambiguous European example. This entanglement contributes both to the persistence of an ideal of generosity and to the appeal of commercial relations. While the affluence of Europeans suggests to the villagers admirable moral accomplishments in the realm of social relations, European society does not provide a single model of distribution and exchange to emulate. On one hand, Catholicism seems to mirror the norms and practices of the indigenous gift economy; on the other, secular European institutions display the practices of a commodity economy.

Catholicism probably not only has heightened an indigenous tendency to read material problems as moral or social problems, it also appears to have influenced ideas about what good social relations are in a number of spheres, including that of distribution and exchange. The ideal of generosity that some villagers articulate may not be so much an autocthonous legacy as a synthesis of compatible indigenous and Catholic themes.

Catholic missionaries brought to Kragur not only a general Christian teaching of compassion but also an explicitly antimonetary bias. Manup tells of a past parish priest who frequently held services at a church that once stood at Bou, who preached that God favored the poor and that it was sinful to be too concerned with money or ostentatiously to display one's monetary wealth. Ibor pursues the same theme in his Sunday messages. Although Ibor himself is among the monetarily more successful resident villagers, he preaches that too much concern with money is an impediment to salvation. On one occasion he proclaimed: "This money isn't something you can take and show to God and he'll say you can enter heaven! This thing is only something for here on earth!" He then went on to caution against following the example of outsiders, like the teachers at the Bou primary school, who, Ibor said, were too greedy for money: "You look at those teachers, their ways are different; you forget about them! Follow our own ways!" Just what Kragur's own ways should be was, of course, open to question at the time, and Ibor himself was also busy criticizing some Kragur customs as obstacles to greater cash incomes. Nevertheless, while the line between acceptable and unacceptable levels of concern with money is fuzzy, the idea that it is not good to allow the desire for "this money" to govern one's behavior is a living part of the perceived message of Catholicism.

The fact is, however, that the Catholic mission in the Sepik has been very deeply involved in commercial enterprises, initially in order to finance and supply its other activities (Huber 1988:47–74; Wiltgen 1969). Many villagers themselves have worked for wages on mission plantations, and for some this was their first experience of having their labor treated as a commodity. Nevertheless, Kragur people still tend to associate the mission with noncommercial values. This is due in part to antimonetary teachings. It also may be due to the fact that, although the Catholic schools on Kairiru do hire some local labor, there are no mission plantations or other predominantly commercial enterprises on the island. The most immediate Catholic presence has been a noncommercial one, engaged almost exclusively in teaching and preaching.

Early Catholic plantations and industries in the Sepik could be construed as "development" activities, although they were not so conceived at the time. Arbuckle (1978:284) points out that Catholic views on the place of development work have changed greatly over the years. Whereas before Vatican II the Catholic mission tended to regard development work as a distraction from its real aims, in the post-Vatican II period it has become a central part of its endeavor. At least some Kragur villagers have noticed a change in the mission attitude that may reflect this shift, although they give it their own significance. According to Brawaung: "[The mission] has changed. They don't talk about Jesus a lot anymore, talk about God a lot. Now they talk about different kinds of business, but before they talked about God's work." By "God's work" Brawaung means Catholic prayer and religious observance. He speculates that the mission has deemphasized such activities because it fears people are coming too close to actual contact with Jesus and the Virgin. In any event, many, like Brawaung, continue to identify genuine Catholicism with the mission's noncommercial aspect and to identify Kragur with such more genuine Catholicism. "Some people don't think about God's work, they just think about business," Brawaung says, "but not us."

Nevertheless, villagers also see the secular side of the European world. Viewed through its secular institutions, the European world is dominated by buying and selling; it is a world in which almost nothing is given away without an immediate equivalent return. As I sat with Mowush one afternoon, eating the citrus fruit known in Pidgin as *muli,* he noted that he had just asked Paypai for the fruit and Paypai had given them to him for nothing. "No European would just give me a muli," he commented. He went on to speak of such customs with approval and criticized contrasting Kragur practices as impediments to progress: "Look here, now you're living here and you give lots of things to us for nothing, and we give lots of things to you. Doing things like this, are we going to change? No! We'll just stay the same."

Approval of the European form of material relations coexists with pride in Kragur's distinction from Europeans in this sphere; but the association of such European practices with European material accomplishment cannot help but recommend them to many people. Some undoubtedly see that curtailing gift exchange is necessary if they want to accumulate goods for sale or money for investment. Given, however, the deep associations in Kragur between material prosperity and morally correct social relations, it is impossible not to surmise that European forms of material relations appeal to many, not just because they are seen as instrumentally effective, but also because their association with remarkable material well-being makes them look *good*. If these new sorts of social relations can bring a new kind and level of material well-being, then perhaps they are a new kind of *good* social relations, better suited to the current era.

Catholicism, on the other hand, provides a European model seen as compatible with familiar indigenous practices. The dual European example thus lends the moral weight of material accomplishment to contrasting forms of distribution and exchange. It encourages villagers both to cling to established ideas of good social relations and to entertain the idea of a new, and perhaps better, form of good social relations. I have already given numerous examples of the disagreement and contrasting viewpoints that have grown out of this ambivalence. The ways in which Kragur people use and think about alcoholic beverages, chiefly beer, provides a final, more detailed example.

The Case of Beer

Alcohol use is not common in Kragur, but almost inevitably when I attended a drinking event someone would point out to me how well Kragur people behave when they drink. They told me that they seldom become obstreperous or belligerent, and that in some other villages the people not only fight among themselves when they drink, they also turn against any outsiders present. Villagers also pointed out that their peaceful and convivial behavior while drinking reflects both their traditional harmony and solidarity and their remarkable adherence to the norms of Catholicism. There is virtually no disagreement that such restrained comportment when drinking is good social behavior by any standard.

There is considerably less agreement, however, on the relative virtues of excess and restraint in the scale of alcohol consumption. Villagers usually drink beer and other alcoholic beverages on traditional occasions for feasting and gift-giving, so alcohol use has been caught up in the larger uncertainty over the virtue of thrift versus that of generosity and extravagance. Some of alcohol's special qualities cast the issue into relief. Unlike taro, fish, sago, and other common items of gift exchange, alcohol is available only in the money economy, so its use in warap or other traditional events inevitably raises distinctly contemporary concerns with material progress. Further, as villagers recognize, drinking is a particularly extravagant form of consumption. Alcohol is, as Schwartz (1982: 395; cf. Schwartz and Romanucci-Ross 1974) has put it, "the ultimate consumable," a strikingly efficient way of turning money into urine (Schwartz 1981).

Kragur people impressed me as moderate in their comportment while drinking and, if not moderate, then something short of excessive in their consumption; but moderation means little unless one specifies the terms of comparison. Kragur drinkers certainly look moderate compared to Saturday afternoon drinkers in Port Moresby, staggering into the street in attempts to halt and board moving buses. Other standards of comparison might, of course, give different impressions. Kragur villagers often continue singing and dancing until dawn when they drink. They also do so on occasions when they do not drink, and even when they drink, the alcohol often runs out before the revelers' enthusiasm runs down. Women, too, often hold on far into the night even though they seldom drink. Nevertheless, the sight and sound of a Kragur party at 2:00 A.M., cartons of empty beer bottles animated by the flickering shadows cast by circles of dancers revolving in the lamplight, voices keening and drums pounding, might inspire impressions of anything but moderation in an observer transported from a university wine-and-cheese reception or one of the Wewak bars frequented by expatriate and Papua New Guinean businessmen and bureaucrats.

For the most part, however, comportment on drinking occasions does not belie villagers' claims about their own behavior. Outbursts of anger or belligerence were rare in all the drinking events I observed. There were only a couple of men who waxed surly and bellicose when they drank, but the other men found it easy quietly to restrain them. I recall listening to a young man bellow his way home in the night, challenging those who had called out to him to be quiet to come out of their houses and fight. Such a scene, however, is not remotely so typical as the spectacle of the leader of village Catholicism and a suspected sorcerer grinning broadly as they faced each other in a stately dance, their left hands on their hips, South Pacific Lager bottles held on high in their right.

Men do almost all the drinking in Kragur. Villagers speak of past events at which some women drank heavily. During my stay in Kragur, however, this was not the case, although many women often were present at the larger events—cooking, serving food, watching, listening, forming their own conversational groups, and joining in the singing and dancing. Men say they do not discourage women from drinking; but the kinds of public events in which alcohol is usually used are those in which men have always taken center stage, and men pioneered alcohol use in their travels as wage workers. Most women seem reticent to draw attention to themselves by intruding into what has always been a predominantly male activity. Part of the value of alcohol in such an event can only be realized by consuming it on the spot. Immediate public consumption enhances whatever valued physiological sensation alcohol produces and the extravagance of the display and distribution. It also tends to exclude women from consumption because they play limited public roles in such events.

In 1975–1976, people did not drink very often in Kragur, and they very seldom drank much. I noted only seven events at which men from more than half of the koyeng drank together.[7] At six drinking events men of only one to four koyeng were present, and small numbers of Kragur men attended four events in other villages. In addition, several times migrant villagers living in Wewak or working on the far side of the island entertained small groups of visitors from the village with alcohol.

The events at which resident villagers consumed alcohol in 1975–1976 were of several kinds, including a leader's apparently unprecedented presentation of a carton of beer to the assembled village men to mark his adult daughter's birthday, going-away parties for men returning to school or work after holidays and leaves, an impromptu celebration of a migrant's return on leave, feasts for those who had helped build new houses, a feast reciprocating aid in settling a sorcery dispute, feasts marking the dissolution of temporary adoptive ties, and commemorative mortuary feasts. Solitary drinking is rare.

My information on how much alcohol was consumed in particular drinking events is not precise, but I can provide a general picture. Most of my observations are of the six events involving more than half of the adult men. Consumption ranged from a single carton of beer shared among thirty to thirty-five men to ten to twelve cartons of beer and four or five bottles of hard liquor shared among the same number.[8] Men over the age of fifty to fifty-five tend to drink less than younger men, and there were as many as fifteen men of this age group at some of these events. To hazard an estimate of individual consumption at an event where ten cartons of beer and three bottles of hard liquor were consumed, older men might have consumed four or five bottles of beer apiece and a comparable percentage of the hard liquor. With thirty to thirty-five men present throughout the event, that leaves eight to nine bottles of beer and a comparable percentage of hard liquor for each of twenty or so younger men. Typically, villagers spread their drinking out over several hours and accompany it with a large meal either before the alcohol is served, midway in the drinking, or both. Usually those who provide the alcohol, or men acting on their behalf, open and distribute the bottles of beer. They often serve hard liquor by pouring each man a shot in a collective glass, which he consumes on the spot, unless he has his own glass or an empty beer bottle. The host then passes on to the next man and pours him a shot, and so on until the bottle is empty. This form of distribution tends to regulate the rate of consumption and prevent radical imbalances in individual consumption, although men will decline another beer or a drink of hard liquor if they wish to drink more slowly.

Alcohol is not readily available in Kragur. Most of it has to be brought over from Wewak. There are trade stores licensed to sell beer in two villages within a mile or so of Kragur, but their stocks are small and their local clientele deplete them rapidly. Kragur people were seldom able to buy beer at these trade stores while I was there. Their small and sporadic cash incomes also make alcohol hard to come by. A number of men do know how to make coconut toddy, a skill learned from Japanese occupation forces, but during my stay in Kragur no one bothered to do so. There are no indigenous alcoholic beverages on Kairiru.

Both men and women frequently call alcoholic beverages by Pidgin names. Beer is *bia* and hard liquor is usually *sitrong*. Villagers seldom use brand names for beer, although South Pacific is almost inevitably the beer they purchase and drink. The most popular hard liquors known by brand names are Johnnie Walker scotch and Bacardi rum. Although the Pidgin term *sitrong* acknowledges hard liquor's special potency, vernacular terms refer to the physical properties of alcohol's various forms rather than its effects. Villagers often refer to both beer and hard liquor as *rian,* the Kairiru term for water. Occasionally, someone may call beer *shubashiep,* a Kairiru word that also refers to such things as foam and spittle. It seems to be the Kairiru equivalent of the American slang term for beer, suds.

Anger and Inhibition

Villagers acknowledge that alcohol produces a characteristic sensation and are aware of alcohol's potential ability to loosen inhibitions. The very importance they attach to lack of violence while drinking is ample evidence that they feel alcohol consumption increases the possibility for violence (cf. Carrier 1982); but in drinking within the village, Kragur people both hope and expect alcohol consumption to have only mild and generally benign effects on behavior. At least with regard to anger and violence, the possible benefits of using alcohol to signal a "time out" (MacAndrew and Edgerton 1969) from normal expectations take a backseat to other concerns.

Alcohol does not loosen inhibitions automatically. Behavior while drinking is shaped by indigenous cultural precedent and introduced models of drinking behavior (cf. Marshall 1979). I know little of possible indigenous precedents for drunken comportment in Kragur like those described by Schwartz and Romanucci-Ross (1974) and Clarke (1973) for other parts of Papua New Guinea. Colonial Europeans certainly provided one model (cf. Poole 1982), and this was not always one of moderation in either scale of consumption or behavior under the influence. The nearby representatives of Catholicism on Kairiru, however, provide an example of moderation, and mission teachings associate uncontrolled anger and violence with backwardness and ignorance as well as simple immorality. Add this to a homegrown concern with controlling hostility, and villagers' pride in their sociable comportment while drinking is easy to understand.

Villagers see their restraint while drinking as both autochthonous and, as one would say in Pidgin, *Katolik fasin* (Catholic style). This Catholicizing of the issue annexes modern significance to indigenous concerns. Yet, when they move from anger and violence to other issues concerning alcohol use, Kragur people find

it considerably more difficult to determine just what exemplary
behavior entails.

The Problem of Alcohol and Progress

Alcohol use can have contradictory meanings in terms of morality
and material progress. It must be purchased with money, and
money is harder to come by than fish or taro. This increases the
value of alcohol in reciprocal giving, but it also lends a special
opprobrium to giving that might be considered excessive.

The capacity to acquire and give goods purchased with money
is evidence of or a claim to prowess in the postcontact social
world. One traditional leader's description of a commemorative
mortuary feast held in about 1971 illustrates alcohol's associations
with success in that world. The sponsors provided unusually large
quantities of rice and alcohol. My informant described the
deceased in whose name the event was held and one of the principal sponsors of the event as men who had been vocal advocates of
greater involvement in *bisnis,* that is, modern commercial activities. On this account, he said, the sponsors conducted it *Yuropian
fasin*—namely, they provided food and drink purchased with
money, as Europeans would, rather than locally produced goods.
Similarly, a village leader and successful trade-store operator,
whose daughter was studying in Australia in 1976, was the only
one in the village to follow the European custom of celebrating a
family member's birthday. Although his daughter was absent, he
marked the occasion by presenting a carton of beer to an assembly
of village men. A final example is a migrant's conspicuous largess
in providing rice and, even more conspicuously, beer and hard
liquor at a commemorative mortuary feast he sponsored while
home on holiday. The sponsor was an older man reputed to have
achieved considerable commercial success in the province of New
Britain. During his brief stay in the village he was prone to stern
criticism of what he saw as the people's lassitude in the pursuit of
bisnis.

The problem is that the moral significance of such largess is
unclear. Although no one took amiss the modest birthday presentation with its symbolism of modern forms of success, both of the
large commemorative events aroused critical comment. In particular, some villagers questioned the propriety of such large expendi-

tures of money primarily on alcohol. Commenting on the Yuropian fasin event of 1971, one man noted that many villagers
thought it inappropriate, for the deceased had not been as successful in his own conduct of bisnis as he had been vocal in his admonitions to others. In Pidgin he branded the event an empty gesture
in which "bigpela moni i godaun long solwara," that is, a large
amount of money was as good as sunk in the ocean. Similarly,
another villager, commenting on the preparations for the commemorative event given by the visiting migrant, said: "We don't
have any business. This is a lot of money . . . enough to help us.
[But] when you drink, in the morning you throw-up and it's all
gone."

Both of these critics, like a number of others, labeled such conspicuous consumption in Pidgin as *samting bilong bipo,* a custom
of the past that is incompatible with contemporary goals and
values. Alcohol does fit well with and enhances the traditional pattern of feasting and distribution because it is an extravagance and
a luxury, calculated to impress and indebt (cf. Warry 1982). Providing alcohol is also a claim to success in the new economic
arena; but many villagers know it consumes at an alarming pace
the money needed to enter the new economy.

A final example shows how alcohol consumption is linked to
the larger issue of the connotations of extravagance and generosity, on the one hand, and frugality, on the other. The pattern of
drinking until dawn has traditional precedent in magicoreligious
rituals involving group musical performance, the efficacy of which
depends on carrying through from dusk until first light. In many
contemporary contexts the capacity to last until dawn also has
connotations of collective potency and worth.[9] If alcohol is part of
an event, then the capacity to provide sufficient alcohol to last
through the night, and to withstand its potentially deleterious
physical effects, may add to its significance (cf. McDowell 1982;
Chowning 1982). When there is not enough alcohol to last the
night, simply finishing all that is available has to suffice.

The same individuals who on some occasions revel in such
accomplishments also profess admiration for what they see as the
abstemious drinking habits of some Europeans.[10] A number of village men speak of their admiration for the drinking habits of certain Australian employers they have known. They say that a single
bottle of hard liquor would last these Australians for days and

weeks; they would pour a drink, then put the bottle back in the cupboard, while the *netiv* (native) does not stop drinking until the bottle is empty. These men feel that the perceived Australian practice is good because it is not wasteful and makes it easier to achieve commercial success. This brings prosperity and affirmation of self-worth. But there's the rub, for such a route to prosperity and affirmation of a flagging sense of worth may violate indigenous and syncretic Catholic notions that generosity, even extravagance, affirms and prepares the ground for moral and material prowess.[11]

Calculation, Compartmentalization, and Redefinition

One well-educated Kragur migrant is extremely skeptical about resident villagers' generosity with their labor and their goods. He acknowledges that they excel in helping local schools and the mission; but, he adds, "They don't like it." He implies they help only in hope of some future reward or because of social pressure and asserts bluntly that their refusal to accept money is primarily an attempt to build up a reservoir of obligation into which they may tap in the future or to precipitate spontaneous reciprocity on a grander scale. Indeed, the giving that takes place in a gift economy is not bottomless charity. Mauss notes early in *The Gift* that the prestations which are the subject of his study "are in theory voluntary, disinterested and spontaneous, but are in fact obligatory and interested" (1967:1). Certainly Kragur people expect that generosity will not flow in only one direction and there will be relatively balanced reciprocal giving over the long run. For the sake of one's reputation, however, it is better to overextend as a giver rather than as a receiver. Those seeking prestige through organizing warap or other large exchanges can tap into the reservoir of obligation to accumulate goods, to be given away once more.

The skeptical migrant, however, implies that, especially in their dealings with mission and school personnel and other representatives of the outside world, Kragur villagers hope that their admirable and cooperative behavior will bring tangible benefits in the near future.[12] In fact, it appears already to have done so, by contributing to the exceptional success of Kragur young people in the educational system—a success probably facilitated by the schools' positive expectations of Kragur children.

Similarly, it is not difficult to find calculation behind the rejection of monetary relations that many villagers advocate. Such a stance makes a virtue out of the unavoidable predicament of poverty. It also constitutes a kind of control over money, although it is not likely that a strategy of control through simple denial could remain satisfying for long. I also find it hard to imagine the majority of Kragur people committed to the nonmonetary path in hope of finding their way to a distant Christian heaven. Many villagers' commitments to the virtues of generosity and nonmonetary relations undoubtedly spring from an interest in being better off here and now. They see good social relations, of course, as the basis of material well-being; but there also may be a more specific logic at work. As I have already pointed out, the successful practice of magical procedures for improving food production requires that the practitioner abstain from sexual activity. That is, he denies his own fertility in order to increase the fertility of the crops. Some villagers may hope that a studied indifference to lucre will somehow lead to a more lucrative future through supernatural intervention.

Nevertheless, one cannot reduce cooperation with Europeans, commitment to a noncommercial ethic, or the competing appeal of commercial practices to calculations of their efficacy in bringing material well-being, because that aim is so tightly bound up with moral aims. The conflation of material and moral aims helps to account for the disagreement and ambivalence on the question of generosity in Kragur. Villagers are puzzling over the claims of contradictory economic logics fused with contrasting moral standards. This is not simply a conflict between those who prefer traditional routes to traditional styles of success and those who have embraced the mores of the new money economy. The discordance is in emotionally laden systems of ideas as well as in relationships among people. Villagers are aware that they cannot accumulate funds for a boat or some other investment if they disperse them in traditional-style giving, and that commercial ventures often founder because obligations to kin eat up capital and profits. Such generosity may be good in indigenous terms, but it leads to failure to achieve the material well-being that constitutes success in the new social world. Unfortunately, while failure by the standards of the wider, postcontact world inspires feelings of individual and collective moral deficiency, villagers persist in judging themselves and others in terms of indigenous notions of individual and collective moral adequacy as well. Of course, if Catholicism is an attribute of modernity, as many Kragur people believe, then failure in the pursuit of modern goals is also a failure in Catholicism. Yet, villagers tend to see Catholicism as affirming many of the indigenous premarket ideals of virtue in social relations. The public disagreement and private perplexity on these issues is not surprising.

Compartmentalizing spheres of behavior may help to ease the tension. The village trade stores are a step in this direction, although rumor has it that they suffer chronically from giving excessive credit rather than insisting on prompt payment: in other words, there is a tendency to let the principles of reciprocity creep into their operation. Younger villagers, however, do seem to find it more plausible that there could be a sphere of everyday behavior, bisnis, that operates according to a distinct moral code and logic. When I returned to Kragur in 1981 I saw evidence of this. The Community Development Youth Club had appropriated as its meeting place the house built for me five years before and hoped to make money by using it as a commercial guest house. They intended to charge a nightly fee for food and lodging to visitors of all kinds, from government agents to students on excursion from St. Xavier's. (Staff at St. Xavier's told me that the club's high rates had scared away a student group intending to stay overnight in Kragur while on a walking tour of the island.) I stayed in my old house myself in 1981. I bowed to the club's proprietorship, although I received a substantial discount. Nevertheless, in 1981 the house once built for a visiting European without money payment for labor or materials had become like the villagers' image of a European's house—that is, a place where everyone pays.

The familiar Good Way had not entirely disappeared, however. Some villagers thought it was wrong that I had been asked to pay anything at all to stay in my old house. Furthermore, the Good Way appears to be flexible. Some of those involved in the club still spoke of the gudpela fasin of their village; and the club offered mission personnel discount rates at the guest house, a policy that might be seen as a more frugal version of the Good Way. If the debate over the merits of competing forms of exchange and distribution is leading toward a redefinition of what constitutes good social relations in this realm, this does not mean that villagers will have to abandon the claim to exceptional goodness. The goodness to which they lay claim can simply be of a different kind. Such a transition, however, will proceed slowly and may never be complete. It certainly will occasion uncertainty and psychic discomfort. It is clear that while many Kragur people want to alter long-standing practices, the desire to do so grows in part from the desire to maintain a sense of moral adequacy. Villagers in general do not wish to adopt materially more pragmatic forms of behavior at the expense of their carefully nurtured sense of being good people.[13] One young man's comment exemplifies the perplexity and ambivalence aroused in some by the effort to cling to goodness while experimenting with new economic forms that have ambiguous moral significance. The confusion Benau ascribes to his fellow villagers is evident in his own words: "We young people should do as the Australians do. When someone comes to the village we can't just give things to them. They should pay rent and things like that. We Kragur people are good people, we're generous and helpful. I think the people of my village are good people, but they're a little mixed up too."

EIGHT

Redefining Good Social Relations: Organizing Time and Work

EUROPEANS COMING TO WEWAK or passing through to points beyond must shed the desire to get things done fast and the expectation that things will happen on a regular schedule. Wewak's airport is a somnolent little establishment. There is no busy stream of taxis between the tiny terminal and the center of town. Unless one has made prior arrangements, getting to town may take considerable patience. Businesses and government offices in Wewak keep regular hours; but the small boats that travel to Kairiru, Mushu, other offshore islands, or villages up and down the coast come into town on unpredictable schedules. They generally leave whenever they are ready—when the cargo has been stowed, when the crew has purchased fuel for the return trip, when everyone has returned from his or her business. The only way to be sure to catch your boat is to haunt the wharf. During the monsoon season all bets are off. Even the St. Xavier's boat, which tries to arrive and depart at regular hours, may be unable to run at all for days at a time. The traveler sits in Wewak waiting for the wind to abate and the sea to calm.

Wewak is a frontier town. Here Europeans meet the unfamiliar rhythms of provincial Papua New Guinea and rural Papua New Guineans meet the novel rhythms of the European world. Once, while I was riding one of Wewak's small buses out to the Copra Marketing Board warehouse, it pulled over to let a middle-aged man off. He looked like a villager on a rare visit to town, his shorts and T-shirt faded and worn to the same nondescript color and texture, his hand hardened by work but hesitant and uncertain as he opened and shut the unfamiliar folding door of the bus. He started to walk away without paying, and the driver—a young man in crisp, clean shorts and sport shirt—called him back. The village man returned to the driver's window looking embarrassed, drew a small coin purse out of the net bag hanging from his shoulder, and fumbled in it for his money. Finally, the young driver impatiently helped him choose the correct coins while instructing him scornfully in Pidgin in the proper way to do things in town. "When you go on the bus you have to do things the way we do! Put your money in your shirt pocket so you can get it quickly. You're wasting the time of all the other passengers!"

The poor man did not have a shirt pocket and none of the passengers really seemed annoyed at the delay, but the lesson was still clear enough: in town, making people wait "wastes their time" and can make them angry. The ragged villager was confronting not only a novel form of transportation; he was also confronting an unfamiliar way of perceiving and experiencing time and events and an unfamiliar idea of good social relations.

In comparison even with Wewak, Kragur at first appears quite isolated from the pressure of clocks and the modern demand for temporal order and regularity in all of life's activities. Nevertheless, the characteristic Western-industrial view of time and mode of conducting activities are making themselves felt. At issue are not only cognitive patterns and modes of behavior but also conceptions of good social relations—in particular, what it means to be cooperative and harmonious. This is being opened to question in the sphere of time, as it is in the sphere of distribution and exchange, by exposure to unfamiliar European ideas and practices.

Just as the novel European way of distributing and exchanging things is based on their cultural construction as commodities, so are the unfamiliar European ways of construing temporal experience and conducting activities based on the cultural construction of time as a commodity. The Western idea of time as an autonomous entity that can be minutely quantified, wasted or saved, plentiful or scarce, is an aspect of its construction as a commodity with exchange value in the market. In practice, it is not time per se that is bought and sold, but the commoditized form of human activity—labor—for which time is the measure. The transformations of concrete human activity into the abstraction "labor," and of the concrete experience of sequence and duration into the precisely quantified abstraction "time," have gone hand in hand in the West (Gutman 1973; Rodgers 1978; Thompson 1967). The Western obsession with doing things quickly and efficiently is a dimension of the transformation of time and activity into entities with quantifiable market value within a political economy focused on increasing material output and accumulation. In this political economy, time is money.

Kragur villagers have witnessed European order, regularity, and obsession with temporal efficiency in conjunction with impressive European material well-being. I will argue that this contributes to a tendency to regard Europeans not simply as technically superior but as morally superior, and to regard their behavior as a spontaneous expression of a higher social harmony. This view of European practices underlies much of Kragur people's enthusiasm—albeit, as I will illustrate, ambivalent enthusiasm—for European ways in this sphere, and it helps to motivate the steps they are taking toward altering their own patterns of behavior and redefining their concepts of good social relations. Unlike the case of distribution and exchange examined in the preceding chapter, here the European example is relatively unambiguous; both mission and secular institutions show much the same face. Hence, the tendency to see European practices as morally superior forms of social relations is much clearer here.

Modes of temporal perception and reckoning are visible in the way people organize and conduct their activities. Although the rigidly patterned and time-regulated European mode of behavior is manifest in virtually all activities in the societies of the developed Western world, I focus in this chapter on the kinds of activities we usually call work. Kragur villagers have gained much of their experience with European time orientations and activity patterns as wage laborers. When they compare their own practices with those of Europeans, they tend to focus on activities most nearly comparable to their tasks as wage laborers—for example, producing subsistence and cash crops—and to invoke plantations or other European centers of commodity production as examples of morally admirable order and cooperation. Before examining that comparison, the conclusions villagers are drawing from it, and their contribution to villagers' integration into the new political economy, I shall set the stage by describing indigenous views of time and patterns of activity in Kragur.

The Indigenous View of Time

Although Kragur is in a period of transition, the indigenous view of time is still dominant for many villagers in many contexts. The key fact about it is that there is no concept of time as an autonomous entity distinct from human and natural events and forming a container or framework into which they fit. A similar view can be found in many small-scale, nonindustrial societies, but Hallowell's (1955:234) classic discussion of Saulteaux temporal orientations provides one of its best formulations. He writes that, to the Saulteaux, "durations . . . are interwoven with, and experienced as, events in all their individuality. Night is darkness, the stars and their movements, sleep, quietness. Day is the light, the journey of the sun across the sky, the round of domestic duties. . . . Any comparison of such durations must be by metaphors and not by exact measures." Hallowell goes on to contrast this mode of experience with the Western experience of time in which "time assumes . . . an autonomous character and we are free to manipulate temporal concepts instrumentally, without constant reference to specific events." Both Kairiru linguistic categories and villagers' descriptions of their temporal experience suggest that indigenous Kragur temporal orientation also contrasts starkly with that familiar in the developed West.

The Language of Time

The Kairiru language does not contain a word equivalent to the English *time* or the Melanesian Pidgin *taim*.[1] One can ask "when," using the interrogative noun *saris;* one can label an approximate point in time; one can speak of a short or long duration; but one cannot speak of time as a thing in itself.[2] There is a term, *abil*, for the sidereal year, marked by the perceived passage of the Pleiades across the sky; I believe *abil* is the name for the Pleiades. The month or cycle of the moon is referred to simply as *kareo,* or moon. There are thirteen kareo. When villagers name them, they describe the weather, condition of the sea, subsistence activities, and, less often, the position of the Pleiades characteristic of each moon. Some of the names of the moons themselves describe such events. *Korraliek korramiai,* for example, means literally "the tide goes and the tide comes," and refers to a moon in which extreme tides are common.

To refer to a single day in the Kairiru language one says *waryang tai*—literally, "sun one," or one sun—or *bung tai, bung* referring to the period of greatest darkness during the night. Although Pidgin allows people to speak of a day—*de*—or days, many also speak of a day in Pidgin as "one sun," *wanpela san,* or sometimes *wanpela san wanpela nait,* "one sun, one night." There are no indigenous terms for the days of the week, nor is there an indigenous unit of time analogous to the week. From the current day *(nembai),* one looks back on yesterday *(numbunai),* and the day before yesterday *(noronai),* and forward to tomorrow *(kagua-nai)* and the day after tomorrow *(malalnai).* That is, days are labeled relative to the extant moment; it is always nembai. As one moves backward and forward from nembai, some of the names for past and future days are identical. While they make clear the number of days from the present, one must determine the direction by context (cf. Geertz 1966:72; Schieffelin 1976:141).

There are a number of terms for successive periods of the day and night, which villagers describe in terms of the waxing and waning of darkness and light. Some of the terms for daylight periods refer to the position of the sun. *Waryang yet,* mid-morning until about noon, means literally "the sun is up." *Waryang atabul,* from about noon until mid-afternoon, means "the sun turns back" or "the sun turns over." *Waryang afus,* sunset, means "the sun goes down." English, of course, contains similar terms denoting loosely bounded durations; but, unlike English, Kairiru does not supplement these loose, qualitative terms with a system of quantifiable units. Although Pidgin provides Kragur villagers with the hour—*aua*—it appears that the primary concept of daily time is the sun's passage and the dispelling and deepening of darkness rather than the flow of uniform abstract units. A number of villagers, primarily young men, do wear wristwatches. Some of their elders, however, refer to that device for reducing the day to readily quantifiable units as a *waryang shawaung,* a ghost or spirit of the sun.

Quite a few villagers sometimes refer to the time of day by the hour. Women tend to be wide of the mark, but men with wage-labor experience, who do this most, often estimate the hour very accurately from the position of the sun or, as some say, the length of their shadows. On dark, rainy days both estimates of clock-time and choices of the correct Kairiru-language term are uncertain and vary widely. Villagers sleep longer on such mornings, and without the sun to guide them they sometimes wonder if it is still *shemeshem* (after dawn, *shemot,* but before the sun begins to rise quickly toward its zenith) or whether it is already waryang yet.

Temporal Experience and Acculturation

For some at least, the sun is not so much a means for measuring time as it is time itself. This is suggested by the way villagers describe their experience of duration, or, as one would say in English, the speed with which time passes. When Kragur people speak of their perceptions of duration they sometimes use the Pidgin word *taim,* but they often speak of the speed with which the moons pass or the sun moves across the sky. As one would expect, the type of activity in which they are engaged affects villagers' perceptions of duration. Ungwang is one of many men I asked about the speed with which the months, or moons, and the years passed in their days as wage laborers. His response is typical. When he was working on a copra plantation, he says, "the work was no good and the moons didn't pass quickly." In contrast: "In the village [the moons] go by fast, because it's your place, you have all different kinds of work, you change from one to another. You don't think it's a long time, it goes fast." When he worked as a crewman on a cargo vessel, Ungwang felt that time passed quickly, much as it does in the village. "It's a lot the same. The ship travels from one place to another, so you feel [the moons] go by fast. If you stay in one place it feels like a long time. But here in the village, one day you go work in one place, another day you go work somewhere else."

Life in the village is not, of course, the same for everyone. Taunur remembers his days on a cargo boat and speaks of how, as he traveled from place to place, he lost track of the days and did not stop to think what month it was. Life in the village, he says, is a lot like working on a plantation, because you are stuck in one place and you mark the days going by. His perception of life in the village, however, is colored by the fact that he is old and ill and can no longer take part in a varied round of activities. Despite his important religious and political roles, he spends many days waiting for people to return to the village from their tasks in the bush and for the midday heat to subside: "Before, when I worked, I thought the days went by fast. Now I'm old, I sit in the house, I think, 'When will evening come? The fucking sun stays and stays and stays.' " Sounding a similar theme, Tarakam speaks of how time dragged during the Japanese occupation of Kragur when he was a young boy: "[The moons] went slowly because we had to stay in one place. You felt that the days went a little slowly and the moon, too, went slowly. It was like putting someone in the guardroom, putting someone in jail."

Tarakam, Taunur, and Ungwang are quite aware that in these cases durations themselves do not change, only their experiences of them. Even some younger, more schooled villagers, however, sometimes seem to fail to make the distinction between duration as experience and the concrete events that constitute the days and the moons. Discussing durations with Bashi, an unmarried young woman with a high-school education, I asked explicitly about the speed of taim, not the speed of the moon or the sun. She told me that when she had been in school, Monday through Friday had passed slowly, but the weekends had gone fast. In the village too, she said, taim went fast; but she speculated that this was because in Kragur the last part of the sun's arc is hidden from view by the slope of the mountain and darkness comes early. Bashi's explanation suggests that she does not always think of time itself as distinct from natural cycles and events.

Some other villagers exhibit an even more distinctly concrete conception of time. Molap says that when he was a migrant laborer on a copra plantation some of his fellow workers knew magic to make the moon wane more rapidly, presumably so they could receive their pay or finish their contracts sooner. Mowur, a much younger man, says that when he worked on a cacao plantation some of the men used magic to make the sun stand still: "When we were working in the cacao, if there was too much to do, we'd go get a special plant, someone would say a spell and stop the sun so it wouldn't move for a while. Then we'd have plenty of time to work."

It is interesting that my only evidence of attempts to *intervene* in the speed of time comes from villagers' days as wage laborers, when their lives were regulated by the calendar and the clock. Examples of a conception of time as events themselves, however, also can be drawn from village experience. One Kragur woman, for example, says, "when you're weeding in the garden, if there is much to do the evening comes fast, but if there is only a little to be done the sun is still well up when you finish your work." A member of a Western industrial society could easily say something like this, using the phrase "the evening comes fast" metaphorically. Yet, when some Kragur villagers speak of such experience of variable duration their intention is clearly not metaphorical. Another woman says: "If you're working and the sun goes rapidly you don't finish much work. If the sun goes slowly you can accomplish a lot. I don't know why the sun goes rapidly. Sometimes it goes rapidly, sometimes it goes slowly."

This villager appears to be projecting her subjective experience onto natural events. Extreme subjectivity may not have been the indigenous norm. Such an "orientation to direct, perceived experience, uncorrected by culturally provided information" (Levy 1973:251), however, is highly compatible with an experience of time as the interrelations of concrete events rather than a thing in itself. It is not compatible with the Western concept of time as the inexorable flow of an autonomous entity that measures and contains events, "time as envelope," as Barden (1973:343) puts it.

Kragur people have been exposed to new temporal concepts and practices through contact with European institutions for decades. Pidgin and English provide them with terms for time in the abstract, the days of the week, and the division of the day into precise quantifiable units. Mission, school, government, and commercial institutions regulate their affairs by the clock and the calendar, and villagers have had to learn to adjust. Village life itself is now structured by the seven-day week, punctuated by Sunday's religious observances. A few younger villagers even wear wristwatches, and the handful of transistor radios in the village make it possible for them to keep their watches coordinated with Greenwich mean time.

Yet, although one can hear a great deal of talk that sounds as though European time is now second nature to villagers, there are still those who puzzle over this new, abstract, and arbitrary demarcation of the temporal pattern of the world. The calendrical months, for example, present a problem for some. Villagers are closely attuned to the waxing and waning of the moon. They are not insulated from it by living indoors, nor do city lights obscure their view of the night sky. On clear nights when the moon is full, they sometimes take advantage of its light to sit outside their homes, smoking and talking far into the night. The thirteen lunar months or kareo, however, do not coordinate with the twelve calendar months. As Sawot puts it, "The moon goes rapidly, but its days don't run out very fast. The moon goes down, but some of its days are still left." Taram observes: "Before, the days and the moons went together. When the moon died, its days finished. But now the days don't end. February has come up in the sky, but the days of January aren't over yet. In the sky it goes fast, but the days go slowly."[3]

Precolonial temporal orientations are plainly highly resistant to change. Surface familiarity with the terms and practices of European time reckoning may mask a highly un-European mode of temporal experience. Pressure on villagers to commit themselves more deeply to European time concepts and patterns ebbs and flows, but it never ceases. The center, however, of the process of acculturation, the dialectic of incorporation into and resistance to the new temporal world, is the sphere of production. Villagers had their earliest and most dramatic exposure to European time as wage laborers, and in the village it is in the sphere of "work" that the confrontation of temporal schemes and the larger institutional orders they imply are most apparent. To understand the process of time reorientation and resistance, then, we must look at the nature of work in Kragur. These questions of time and work will bring us back eventually to the definition and redefinition of good social relations and the pursuit of moral and material progress.

The Nature of Work

Like time, work is not a culturally universal category. Schwimmer (1979:287) suggests that the modern Western idea of work is a product of the wholesale transformation of labor into a commodity during the industrial revolution: "Work as a concept is based on the assumption that, from a certain viewpoint, all economically useful activities are fully comparable by a single yardstick transcending their diversity, in other words, that labor has become a commodity and that the technical and administrative direction of that labor has become part of the same kind of commodity." In Kragur, as among the Tshidi described by Comaroff (1985:126), "both 'work' and 'time' remain immanent features of the social process itself." What the European observer would call work in Kragur is neither as conceptually, temporally, or spatially distinct from the rest of life, or from "life" itself, as it has become in the industrial West (cf. Levy 1966:49–50; Marx 1974 [1844]:125). This is evident to some extent in linguistic categories and is vividly apparent in the significance accorded the moral dimension in any important endeavor in Kragur. Further, in typical activity patterns, what appear to Westerners as discrete activities intermingle in time and space. This is highly consistent with a system of time reckoning that does not encourage allocation of time to separate tasks in carefully measured units. It is also consistent with a conception of productivity in which morally correct behavior is as essential as physical effort.

Varieties of Mol

It is easier to locate something like what the West knows as "work" in Kairiru linguistic categories than it is to find anything like time, but there is still no neat reflection of familiar Western concepts. The Pidgin translation of the English *work* is *wok*. Kragur villagers readily translate *wok* into the Kairiru language as *mol* and appear to use the terms interchangeably. From observation of common usage, however, it is clear that both *wok* and *mol* convey something somewhat different than the English term. In some contexts both *wok* and *mol* seem to be used as generic terms for almost any kind of exertion. For example, when I asked Manup to name some activities that were not mol, he replied (in English): "I don't think there is [*sic*] any, because they're all a job. If you have no job you have to sit down and sleep and do nothing. Fishing or praying is a job, you have to think."

Wagner (1981:24–25) suggests that such a broad conception is common throughout Melanesia, that "For the Melanesian, 'work' can be anything from weeding a garden to taking part in a feast or begetting a child . . ." (cf. Schwartz 1973:161). This interpretation has to be qualified, however. Kragur villagers often apply the

terms *wok* and *mol* to activities that native-English speakers might
not label as work; but not all agree on the exact range of application. They also commonly distinguish from wok or mol a variety
of activities that look very much like work to the Western observer.

Many villagers refer to ritual activities (cf. Firth 1967:27–28),
public gatherings for settling disputes or curing illness, or formal
occasions of exchange or prestation as wok or mol, but they do
not do so invariably. Some such activities entail considerable
expenditure of effort—including growing, harvesting, and cooking food—and all have claims to importance in maintaining the
community's well-being. Whether they are designated as wok/mol
depends to some extent on the speaker's role in the event. On the
day of a commemorative mortuary feast in a nearby village, Brawaung was busy assembling smoked fish to contribute to the proceedings and was concerned that the event be handled properly. It
was not only wok, it was, he said, "bikpela hatwok"—that is,
"big, hard work." However, Benau, a young unmarried man less
concerned with the ramifications of such undertakings, referred to
the event, in Pidgin, as a *de bilong malolo,* or day of rest. Loss of
faith or interest in an undertaking also can cost it its status as real
wok. During the weeks the fish assemblies were going on,
Korayet, an older but still very active woman, commented on
them. "This is important, its rather hard work. The lazy men say,
'Never mind, I'm tired of meetings.' [But] fish are a good thing, an
important thing." Misiling, however, was of another mind. While
her husband, Brawaung, was answering my questions one night
about the assembly that had taken place that day, she interrupted
angrily: "You [men] just stay in the village and sleep and have
meetings! When are you going to do some work!"

There is wider agreement that a variety of other activities are
not wok. Many of these would fit at least some Western industrial
definitions of work, as they are essential subsistence activities—for
example, harvesting garden produce, gathering other vegetable
foods, gathering firewood, or even hunting small game. Sogum's
view of such activities, however, is not uncommon. "Some lazy
men," he says, "don't think about work. They just wander around
in the bush looking for game."

Villagers have adopted the custom of abstaining from work on
Sundays. Although interpretations of what this requires differ,

what villagers agree on provides insight into their views of work. Virtually everyone agrees that it is acceptable to harvest garden produce or gather wild greens, tasks usually performed by women. Women also feel free to fish from shore with hook and line and men sometimes go out fishing in canoes. Women cook and men help if they are preparing pounded taro. Men often head for the bush in the afternoon. Although some undoubtedly do more serious work than they will admit to, they often simply inspect their gardens and tree crops, search for materials to be used later in construction, look for signs of wild pigs, or hunt small game.

Rosch (1975:191) suggests that in trying to delineate cultural categories it may be more "universally fruitful" to ask "which 'x's' are more 'x-like' "—that is, to look for prototypical exemplars of a category—than to look for explicit formal criteria. Kragur villagers almost always speak of some activities as wok, and these may serve as such exemplars. They consistently speak of making and cultivating gardens as wok or mol and distinguish this from other important subsistence activities. Brawaung told me how once he went fishing and told Misiling to go gather firewood because he was sure to bring back fish. She, however, ignored him and went to plant and weed in their gardens. "She didn't believe me," said Brawaung. "She didn't go get firewood, she went to work." Villagers probably agree that gardening is wok because it is a relatively arduous task involving both men and women, it provides not only a significant portion of the daily diet but also goods vital to prestation and exchange, and it is an activity that dictates and constrains the conduct and scheduling of other activities; in many ways life revolves around it. Villagers also regularly speak of sago production as wok, although they do not speak of it as often as they speak of gardening. Other activities undoubtedly could be added to the list. Moving away from this stable core, however, things become less indisputably wok-like and more susceptible to redefinition depending on speaker, social context, or the comparison in question.

The Essential Moral Dimension of Work

I already have discussed the importance of supernatural assistance and favor to the success of subsistence activities. This is illustrated

at length in Chapter 5, on the konan rituals. In many Kragur villagers' eyes, the meetings at which they petitioned the Virgin and
the ancestors for assistance and sought to gain their favor through
creating and displaying social harmony were not a distinct activity
conducted in support of the real work of fishing; they were an
essential part of the same endeavor, because they helped create the
indispensable moral climate for abundance. Schwimmer (1979:
301–302) makes a similar observation about gardening among the
Orokaiva of Papua New Guinea's Northern Province. "It is the
demigods of the various crops and the ancestors who do the actual
producing in the gardens, and all that is expected of man is to
clean, to plant and to protect against magical and technical dangers. . . ." Hence, success in gardening depends less on physical
prowess than on "warding off . . . sorcery and hence on ensuring
one has no dangerous enemies," "harmony in the family," and
"avoiding straying pigs, not just by building fences but by being
the kind of person into whose garden one does not want one's pigs
to stray." Given the importance to productivity of good relations
with others, "Time is . . . a highly inappropriate measure of useful activity in Orokaiva gardens."

The equivalence of what Westerners might see as expressive
religious activities and instrumental technical activities is also seen
in villagers' concern with the *way* in which they carry out the mundane, technical aspects of tasks. People were disturbed and feared
for the success of the enterprise when Tarakam sat aloof from the
main body of men in one of the last konan meetings. Similarly, villagers expect everyone to show up to help build houses or undertake other communal tasks. Full participation is expected whether
or not everyone actually contributes much actual labor. One
young migrant once complained to me at length about the inefficiency of this practice, saying, "People just show up and count that
as having done their part." In a way, they have.

This is most obvious when someone fails to show up. On one
occasion the village men gathered in the morning in a glade near
the church to prepare a large bundle of sago to present to the
neighboring village of Shagur as settlement of a dispute. This
involved molding the contents of five or six ordinary bundles of
sago into one fat cylinder, binding it with sago leaves, and deco-
rating it ornately with woven palm fronds and red and orange
fruits. The sago bundle, fashioned to resemble a pig trussed and

decorated for a ceremonial occasion, was then hung from a sturdy pole to be carried. At one point Moke intoned a magical spell to cause the small bundles of sago to fill the large mold more rapidly. All this took the better part of the day and the labor and skills of a number of men. Yet many men present were almost completely idle throughout the day, passing the time observing, talking, smoking, and chewing betel nut in the shade of a large mango tree. That evening I sat with a group of men, discussing the day's events. Someone commented on how much manpower was wasted when people came to help in such a task and there was nothing for them to do; but he also joined with others in criticizing a man who had gone to work in his garden and had been conspicuously absent. One man wondered aloud, "What kind of man is he?" and another answered that he was a "man bilong bikhet"—that is, someone who indulges his own self-interest without heed of the group. The others muttered their agreement.

In the end, all went smoothly. The sago bundle turned out solid and handsome and was delivered to Shagur a few days later without mishap. Had there *been* a mishap, however, had the bundle fallen from the pole or the sago mysteriously gone sour, there would have been a great deal of postmortem discussion. Much of that discussion undoubtedly would have focused on the possible supernatural repercussions of one man's absence from the sago preparation gathering.

Work Patterns

In 1975–1976 I collected data on how Kragur villagers spent their time—to use a Western metaphor that equates time with money—during eleven weeks spread over eleven months. This involved monitoring the activities of the members of one or two koyeng at a time, twelve hours a day for a seven-day week. I also accompanied individuals or groups for entire days in the bush or the village, taking detailed notes on what they did. Such data on the quantities of time people devote to various activities can be useful, although they must be used with caution. A major problem is that if one uses Western categories to distinguish activities in order to measure their duration, one will probably impose distinctions meaningless to the people of a community like Kragur. It is also easy to misconstrue the nature of activities entirely. For example, education, settlement of disputes, diagnosis of illness, preservation of cultural history, and philosophical speculation are conducted in the industrial West by specialists, in formal, marked contexts. In preindustrial communities, many take part in such matters in informal contexts that sometimes look a lot like people just taking it easy around the fire (cf. Jones 1969:278).[4] Perhaps more important than the time-use data I collected was the fact that gathering it forced me into contact with the pattern and organization of activity in Kragur.

My time-use data show that Kragur people spend many hours doing things that Westerners might regard as work (see Appendix). They often do them, however, in a way that may appear haphazard and unorganized to Western eyes. In brief, the pattern and rhythm of larger events and the conduct of particular activities tend to be irregular and to lack temporal coordination. In such collective activities as house building or copra shelling, participants drift to the work site one by one and gradually engage themselves in the task at hand. The level of activity and participation builds to an intense burst of coordinated effort that runs its course and ebbs by degrees rather than reaching a dramatic conclusion. An assembly of village men intended to begin "right away" (in Pidgin, *nau tasol*) may begin after a leisurely process of assembly lasting more than an hour. The time coordination of work groups is loose. Although members of different households or a single household may agree beforehand that they will work together on a particular task on a particular day, they often set out for the work site at their own time and pace. If those who arrive first can begin, they do so. If the presence of the others is necessary, the early arrivals seldom display much interest in the fact or the cause of their delay unless it is extreme.

To reach their work, villagers often must climb the steep trails to gardens, sago-palm groves, timber stands, or other sites distant from the village. On their way they pause frequently to rest, talk, smoke, and chew betel nut, or perhaps to gather betel nut and betel pepper near the trail. The individual members of a work group typically intersperse their labors with pauses to rest, chew betel, smoke, and prepare and eat food at more or less their own discretion, depending on the degree of coordination of effort and constant application a particular task requires. Seldom does anyone seem to be giving anyone else directions.[5]

The best way to convey the flavor of activity patterns in Kragur is to recount briefly the events of some of the ordinary days I observed closely. The first was a day spent mostly in a taro garden with the Brawaung family; the second, a day spent with Kabwam and others, cutting a timber and making thatch for a new house.

A Day with the Brawaung Family

Although no day is typical in all respects, this one has some very common features. It is common, for example, for members of nuclear families to work together. (Work groups, however, frequently embrace more distant kin, including those in the wide network of affinal and koyeng ties.) The pace and manner of organization of this day of gardening would be familiar to anyone who has ever lived in a rural community only marginally involved in the market economy. Other tasks are interspersed with planting and weeding; there is no break for a midday meal, but people pause to rest at will; no one gives anyone else much, if any, obvious direction; and there is little sense or appearance of urgency. It is August 31, in the middle of the dry season, so rain does not interrupt work and travel. The sun blazes until late afternoon, and walking to and from the garden plot and gardening on the steep, exposed mountainside make one drip with sweat.

Just after dawn I see Brawaung walking along the top of the cliff looking for signs of a school of konan. When I arrive at the house at 7:30 A.M., Brawaung is sitting smoking, and I join him. Misiling and their two oldest daughters, Bashi and Mokayu, have gone to the stream to wash dishes. They return shortly. Brawaung and I sit and smoke a while longer, then we set off on the main trail up the mountain at about 8:30. We walk slowly but steadily for half an hour to a garden site called Ulamyan, a short distance off the main trail just below the old village site at Kafow. Brawaung walks around the garden inspecting the young cacao plants, then we sit down on the trunk of a felled tree to chew betel nut. While I sit and write notes, Brawaung goes to the other side of the garden to get some taro cuttings cached there, returns, sharpens a digging stick he has picked up, sits down, and rolls a smoke.

After ten minutes or so Brawaung gets up and begins planting taro, making holes with the digging stick for the cuttings

and tamping the soil around them. He works steadily for an
hour, until 11:30, then joins me again to sharpen his digging
stick, open a green coconut to drink, roll another smoke, and
have another betel nut. We chew and talk until about 12:00,
when Brawaung begins planting again.

Misiling, Bashi, and Mokayu arrive about fifteen minutes
later. They are carrying sago pounders and bark baskets for
sago pith, and they are annoyed. Misiling says Brawaung told
her they were going to make sago today, so she and their
daughters went all the way to Iupulpul, near the top of the
mountain, and waited for him until they finally gave up and
came back to the new garden. As long as she was at Iupulpul,
she has brought down a cylinder of finished sago that was
stored there. She and her daughters start working almost
immediately. Bashi begins weeding the established part of the
garden, Mokayu is digging holes for taro planting, and Misiling is piling brush cleared from the new garden for burning.

Brawaung stops planting at about 1:00 P.M., makes his
way down the steep slope from the top of the garden to where
I sit, and rolls a smoke. He says Misiling just assumed they
were going to make sago, he never told her so.

At 1:30, Misiling and Mokayu stop planting and descend
to where Brawaung and I sit. After resting a few minutes,
Misiling climbs the straight, slender trunk of a nearby betel
palm to pick a bunch of the nuts. Mokayu spends a few minutes cutting the brush around the base of a *muli* tree with
her bush knife. Brawaung gets up and walks over to a sago
palm visible close by and begins cutting the leafstalks,
called *bangal* in Pidgin, which are used to make the walls
of houses. Mokayu goes off in another direction to do the
same, she says.

By 2:00 Brawaung and Mokayu have both returned with
small bundles of bangal. Brawaung breaks open a dry coconut and eats the meat. Bashi stops weeding and comes to sit
with us, Mokayu disappears for a few minutes to drink at a
stream, and everyone has a smoke before starting back for the
village at about 2:30.

Brawaung and I go on ahead and get back to the village by
3:00, where he gathers up the tools he needs to make a spear

for hunting sea turtles. Misiling, Bashi, and Mokayu are not far behind. When they reach the house Misiling says she does not feel well and goes inside to lie down.

Brawaung and I go up to my house, where he sits in the shade and works on the spear. I go bathe in the stream and then work on my notes in the house. Brawaung keeps at the spear until 5:30, then sits and smokes until 6:00, when we go back down to eat the sago the women have prepared. Brawaung has been talking about going turtle hunting that night, but decides against it because now it looks like rain. We talk and smoke and chew betel for awhile, then go up to the center of the village for evening prayers. After prayers, many of the adults stay to discuss a dispute between some Kragur men and the teachers at Bou school. People, Brawaung among them, are still talking—sitting about on bark mats, on Saulep's veranda, and on the long bench on one edge of the clear space —when I go back to my house sometime after 9:00.

A Day with Kabwam

September 7—another dry, sunny day—is a day of communal work at least nominally directed by the village councillor. I am spending the day with Kabwam, a vigorous unmarried man in his late twenties. Kabwam complains a bit early in the day of having to wait for others, but the overall pattern of activity is loose and unhurried. The several men involved seem at ease with this and Kabwam, too, makes nothing of it after his early remarks. Some garden work is interspersed with the main task, and there are many pauses to rest, smoke, gather betel, and so on. Notice that, although Kabwam does not fill the daylight hours with labor, he works until far into the night. (Remember that Brawaung had planned to hunt turtles at night, weather permitting.)

The councillor rings the village bell—an empty gas cylinder, detritus of the war, that hangs from the trunk of a coconut palm—at about 7:00 A.M. and people begin to assemble in the center of the village. By 7:45 Saulep has led them in prayers and the councillor has announced the day's tasks. The men are to work on Aram's new house and the women are to clean the village grounds and prepare a meal to mark the end of the day's labor on the house. This probably has been discussed before and comes as no surprise to anyone. Kabwam is to go with several other men to cut a timber for the house.

After the councillor has made his announcements the women disperse. The men hang around a while longer, talking about house building and unrelated topics, then begin to drift away. I have lost track of Kabwam, but I find him at about 8:30 sitting on his veranda eating galip nuts with his mother and sister. He says we should wait for the others before we leave, but grumbles about the delay after twenty minutes or so have passed. Karum arrives at Kabwam's at about 9:00 and we set out, although Karum immediately disappears.

Within a few minutes we reach the first stream crossing and stop there to wait again. Kabwam says we have to wait for the others, to find out which tree we are going to cut and where. By about 9:30 Karum and Urasup have joined us and we all walk up to Kafow, where we stop, pick a ripe papaya, and divide it among us. Aram catches up with us at about 10:00 and we move on. Fifteen minutes farther up the trail, just below the place called Wup, Karum and Urasup turn off on a side trail to go see Mangoi at his garden at Ribaiyet. We stop and wait a few minutes, but go on again at about 10:30. Kabwam and Aram grumble a little about how slow the others are. Kabwam says that if one gets started first thing in the morning you feel strong, but by midday everything is harder.

The tree we are going to cut is only a few minutes walk off the main trail. When we get there, Kabwam and Aram immediately start to clear the brush at the base of the tree with their bush knives. Taram arrives and lends a hand. When the trunk is accessible, Taram begins chopping. He is a young and very muscular man and, like most other Kragur people, he handles an ax expertly. The tree—about fifteen inches in diameter with a long, straight trunk—falls in five or ten minutes.

Karum, Urasup, and Mangoi arrive just after the tree falls, at about 11:00, and everyone pitches in to free it from the brush and another tree on which it has fallen and to cut off the top and some lateral limbs. Then they drag the log down to the main trail. After a brief discussion, they begin shaping it into a thick, rectangular beam, taking turns with ax and adze.

By 12:30 they have finished and everyone sits down on the log to rest. A couple of the men get up again, sweep the wood chips off the trail, then sit again to roll smokes and talk and joke. Karum goes off to Wup for a few minutes to see his wife, then returns.

A little after 1:00 P.M. we leave the log on the trail and go down to Ribaiyet. We pause to rest at the garden house there, then proceed along a path between slopes covered with taro plants to an unplanted garden plot belonging to Mangoi. We share a papaya picked there, and Kabwam scales a betel palm for a cluster of nuts. Everyone sits to smoke and chew betel, except for Mangoi and Urasup, who start trimming logs lying in the garden and positioning them to serve as the low walls of steep terraces. The others soon join in and all work until about 2:15. Coming back to the bottom of the sloping plot, they all sit, smoke, and talk until about 2:30.

There are still logs to trim and move, but we leave now for the village, pausing briefly between Ribaiyet and Kafow to pick up the timber cut earlier and wait while Urasup and Kabwam climb for betel nut. Karum, Kabwam, and Taram take turns shouldering the timber two at a time. Kabwam tells me later that Aram and Mangoi have bad knees and cannot carry heavy loads on the mountain trails. Aram, Mangoi, and I come behind with the axes, the bush knives, and the adze.

We take a half-hour break at Kafow. Urasup goes off to pick some betel pepper and returns. Everyone chews betel and talks of the coming singsing at St. Xavier's to dedicate the school's new library. The men break into random snatches of traditional songs. We set off again and stop at Plos, by the church at the east end of the village, at about 3:30. Kabwam climbs a coconut palm for green nuts, which we all drink. At 4:00 we go to the nearby men's bathing place and wash in the stream.

I am already at the site of Aram's new house about fifteen minutes later when Kabwam and Taram arrive with the log. About thirteen other men are also there. They are just putting down their work when I arrive. Everyone sits and talks until

about 4:30, when Brawaung begins shaping timbers other
groups have brought down. Kabwam leaves. I go to his house
at about 5:00 and find him sitting outside making sections
of thatch.

He is still working at around 6:00 when his sister,
Manshir, tells us that the collective evening meal is ready.
Kabwam and I join the other men at Aram's unfinished
house. My house is right next door and women are converg-
ing there from all parts of the village, leaving plates of food
on the large veranda and going off again. A young boy is
standing over the plates of food, which cover almost half the
floor, waving a palm frond to keep off flies. When everything
is ready the men drift over and sit down to eat. Most reach
into their baskets or net bags for their own utensils, either
metal forks and spoons or curved spoons carved from coconut shell.

Kabwam eats quickly and goes back to work within a half-
hour. With occasional pauses to smoke, he works steadily by
moonlight, adding to his growing pile of sections of thatch.
I go off to visit others or to make myself a cup of tea a few
times, but by about 11:00 P.M. I am tired out and go home to
bed. A number of men and women are still sitting outside
making thatch, taking advantage of the light of a huge full
moon. The next day Kabwam tells me that he worked until
about 2:00 in the morning. He bases his time estimate on the
crowing of the village roosters. "I finished work and went to
sleep. I'd only slept a little while when the first rooster
crowed."

Work Preferences and Comparisons

Kragur villagers sometimes speak wistfully of the life without
effort promised in cargo-cult lore or versions of Catholic teachings
about heaven, but in daily life they greatly dislike idleness. Some
of the activities they commonly speak of as rest or leisure (in
Pidgin, *malolo* or *limlimbur*)—such as gathering greens in the
bush, hunting, or scouting for timbers suitable for house or canoe
construction—are useful and strenuous. Healthy people sometimes stay in the village for a day to rest sore muscles and aching
joints. Usually, however, when inactivity is forced upon villagers,

it does not agree with them. One rainy day, for example, Mowur complained to me of his boredom. "When the weather is good I'm always out in the bush. Now the rain has me trapped here in the village. I'm tired of just staying here in the village."

Others complain that inactivity makes them hungry. Ibor says one banana is enough to satisfy him in the bush, but in the village he needs a lot to eat. Tarakam feels the same way. One sunny day his wife and oldest daughter left the younger children with Tarakam and went to carry beach sand to the top of the mountain to mix concrete for the Virgin's pedestal. In mid-afternoon Tarakam sat near his house, carving a bamboo comb and complaining. "This isn't right. I like to work, to go to the bush. When I sit around the village I'm hungry, but not when I go to the bush."

There is sometimes much activity in the village—building houses or canoes, or taking part in curing sessions, religious activities, or other gatherings. Simply being confined to the village, however, wears on many Kragur people. Many say that it makes them physically tired and their blood sluggish or congested (in Pidgin, "blut i fas"). That is one reason Kanim does not care much for the authority of the councillor. "The councillor is always keeping us in the village for something. When I just sit around like that I feel tired, like I'm sick, my blood is sluggish. If I'm moving around it's okay; but just staying around the village isn't right." Similarly, even though when Ungwang worked as a truck driver on the mainland he was not idle, the job was not active enough to suit him. "I didn't like being a driver," he says. "You sit and sit and your blood gets congested and you get sick."

Women usually have more to do in the village than men, for most of the work of child care, cooking, and cleaning inside and outside the house falls to them; but they, too, like to do more. Narawai, for example, does not like staying in the migrant settlement on Kreer beach. The men living there have jobs in town, but there is no land to garden and the women have only domestic chores to occupy them. "I don't like it," she says. "I don't feel very well." Semai's husband once worked in the mainland goldfields at Wau. She lived there with him and their two children for two years and says it was a bad place. They could not see the ocean and sago was hard to come by. In addition, she was bored "We women didn't have much work. We washed clothes, swept, cut the grass, cooked, planted some sweet potatoes." They did not have space for large gardens, however, nor did they have most of the other tasks that take them over the trails and into the bush around Kragur. Consequently, "the months went by very slowly. I wanted to hurry back to the village."

In short, Kragur people like to work. Yet they do make distinctions among kinds of work. As mentioned earlier, garden work enjoys a special status because garden produce is central to the diet and the exchanges that create and maintain social relations. Villagers regard most food production similarly. It is, as Paypai puts it, "work that helps us. Your family is happy, you're happy. Other work is rubbish."

Other types of comparison are also interesting. Although the overall pattern of activity in Kragur is extremely flexible and uncoercive by Western industrial standards, villagers are sensitive to the degrees of constraint that specific tasks entail. After hearing several people speak of this or that task as especially difficult, I pursued the question further by asking thirty-eight adults to judge the relative "ease" or "difficulty" of major kinds of work—gardening, sago production, hunting and fishing (referred to jointly in Pidgin as "painim abus"), copra production, and council work. Such context-free comparison neglects the rhetorical purposes of many spontaneous remarks on the ease or difficulty of kinds of work, but the results are still illuminating. The thirty-eight people I asked gave 169 explanations for their judgments, and these exhibit a pronounced concern with the degree of autonomy and flexibility activities allow.[6] As Table 2 indicates, a very common reason, making up 20 percent (33) of the total, for judging one activity more difficult than another was that it demanded a more regular pace and more coordinated efforts. For example, people invariably judged sago processing as more difficult than gardening. Once one has opened a sago trunk, one has to work at a steady pace from morning until late afternoon, sometimes for several days in a row, so that the palm pith or the sago powder being extracted does not start to spoil. This also requires coordinating the efforts of a crew of several people. In contrast, most phases of garden work require neither such sustained application nor such close coordination of individual efforts. Monai, a woman in her late twenties, says, in Pidgin, that garden work is easier than sago processing because you can do it "long laik bilong man tasol"—

Table 2
Characteristics Mentioned When Judging Comparative "Ease" or "Difficulty" of Village Activities

REASON	NUMBER OF TIMES GIVEN	PERCENTAGE OF TOTAL*
Duration (greater duration makes activity more "difficult")	44	26
Number of people involved	37	22
More people make activity "easier"	17	10
More people complete activity faster (make activity "easier")	6	4
More "difficult" because requires more people	14	8
Demand for regular pace and coordinated efforts (makes activity more "difficult")	33	20
Physical effort or discomfort (makes activity more "difficult")	22	13
Certainty of material return (makes activity "easier")	15	9
Immediacy of material return (makes activity "easier")	15	9
Working under orders (makes activity more "difficult")	3	2
Total	169	101

*Percentages do not add up to 100 because of rounding.

that is, at your own discretion. "If there's still work to do it can wait until tomorrow." In 26 percent (44) of the explanations given, villagers said simply that the relatively longer duration of one activity made it more difficult than another. This also suggests sensitivity to restrictions on autonomy and flexibility, for one cannot easily abandon such activities—for example, sago processing or deep sea fishing—in favor of others.[7]

Through noting spontaneous comparisons and making some special inquiries I also collected the opinions of thirty-one adult villagers with wage-labor experience about the relative ease and difficulty of village work and their work for wages. Here flexibility and autonomy also were significant factors in people's judgments. When they elaborated on the differences between village work and wage work it was also clear that they felt a strong aversion to the greater constraints imposed by wage work.

My thirty-one informants offered forty explanations of comparisons between village work and their wage-labor experience. In 25 percent (10) of these, they spoke of the quantity of work, noting the number of tasks or, more often, without specifying the measure of quantity. Those who spoke of quantity all found wage work "easier" because it involved less work in some way. In 17.5 percent (7) of the comparisons, villagers focused on the degree of physical effort or discomfort involved, in most instances (5) finding wage work "easier" because it involved less physical effort or discomfort. In 12.5 percent (5) of the comparisons, they spoke of the certainty (10 percent) or size (2.5 percent) of the material return on their efforts, and all found wage work easier in this respect. But whenever people spoke of the nature of temporal organization and authority in the labor process, which they did in 30 percent (12) of the comparisons, they invariably found wage work more "difficult," because as wage workers they could not work at a pace and pattern of their own choice.

They spoke of this contrast with color and feeling. "The town is okay," says Numbushel, a young carpenter home on leave, "but you have to be afraid of the boss. In the village you work the way you want to." Another man, now quite settled in the village after several years as a wage worker, paints a vivid picture of the difference. As a wage worker, he says, "You just work and work and work. In the village you work the way you want to. If you feel a little tired or if you're a little sore, you can rest a day or two. Or if you're tired of working in the bush and the sea is calm you can go fishing. That's what our work is like." And, finally, the words of Tarakam, a former laborer in the gold mines at Wau; he finds his work as a villager easier because he can rest when he feels like it, whereas at Wau "we worked as though we were in jail."

To use typical Pidgin phrases, in the village one can *wok long laik*. That is, one can conduct and organize one's activities according to one's own preferences. Wage labor is *wok long taim stret,* or work according to a rigid time schedule. At its worst, wage work is *wok kalabus,* or work that is like being in jail. Wage labor, of course, is not all the same. Many men say they prefer jobs that are more varied in some way. Recall Ungwang's comparison of the tedium of work on a cacao plantation with the rapid passage of the months on a cargo vessel.

The Problem of How to Work

One morning, as Kragur men and women assembled in the village center to prepare for a day of copra processing, the talk turned to the poor returns on all their efforts to make money. "We have to think hard and figure out how to work!" Ungwang proclaimed vehemently.

How to work definitely has become an issue. Some villagers occasionally say that their parents or grandparents worked much harder than people today; but the contrast with the European way of working is most responsible for the present concern. As in the case of forms of distribution and exchange, the materially successful European example has made Kragur people self-conscious about their own practices and has inspired much self-criticism.

Working For vs Like Europeans

As noted above, villagers often judge working for Europeans for wages easier than making a living in the village because it involves less work and physical discomfort and yields a surer return. These are not, however, the features of European work that they most admire. Rather, they admire its temporal coordination and regularity. Both privately and in public, Kragur people often compare their own style of conduct and organization unfavorably with an ideal of European-style coordination and regularity.

For example, at the New Year's meeting in December 1976, one young householder vigorously criticized the prevailing sporadic pattern of copra production. He recommended, in Pidgin, that they "wok olosem long stesin," that is, as European-owned plantations do, by collecting, shelling, and smoking copra at regularly scheduled intervals. Some villagers are also beginning to grow impatient with the loose coordination of effort in subsistence activities. As Kabwam and I sat waiting for the others to join us to cut timbers for Aram's new house, he eventually was moved to complain of the delay: "It's wrong for us to have to wait like this. They understand the way of the whites, but when they come back to the village they just sit on their bloody asses!"

Furthermore, villagers often comment on the perceived willingness of Europeans to accept the decisions and directions of the "boss" of a work group. They contrast this with what they see as the tendency of Papua New Guineans to follow a leader's directives only if it suits their fancy. Herein, they assert, is one source of their inability to work and live in a more regular and coordinated way.

The underlying concern is that a major reason they are so much poorer and politically weaker than Europeans and the emerging Papua New Guinean elite is that they have failed to achieve a comparable level of regularity, punctuality, and cooperative obedience to authority. One day in 1976, I sat with a group of Kragur men and women while we waited for a special event to begin at Bou school. Nearly two hours had passed since the school bell had announced the gathering, and many in the crowd from several villages had begun to complain loudly of the delay. Although there were some obvious reasons for this particular instance of temporal imprecision, at least one of my companions chose to view the matter in a larger and more self-critical framework. "Look at this," he muttered. "We're not ready yet. We can't do anything right."

Such admiration for the European way of conducting work and other activities seems curious at first glance, because villagers who have worked for Europeans find doing so difficult and distasteful precisely because such work is tightly regulated by the boss and the clock. This apparent contradiction dissolves if one distinguishes working *for* Europeans from working *like* Europeans. Kragur people know that Europeans *impose* order on their Papua New Guinean employees; but many appear to suspect that among Europeans themselves coordination and regularity in work occur spontaneously, or at least with minimum coercion. Only rarely does anyone take note of the fact that European workers must obey the boss readily and pay attention to the clock because they cannot afford to lose their jobs. (In Kragur, of course, there is no class of persons who are obliged to work for others because they have no productive resources of their own.) Instead, villagers say that they, and other Papua New Guineans, do not heed their leaders and are not punctual, regular, and coordinated in their work because they are "not ready yet" or because, as Manup puts it, they are "still wild."[8] Such statements imply that order in European work is based on moral superiority, not economic necessity and coercive authority. Even without deliberate European promotion, such a view would not be surprising given the prevalent view that material prowess is evidence of moral superiority. In the indigenous view, external order alone does not ensure prosperity; hidden anger is as dangerous to material well-being as public conflict. Hence, external order coupled with material wealth suggest deeper harmony.

This is not to say that no one in Kragur admires and wishes to emulate the time-conscious, rigidly paced, and coordinated European style of work in order to improve efficiency in the Western instrumental sense. Even those who do, however, probably do not clearly understand the roots of this kind of order and regularity. For many, the desire to be more efficient in the Western sense is undoubtedly fused with the desire to demonstrate the moral worth that European domination has called into question and with the hope that this will enlist the aid of whatever supernatural powers are attending to their performance.

Pursuing the Ideal, Resisting the Reality

Despite widespread admiration for the European way of working, attempts to institute European-style practices in the village often meet with lack of enthusiasm and downright resistance. This is due to many villagers' lack of full acculturation to the European concepts of time that figure in both the rationale for and the practice of European work order, as well as to the strength of indigenous habits of autonomy in the conduct of daily activities. As suggested above, those who try to introduce greater temporal coordination and regularity are probably moved by the desire to achieve a superior form of social harmony in addition to using time more efficiently. Nevertheless, they apply the methods they have learned from European employers, teachers, and missionaries; that is, they try to tell other villagers what to do and when to do it. Long accustomed to great autonomy in their daily activities, many Kragur people resent this.

The village councillor is one of the chief proponents of greater temporal order. People's reactions to his efforts illustrate the con-

flict between the reality of such attempts at discipline and deeply
ingrained habits and attitudes. Many of the tasks now organized
under the councillor's authority would have been undertaken in
the past on a more irregular basis at the discretion of individuals
or as initiated by customary leaders. Some council-work tasks are
new, such as maintaining the buildings and grounds of the primary
school at Bou. Villagers appear to resent the imposition of the
councillor's authority, however, even where the ends are clearly
beneficial and the work would have to be performed at some point
under any circumstances. One incident among many I observed
illustrates this. The councillor had designated several days for
communal house construction, as is his prerogative. On one of
those days the task at hand was making thatch for one of the new
houses. There were not enough sago-palm leaves on hand, so that
morning the councillor sent several women to the bush to gather
more. Arriving back at the village in mid-afternoon with a heavy
load of sago leaves, a middle-aged woman sighed with relief and
lowered her bundle to the ground. She sat down wearily near a
young man who was weaving sections of thatch and began to complain: "He [the councillor] forces us to go to the bush. He rounds
us up as though we were wild pigs or cows." The young man
replied: "You may be a cow, but I'm a man. He can't force me to
work."

Similarly, on another day of council work, the secondary
elected leader, the committeeman, took the occasion of morning
work assignments to reprimand the assembled men and women
for coming late to the place of assembly and for not working hard
enough on previous days. A young man muttered angrily to those
near him, "We're not bloody stupid." An older, bolder man replied
to the committeeman for all to hear: "You give us lectures and lectures and lectures. That's wrong! We're not pigs! We're not dogs!
We know how to work!"

The councillor does not help his cause by adopting a high-
handed style. The first order of business at many council-work
assemblies is a lengthy tirade on the futility of efforts to improve
Kragur's lot if people continue to take their time responding to the
bell and beginning work. One early morning, the councillor,
unusually aggravated by the leisurely pace of response to the bell,
stood in the village center shouting for people to leave the out-
houses, hurry to the assembly, and "hold your shit" if necessary.
This kind of behavior is not popular.

A new, more restrictive form of council-work organization introduced in 1976 also won little favor. Previously, one or, if necessary, two days a week—usually Monday and Tuesday—were allocated to council work. In 1976, however, an assembly of village councillors from Kairiru and Mushu, meeting in the south coast Kairiru village of Yuwun, adopted a new system. In this, one full week out of every four (in Pidgin, *kaunsil wik*) was allocated to council work, one week *(bisnis wik)* to individual or collective cash-cropping (or such other commercial activities as replenishing trade-store stock), and two consecutive weeks *(pipal wik*—that is, "people weeks") to individual or household discretion. Villagers were to spend the latter two weeks in garden work and other subsistence tasks so they could concentrate on council work and cash cropping in their designated weeks. Allegedly, the Kragur delegation to the Yuwun meeting arrived after the other councillors had already agreed to try the new schedule. They acquiesced in part so that Kragur people would not be out of sync in activities involving relations with people in other villages. Proponents of the plan said it would allow people to organize their own activities, including trips to Wewak or other villages, so that they did not interfere with council work, and vice versa.

The new system's few defenders in Kragur claimed that it would work well if people spent their discretionary weeks wisely. Most villagers were not so sure. Some merely proposed that the discretionary weeks be alternated with the council and cash-cropping weeks. Others, however, complained pointedly of the inflexibility of such a scheme of work organization, its incompatibility with both the technical demands of certain activities and the exigencies of personal needs. One man complained that if he harvested taro during the council week he did not have enough time to replant the sprouts and some of them spoiled before the discretionary weeks rolled round again. Another complained that good fishing weather could not be counted on to wait for the discretionary weeks. A woman said that it was easy to get through the council and cash-cropping weeks if you had a supply of sago (which keeps longer than taro) in the house; but one of her small daughters much preferred taro, and she had to make an extra effort to get to her garden to keep her child happy and well fed. By 1981 such discontent had led to the demise of the new council system.

Customary leaders also lecture and berate the rank and file on occasion, and complaints that one or another big man is presuming on his position are frequent. Their exertion of authority, however, is accepted more readily, for it is sanctioned by tradition and based in part on strongly reciprocal intravillage social relations. Councillors and committeemen cannot operate without reciprocity either; but they also derive authority from a strongly hierarchical political structure with its roots outside the village and from the threat of legal sanctions brought to bear through the village local court system. At best, many regard the councillor's authority as an additional burden; at worst, they regard it as an extension of the power of a central government that villagers are not at all sure has their interests at heart. Further, while it is nothing new for leaders to intensify activity—a ramat walap did so to mount feasts, trading expeditions, men's cult ceremonies, and other events—the idiom of time scarcity that the councillor and other new leaders employ is not entirely convincing, and attempts to rigidify activity patterns are an unaccustomed trial to villagers.

Time Scarcity and Attitudes toward Authority

The progress of the idea of time scarcity in Kragur deserves special attention. In developed Western societies not only can time be measured, saved, and allocated carefully in order to maximize return on one's efforts, people feel that they *must* measure and allocate with care because time is scarce. Those villagers who appear to think that they sometimes cannot get much done because the sun moves too fast are not conceptually equipped to think of time as an autonomous entity in short supply. Although economizing calculation is not impossible using indigenous Kairiru categories, there is little similarity between that kind of calculation and the kind one can easily make using the modern Western system of detailed, quantitatively interrelated units fixed in relation to human events. Kairiru categories certainly do not lend themselves to the construction of an image of time scarcity that penetrates into the minutiae of daily conduct, its half-hours, quarter-hours, minutes, and seconds.[9]

Kragur villagers' behavior often suggests an indifference to the passage of time inconsistent with a developed sense of time scarcity. Many will wait for boats or census agents to arrive, meetings to begin, or others to join them before setting out for the bush with an equanimity that would be remarkable to many Westerners. Similarly, when they are engaged in one activity, villagers seldom seem to be in a hurry to get on to the next. As a well-educated Kragur migrant puts it in English, people in Kragur feel: " 'If we don't finish work now we'll do it tomorrow.' The work they're doing now they see as the only work. While you're doing it you're free from moving from one point to another. Time is sort of all partitioned." This attitude is sometimes referred to in the literature as task orientation, in contrast with time orientation (Moore 1963). Within such an orientation, as Barden (1973:343) writes of Australian aborigines, "The business at hand dictates its own duration: sufficient for the day is its own work."

Kragur is, however, in a period of transition; the partitions of temporal experience are beginning to come undone. Scattered throughout speeches and conversations in the Kairiru language one sometimes hears such Pidgin phrases as *westim taim* (to waste time), *westim bladi taim* (to waste bloody time), *taim i sot* (time is short), or *taim i no nap* (time is insufficient). When villagers refer to time scarcity they often speak of it as an occasional and circumstantial problem; it is something that occurs on particular days or in relation to particular tasks and is not a pervasive and continuous problem. People may say, for example, that if they do not begin work early enough in the morning, if there is a particularly large task to be accomplished, or if the work site is a long distance from the village, they will not have time to accomplish much. Others, however, seem to see a more persistent problem. One young man, for instance, suggests that all gardens should be closer to the village to cut down permanently on travel time.

There is some talk among villagers of having too little time or, more often, too much to do. They do have many demands on their time that their parents and grandparents did not, such as church activities, council work, school meetings, copra production, and so on. One cannot be sure, of course, if there are *more* demands on their time than in the past, for such things as warfare, men's cult activities, and overseas trade have dropped from the repertoire. Yet, despite what sounds like talk of time scarcity, even many who are adept with hours and minutes seldom seem to regard their passage as the dissipation of a precious commodity. Given the nature of indigenous categories and the perceptions that clearly persist in some quarters, it is wise to regard much expressed concern that taim i sot with caution. The rank and file are bothered as much by leaders' attempts to impose greater temporal regularity as by the alleged problem of scarcity these attempts purport to address. When nonleaders say that in these days there is too much to do, they may well be complaining more of unaccustomed impositions of authority on their patterns of activity than of a changing ratio of tasks to available temporal resources (Smith 1982a).

The councillor, the leader of village Catholicism, and other occupants of new, nontraditional positions of leadership are the principal proponents of new temporal practices and values in Kragur. Any kind of leader, whether ramat walap or councillor, is more constantly involved in a wider range of activities than the average villager (cf. Oliver 1967[1955]:396–397). This may make leaders in general more susceptible to the ideology of time scarcity. The words of one councillor, who also has traditional claims to status, to a meeting of Kragur men suggest this: "You unimportant men, you think time is long. But for those of us who run things, men with ideas, no! Time is short!" In addition, many of those who aspire to the new positions of leadership are probably especially concerned with emulating European ways in order to achieve progress in the village, and their participation in church and local government council activities outside the village exposes them to additional acculturative pressures. Purveying to other villagers novel temporal practices and values may also help to legitimate and, perhaps, expand the new leadership space they occupy. The councillor and Catholic leader, in particular, tend to treat Western concepts of time and temporal efficiency as a valuable innovation of which they are the sponsors.

It might be a mistake, however, to present the conflict over new forms of temporal order and discipline as primarily a conflict among villagers. Many villagers who on some occasions complain loudly of inefficiency, on others complain loudly of new temporal constraints. Similarly, many efficiency boosters—including the councillor, committeeman, Catholic leader, and other vocal proponents of progress and change—often behave as if they were either rich in or ignorant of time. The conflict *between* new leaders and the rank and file mirrors a conflict *within* all Kragur people: a conflict between deeply ingrained habits and new practices and values with an aura of superior moral worth. The conflict between new leaders and other villagers is, however, highly significant because it reproduces within the village the link between new *ideas* about time and the *enforcement* of new ways of working and conducting daily life that is characteristic of the growth of capitalism.

Resistance, Misperception, and Redefinition

The preaching and admonitions that accompany attempts to institute elements of European temporal order in the village may, in themselves, contribute little to acculturation to new temporal concepts and values. As local leaders and external institutions actually change the time pattern of daily life, however, the need to adapt to more rigid patterns will further acculturation by making new concepts and values more plausible and useful. In this way, church activities and the council-work schedule, for example, have made the progress of days within weeks seem natural and familiar. Nevertheless, calendrical as opposed to lunar months still puzzle some villagers, and most pay little attention to the detailed Western divisions of the day. Acculturation has not proceeded very far. When, as migrant laborers, they use magic to slow the speed of the sun or hasten the cycle of the moon, when they respond to the village bell at their own convenience, and when they shout their objections to the councillor's lectures on punctuality, Kragur people are still fighting against time rather than about it, to borrow a phrase from E. P. Thompson's description of early resistance to the forcible alteration of the temporal habits of the English working class (1967:85).

Despite this, European work order still exerts a strong pull. Early Catholic missionaries in the Sepik were explicitly concerned with the work habits and attitudes toward time of the indigenous people. In 1900, Father Eberhard Limbrock, the first Society of the Divine Word Prefect Apostolic in German New Guinea, wrote to a member of the German Reichstag in defense of his appeal for more land for mission plantations. He argued that "through cultivation the land will become healthier and more productive" and "the people will learn how to work and have order in their lives . . ." (quoted in Wiltgen 1969:337).[10] Faced with the councillor's demands, many Kragur villagers may feel that, not being pigs or dogs, they already know how to work. Nevertheless, the spectacle of the temporal regularity and coordination of European work and life in general, in conjunction with its material wealth, suggests to them its moral as well as technical superiority and stirs doubts about the moral value of indigenous practices.

The characteristic order of Western labor processes does rest in part on shared normative orientations (cf. Carrier 1992:202–203); but it also is based on the power impersonal bureaucratic organizations hold over individuals and, more fundamentally, the power of capital over labor (cf. Braverman 1974; Edwards 1979). Western workers do not work by the clock, pay attention to the boss, and coordinate their efforts simply because they feel it is right. However they may feel personally, at bottom their livelihoods depend on their adhering to the pace and pattern of hierarchically controlled labor processes. In order for Kragur villagers to idealize Western work, perceiving its order as a manifestation of deeper social harmony, they have to discount their own experience of coercion when working for Europeans. Their more general perception of superior European social harmony, and their presumption of the inseparability of material and moral accomplishment, lead them to assume—mistakenly—that Europeans themselves cooperate spontaneously.

To Kragur villagers, the surface appearance of European temporal coordination and regularity probably seems a more obvious demonstration of superior social harmony than the reality of European commercial exchange and distribution. As discussed in Chapter 7, perceiving the latter as morally superior to indigenous practices requires strenuous deduction and leaves significant contradictions unresolved. Perceiving European temporal order as morally superior may be somewhat easier. It too, however, requires deduction from the principle that material success is inextricable from moral success; and it entails substantial redefinition of the substance of good social relations, imposing a radically new criterion—temporal coordination and regularity—for harmony and cooperation. This redefinition is still a matter of debate and conflict.[11] The temporal pattern of life in Kragur and villagers' sense of time will probably change very slowly, unless the community becomes much more deeply involved in commodity and labor markets. Nevertheless, to the extent that Kragur is drawn deeper into the new political economy, the moral aura that villagers themselves have helped to create around European patterns of work and temporal practices, and the redefinition of good social relations this entails, could help to ease new ways of living into place.

NINE

The Future, Hard Times, and Visions of Goodness

ASKED POINT BLANK what they think Kragur will be like in a few years, whether it will change and how, many villagers say they have no idea. Others say it is up to the kastom or the councillor, not them. As Sakun puts it: "Business or whatever kind of work, that's up to the kastom or the councillor. The people can't do anything themselves. Everything has to come from the kastom and they have to reach agreement with the councillor."

Most, however, have more to say. There is a strong tendency, also suggested in Sakun's statement, to speak of Kragur's future in terms of prospects of replacing subsistence production with cash-crop production or other bisnis and enjoying the fruits of cash income, such as houses made of milled lumber with corrugated iron roofs, plumbing, and electricity.

Many do not think such a transformation is likely in the near future. As might be expected, some say that significant change is unlikely because Kragur people are unable to reform their contentious and uncooperative ways. Those who do entertain optimistic visions of Kragur's future tend to place their faith in the younger generation, which, they hope, will bring new ideas and skills to the village. It is not surprising that some younger, better-educated villagers feel the future is in their hands. Manup, for example, says, in English: "[The village] will develop if all the young people like me who are educated, who can give them ideas how to run the thing, or business [do so]. If we let them do it themself [sic], I don't think it would [sic]. It would fail."

Many others—old and young, men and women—agree. Although Taunur takes great pride in his status as a ramat walap and his knowledge of important magic, he too sometimes speaks as though the days of his kind of leadership are over. "I tell the young men, the past is past, you have to change your ideas, you have to talk about business. Don't think about taro; taro is finished. I say to them, forget about me, I'm through, the ways of our fathers and grandparents are through. You follow the ways of school."

"The ways of school," "new ways," "the laws of the whites"—all these phrases are used to describe what new generations could bring to Kragur. They can refer to things as mundane as knowledge of business practices and as sweeping as new forms and standards of solidarity and cooperation. Elsewhere in Papua New Guinea, as Vulliamy and Carrier (1985) point out, it has been difficult for young people to bring "the ways of school" or "the laws of the whites" back to the village. They often face pressures, including fear of sorcery, to conform to long-standing social norms; if too young, they cannot make serious claims to leadership; and the ways of school, however much admired in the abstract, may conflict with village social realities. For example, sound business practices according to the ways of school may run up against local ideas of business that privilege distribution of wealth over production of profit.

In Kragur, older villagers appear to pay little attention to the ideas of young people still in high school or even university, and these young people have little or no voice in public discussions. Educated young people working in urban areas did play a major role in establishing the Village Development Fund and the Community Development Youth Club, and older villagers supported these efforts, although they eventually foundered. Some villagers, however, feel that educated migrants have lost touch with the realities of village life and regard their suggestions with skepticism (Smith 1985:14–15). It remains to be seen what influence migrants who return to settle in the village may have in years to come.

What some Kragur people envision, however, is not piecemeal alteration of village life under the influence of a few educated young people, but the eventual wholesale replacement of older generations. Says Kelmiai, a woman in her thirties: "If the old people all die, I think the new ones who are in school will make new laws and leave behind the ways of their parents and grandparents." Some of the older leaders, like Mangoi, agree: "When we big men die, the children will put their efforts into business."

The older generations surely will die, but several factors may complicate the scenario. Younger villagers do seem more open to expanding the sphere of monetary relations than their elders. Recall that some young men say they would have approved of receiving wages for building my house in 1975–1976 and that in 1981 younger villagers were promoting the idea of using my former house as a commercial guest lodge. Some are also versed in the uses of bank loans, government grants, and other financial resources. Younger villagers, however, seem no more certain than their elders about the degree to which money should be allowed to enter transactions among villagers themselves, in contrast to transactions with outsiders. Similarly, while to many villagers of all ages *lo bilong waitman* means some form of superior cooperation, they do not agree on its specific form. Many continue to push for better village-wide cooperation. Some, however, have noticed that European business ventures are often owned and run by individuals or families of limited extension. In short, the young have some of the same difficulties as their elders in defining a "new way."

Also, many villagers are concerned that, rather than replacing the older generations, young people will continue to leave in significant numbers and will not come back. "No more young men stay here," says Morauk. "They go to school, then they go off somewhere else and they're gone for good. Sooner or later we'll die and there'll be no one left to work." Morauk exaggerates; in 1975–1976 there were a number of young men in Kragur who had recently returned from stints as migrant workers. In 1981 some of these had married and settled into village life, and a few others, absent as migrants during my first trip to Kragur, had also returned and spoke of staying on. Nevertheless, the hourglass age distribution of the population does reflect substantial attrition among young men.[1]

Resident villagers view attrition as a moral problem as well as a material hardship. No one expects migrants to sacrifice successful careers to return to the village, and successful migrants are valued for what they contribute to the village in money and influence in external institutions. Many villagers, however, claim that numbers of male migrants have no permanent employment and merely drift from temporary job to temporary job, living off their

employed friends and kin in the interim. These are accused of
shirking their responsibility to help the village in favor of leading
easy and selfish lives in urban centers. On the other hand, some
resident villagers at times blame themselves for these migrants'
reluctance to return. If, they reason, they were to show more initiative in developing cash production, it would attract migrants
back to the village. They often blame their failure to exhibit more
initiative on lack of cooperative spirit, failure of leadership, failure
to follow leaders, and so on—in short, on failure to be good people in terms of an ideal of cooperation based on disinterested, positive sentiment.

Village and Nation

Economic and social forces outside the village will play a central
role in determining the rate of migration and return and what new
generations in Kragur will be able to accomplish. Currently, the
prospects are not encouraging either for developing village cash-
crop production or for success in the urban labor force. The Papua
New Guinea economy has grown slowly since independence, and
per-capita income has increased only marginally, according to a
recent report of the Australian International Development Assistance Bureau (AIDAB 1989:1). Growth outside an "enclave" min-
ing and oil exploration sector has been particularly weak, and this
sector itself is troubled by significant political unrest (AIDAB
1989:17–20; May and Spriggs 1990; Wesley-Smith 1991). The
vast majority of the population is concentrated in subsistence production and self-employed cash-crop production. Copra prices fell
from 1980 to 1989, and prices of most export crops are expected
to rise only slightly in coming years (AIDAB 1989:22; cf. Wesley-
Smith 1991:192).

Unemployment in the small wage and salary sector was about
15 percent in 1986, and as high as 25 percent among those fifteen
to twenty-five years old. In 1989 further increases in these rates
were expected (AIDAB 1989:6–8).

A serious crime problem in urban areas makes life there less
attractive to migrants. When I visited several provincial capitals in
Papua New Guinea in 1989, talk of armed robbery, break-ins,
rapes, and killings was on everyone's lips. Guests in hotels were

advised not to go out after dark except by taxi direct to their destinations. Scanning recent issues of the country's major newspaper, the *Papua New Guinea Post Courier,* in 1991 I see that crime dominates the news. Recent newspaper reports also indicate that Wewak has its full share of crime problems. In 1981 as well, Kragur villagers staying at Kreer were wary, with good reason. Shortly before my arrival that year, for example, a young Kragur woman was robbed at knife point in broad daylight while returning from a nearby store to the Kragur settlement at Kreer.

Crime, of course, feeds on lack of economic opportunity and could in turn inhibit economic growth in Papua New Guinea by discouraging foreign assistance and investments, and even local business activity (O'Callaghan 1991; Senge 1991). Such difficult social and economic circumstances may force younger villagers back into their home communities, where market opportunities will continue to stagnate.

There is a variety of opinions on the extent to which national development policy in Papua New Guinea has promoted increasing inequality among Papua New Guineans. Goodman, Lepani, and Morawetz (1985:42–43) find that, since independence, indigenous Papua New Guineans are receiving an increasing share of the country's gross domestic product and some government services are being distributed more equally, as is access to educational opportunity. On the other hand, while wage and salary differences within urban areas have been declining, the wage gap between unskilled urban and rural workers has increased, and rising unemployment exacerbates inequality. Further, opportunities for successful cash cropping vary greatly among the country's regions, so some have moved more rapidly and successfully into the money economy. However, Goodman et al. conclude, rather optimistically: "This increasing disparity of incomes is observed in most countries at the earliest stages of development. The disparities observed to date in Papua New Guinea are still small by the standards of many countries (e.g., in Latin America)."

Other observers are less optimistic. Amarshi et al. (1979) paint a disturbing picture of the development of enduring class differences in independent Papua New Guinea, and Good (1986:9) describes the prevailing model of economic development followed since independence as one that "acts against the interests of the poor majority."[2]

Many Papua New Guineans do appear to notice and react against increasing economic disparities (Amarshi et al. 1979:140–148; Townsend 1980:10). Kragur people have a pronounced sense of the distance that separates them not only from the indigenous governmental elite but also from urban wage earners who, as some put it, just "bloody sit on their asses and work for their bloody fortnightly wages" or "sit drinking tea and enjoying themselves in Moresby." At the same time, according to some observers, better-educated, more well-to-do Papua New Guineans tend to be rather protective of their privileges and "possess generally paternalistic and elitist attitudes towards the uneducated masses" (Young 1975:39). In my own travels in Papua New Guinea I have met professionals and bureaucrats who do not exhibit such attitudes, but I have also met others who do.

The Fate of the Good Way

One can only speculate on the influence of generational change and extravillage economic and social trends on Kragur's ideology of moral distinction. Contracting or stagnant opportunities in the cash economy and new kinds of inequality are good reasons to continue to assert a positive moral identity and to continue to define good social relations in terms of standards that villagers can achieve within the framework of precapitalist relations of production and distribution.[3]

However, were opportunities in the cash economy to improve significantly—a prospect that seems unlikely in the near future—opportunities for individualistic endeavor also would increase, as would possibilities for widening the sphere of monetary relations. Increasing monetization of social relations—use of money in marriage or funerary exchanges or in quotidian distribution of subsistence goods—would bring profound change in social relations, rendering them less personal (cf. Errington and Gewertz 1987:125).

Would such changes mean the end of the Good Way? Not necessarily. One of the main points of this book is that, while there is broad agreement that Kragur excels morally in general terms, opinions about the specifics of good social relations are diverse and debate and speculation are rampant. Like conceptions of good social relations, the Good Way as an ideology of moral distinction also appears to be malleable. Individuals can interpret the exceptional harmony and generosity to which it lays claim in their own ways and adapt their interpretations to fit new circumstances. For example, young migrants eager to make their way in the cash economy and to avoid their families' financial demands still speak warmly of how supportive and helpful Kragur people are. The Good Way, in various guises, probably will persist for some time, unless future generations radically reject the assumed linkage between moral and material issues. This latter possibility seems unlikely, not only because of the strength of the bond created by the meeting of indigenous tendencies and exogenous influences, but also because of the deep implications of virtue that secularized capitalism finds in material prowess. Hence, success in the capitalist world could bolster feelings of moral worth, and failure could make defensive moral self-assertion necessary.[4]

The Good Way, Catholicism, and Capitalism

What role might Catholicism play in a reformulated Good Way? Villagers' attitudes toward Catholicism have not remained constant in the decades since its introduction. Some are disappointed by its failure to fulfill what they saw as its initial promise of radical transformation. Villagers have also seen Catholicism itself change its shape over the years. For example, they have noticed that religious observance is no longer compulsory for students at St. Xavier's, and that the mission's militant campaigning against all indigenous magicoreligious practices has given way to tolerance and even encouragement not to abandon what is "good" in precontact religious customs. Much of what they have observed has been part of a trend in the Catholic church as a whole toward less emphasis on religious rites, artifacts, and individual conversion, and more emphasis on integrating Catholicism into community life, a trend made manifest in the Vatican II Ecumenical Council of 1962–1965 (cf. Arbuckle 1978; Armstrong 1990).

In addition, many new religious and secular institutions have appeared in the postcolonial landscape, and Catholicism no longer dominates villagers' view of the European world as it once did. All this has led a few Kragur people to regard it as perhaps less central to the project of social transformation and a less solid rock on which to build their hopes for the future (Smith 1988). Nonetheless, Kragur people have done much to make Catholicism their own and might maintain a strong positive identity as Catholics apart from their feelings about Catholicism's official doctrines and institutions. I think it would be difficult, for example, for the official church to undermine the sense of an independent religious charter that villagers build on, or express in, Masos' meeting with God before the first missionaries arrived.

The place of Catholicism in Kragur identity has no simple, predictable relationship to that identity's compatibility with capitalist forms of production and distribution (Smith 1990). For example, although it contributes to idealized perceptions of characteristically capitalist forms of production and distribution, Catholicism is also seen as legitimating indigenous nonmonetary traditions.[5] Thus its relationship to indigenous and European practices is ambiguous and helps account for villagers' perplexity about the nature of good social relations in the contemporary world. This should not be surprising. Christian missions throughout the world have been an integral part of colonialism, but their role has often been indeterminant. As Comaroff and Comaroff (1986:1) note, to phrase the question of the missionary role in colonization in such terms as "Whose side was the missionary really on?" is to risk oversimplifying a complex issue. Burridge (1978:21) points out that European Christian missions have always experienced a tension between the task of creating Europeans and that of creating Christians, between what is often an interest in acclimatizing their clients to a new political and economic order and Christianity's concern with, and imagery of, liberation from worldly oppression. This tension within Christianity helps to account for Catholicism's diverse uses and functions in Kragur and suggests that it could remain an important element of a positive moral identity in Kragur under a variety of political-economic circumstances.

Redefining Good Social Relations: Prospects and Implications

I have tried to show how Kragur people's efforts to understand the roots of European prosperity may be leading them to redefine good social relations in a manner more compatible with life in a capitalist political economy in which the commodity form of material things and human effort dominates. I have argued that, while European institutions make conscious efforts to instill new ideas of social order and new economic practices, Kragur people are also making their own active contribution. The cultural and historical circumstances of Kragur's encounter with European institutions have led some villagers to elaborate a vision of European moral superiority that calls indigenous criteria of good social relations into question, even while they continue to assert their community's moral distinction. The strength of explicit European efforts to undermine the moral authority of existing standards and practices does not seem to have been sufficient in itself to generate such intensity of self-criticism, debate, and speculation as I observed in Kragur. Neither secular nor religious Europeans could have anticipated the sparks given off by the collision of their example and teachings with indigenous understandings of the interpenetration of moral and material issues.

I am more concerned with the possible implications of Kragur perceptions of the roots of material well-being in the contemporary world than with the relative weight of indigenous and European contributions to the development of those perceptions. To a great extent, the influence even of explicit European attempts to instill new views of virtue, order, and harmony has been determined by the indigenous culture of Kragur and the circumstances of its encounter with European institutions—in particular, the geographic circumstances that long kept Catholicism in the foreground of the European world as seen from Kragur. The belief systems of the Europeans in Papua New Guinea, Catholicism, and indigenous Kragur are like all belief systems, in that each encompasses diverse tendencies and potentials. As in a chemical reaction, their meeting under particular conditions has stimulated all parties to the interaction to emphasize and elaborate some possibilities and neglect others (cf. Smith 1990:150–151).

Keesing (1989:23), following Gramsci, argues that even "counterhegemonic discourse," such as Kragur's positive moral self-image, "pervasively incorporates the structures, categories, and premises of hegemonic discourse." More concretely, for example, he argues that many Pacific Islanders incorporate missionary dichotomies between "Christian light and heathen darkness, God and the Devil, good and evil" into their own definitions of self and culture, and that colonized people select those elements of their own cultures to emphasize which "most strikingly differentiate them from Europeans" (cf. Babadzan 1988; Brison n.d.; Linnekin 1990; Thomas 1991:203–204). Yet, even if one could weigh accurately the respective contributions to Kragur people's perceptions of morality and material well-being, the roots of an idea do not necessarily determine its implications. This is abundantly clear in the way in which Catholicism has contributed to both accommodation and resistance to capitalist incorporation in Kragur. The institutions of the new political economy, however, do wield more power in the larger arena than Kragur villagers; they have more control over the conditions of the encounter, and their members suffer less when their intentions go awry. Neither do villagers have the option of turning their backs on the new social, political, and economic structure emerging around them.

In Chapter 1, I characterized the historical process in which Kragur villagers are involved, using Comaroff's (1985:1) phrase, as a dialectic "between the dominant and the subordinate in the colonial encounter." I also spoke of the potential for both resistance and accommodation to domination in actors' struggles within constraining social and historical circumstances. Elsewhere (Smith 1990), I have characterized Kragur people's efforts to cope with the problems of the new social order as a drama of capitalist incorporation and resistance. Perhaps such dichotomies are too stark. Clifford (1988:343–344) writes:

> Along with the history of resistance we need a history of hesitations. Stories of cultural contact and change have been structured by a pervasive dichotomy: absorption by the other or resistance to the other. . . . Yet what if identity is conceived not as a boundary to be maintained but as a nexus of relations and transactions actively engaging a subject? The story or stories of interaction must then be more complex, less linear and teleological.

Kragur people themselves do not speak of incorporation, resistance, or hesitation. They speak of the difficulties of achieving good social relations to meet new material challenges, and they wonder aloud what the criteria for good social relations in the contemporary world should be. They want to be more deeply involved in the new world as they understand it, but not in a chronically inferior position. They wonder aloud how much that is familiar they may have to relinquish to achieve that.

One can find some "hesitation" here, but one can also find phenomena easy to describe in terms of incorporation and resistance.[6] Some are obvious. Many villagers, for example, are quick openly to resist efforts to impose rigid Western industrial temporal styles and activity patterns on daily life. More subtly, Kragur people's insistence on their loosely defined tradition of exceptional moral worth is hard not to see as a bulwark they are erecting against the implicit and explicit devaluation of indigenous practices and standards by European practice and teaching in a context of domination. The nascent redefinition of good social relations is a potentially strong force for incorporation. To the extent that it proceeds, it prepares the way for expanding the sphere of market relations and accepting the temporal discipline of life tied closely to capitalist markets.

Specific conceptions of good social relations aside, the larger tendency to interpret material success or failure in the new political economy in moral terms that has emerged from the circumstances of Kragur's colonial encounter also has tremendous potential for facilitating deeper incorporation. In itself, it does not prepare people to adopt practices more compatible with a new political economy; but it does divert them from questioning the justice and reason of the new political economy by painting economic marginality as moral failure and inequality as just deserts. Sahlins (1991) suggests that "humiliation" may be a necessary stage in economic development. Their own doubts about their individual and collective self-worth may be the strongest single motive pushing Kragur people toward what they understand as *divelopmen;* but it is their desire to maintain their self-worth that also fires their resistance to many of the demands of that divelopmen.

Rapid or steady movement toward deeper engagement in the cash economy is by no means inevitable. The most obvious obstacle to such a "linear and teleological" course in Kragur is the tenuous economic situation of the nation as a whole (cf. Errington and Gewertz 1987:126; Townsend 1980). Kragur people indeed appear to be in a bind. Even successful development, were it within their reach, would bring changes in the nature of social relations

that they cannot anticipate rather than realization of familiar ideals on a new scale. Their position on the margins of the new political economy will continue to raise painful self-doubts about their
moral worth, as well as to deny them a host of new—albeit dou-
ble-edged—economic, political, and cultural opportunities. It may
be as important, under these trying circumstances, that they retain
a sense of their moral worth as that they increase their incomes,
although—given their own tendency to intertwine the moral and
the material, and Western capitalism's secularized tendency to
read poverty as the fault of the poor—this will not be easy. The
worst outcome would be "humiliation" (Sahlins 1991) without
development, whatever surprises the latter might bring.

In the face of many obstacles to development, Kragur people
also grapple with the specter of moral inferiority. Their adaptation
of Catholicism, the religion of the dominant, adamantly affirms
the value of practices rooted in the precolonial past; and they stub-
bornly continue to lay claim to a moral distinction potent yet flexible enough to endure their own private doubt, public disagreement, and social experimentation. They work to remain good
people in their own eyes, even as they struggle to understand what
it is to be good in a difficult and confusing new world.

Appendix: Time-Allocation Data

As pointed out in Chapter 8, time-allocation data should be used with some caution. Nevertheless, systematic time-allocation study can give an idea of the pattern of activity and distribution of effort in a community not apparent to casual observation, and it can reveal a great deal about the division of labor among categories of people. Also, in a community like Kragur, the irregular pattern and often unhurried pace of activities can make it difficult for an observer from an industrial society to comprehend how active and industrious people actually are. Time-allocation study helps correct for this.

I collected eleven weeks of time-allocation data. In each week I observed the activities of the households in one or two adjacent koyeng for seven days, from 7 A.M. to 7 P.M., the hours of daylight activity. I visited each household each hour, noted the activities of the household members present, and asked what those absent were doing. When they returned, I asked household members absent earlier what they had been doing. I also observed people's comings and goings between hourly observation points when possible. I included in my observations all active household members above primary-school age, many of whom were in their fifties and sixties.

I did not collect systematic observations of nocturnal activities. Since much activity of all kinds—such as fishing, hunting, meetings and ceremonies, craftwork, and household tasks—does take place in Kragur after dark, my data understate the amount of time spent in several categories of activity (cf. Scaglion 1986). I also did not keep a thorough account of time spent caring for children as a discrete activity. Kragur people usually keep an eye on their young children while they are engaged in other activities, although those too old or too young for heavy physical work, or adults in their prime who stay in the village because of illness and fatigue, often appear to devote themselves exclusively to watching infants. It is common, however, for entire households to go to gardens to-

Table A-1
Average Daylight-Activity Hours per Seven-Day (84-hour) Week

ACTIVITY	WOMEN	MEN
Food production	23.59	16.45
Construction and crafts	1.26	8.33
Household tasks	12.74	.98
Illness and curing	5.04	7.98
Meetings and ceremonies	2.87	7.00
Visiting	8.75	5.32
Moneymaking	4.34	7.63
Purchasing	.07	0
Council meetings and council work	1.40	2.31
School activities	1.26	3.15
Church activities	1.19	1.40
Dealing with external agencies	.14	.28
Enforced idleness	3.50	5.88
Other leisure	17.92	17.43
Total	**84.07**	**84.14**

NOTE: Totals do not add up to 84 because of rounding.

gether, taking even infants who are still nursing. Only mothers with newborn infants habitually refrain from work outside the village. Although men and older children take some part in child care, women with children too young to attend primary school are likely to be occupied with them in some way almost constantly.

Table A-1 shows the average daylight-activity hours for men and women for a seven-day week for fourteen categories of activity. The categories are loosely adapted from those used by Waddell and Krinks (1968). They are explained below.

Food production: This category includes gardening, fishing, hunting, gathering, and sago production. Fishing includes gathering shellfish along the beaches as well as fishing with hook and line from shore or deep-water fishing. Cultivating and harvesting tobacco, betel nut, and betel pepper are also included under food production.

Construction and crafts: This includes building and maintaining houses, outbuildings, canoes, and such necessary tools of building and food production as axes, knives, nets, string bags, bark baskets, and spears for fishing and hunting.

Household tasks: This includes cooking, washing and mending clothes, washing cooking and eating utensils, fetching fresh and salt water for cooking, cleaning inside the house, cleaning and weeding the grounds around the house (if this is not explicitly a council work assignment), and gathering firewood if pursued independently of other activities.

Visiting: This is a broad category. It covers time spent with members of other households within the village if the people involved are not engaged in some obvious task or clearly demarcated social activity. Hence, it could include anything from discussions between village leaders in which major policy questions are at issue, to people making plans for the day's work, to simple conviviality. When conducting a survey, however, it is difficult to distinguish among kinds of visiting, and they seldom occur discretely. This category also includes visiting in other villages or on the mainland.

Meetings and ceremonies: This includes more clearly demarcated social occasions, for instance, meetings held to control the konan, dispute settlement meetings, mourning and burial proceedings, and exchanges within and outside the village. Communal meals following communal work sessions are also included. Some individual magicoreligious activity is included because it was performed as part of a larger communal ritual endeavor.

Illness and curing: This includes recovering from personal illness or injury, caring for others, trips to the medical aid post, and communal curing activities. When a person confined to the village or the house by illness was performing household tasks or doing craft work, the latter activities were given precedence.

Moneymaking: This includes copra cultivation, processing, and marketing and what little time is spent on coffee and cacao cultivation. It includes time spent tending and stocking trade stores and selling produce at St. Xavier's or St. John's. Meetings to discuss copra production, collect contributions to the village development fund, or assign work on business-week days are scored here, as is attending cooperative society meetings in Shagur.

Purchasing: This category includes making purchases at trade stores or the cooperative store in Shagur or travel elsewhere for the specific purpose of making purchases.

Council work and council meetings: A number of different activities fall under the heading of council work, such as maintaining the main trails branching out from the village, cutting the grass at the aid post, and weeding and cutting grass inside the village. These activities are usually reserved for council days. Villagers often build houses on council days, but I did not categorize this as council work because it is more closely related to basic subsistence needs than to the demands of the councillor's authority. Council meetings include those at the beginning of each day of council work and occasional meetings at which the councillor passes on news from recent Wewak-But Local Government Council meetings.

School activities: This encompasses adult involvement with schools, meetings at Bou, building and maintaining Bou school buildings and grounds, and preparing for and attending special events at Bou and St. Xavier's.

Church activities: This includes Sunday services, maintaining the church building and grounds, and building and maintaining the statue of the Virgin.

Dealing with external agencies: This includes such activities as attending proceedings conducted by a visiting village court magistrate, public health nurse, or local government council tax collector.

Enforced idleness: This category includes idleness enforced by inclement weather, fatigue following a period of unusually intense exertion, or the physical or ritual restrictions of menstruation. When other activities took place during periods of enforced leisure—such as cooking, making string bags, or repairing tools—these were given precedence. All leisure on days following nights spent fishing, in curing meetings, tending the copra smoking house, or at social events also was included.

Other leisure: This includes all idleness not enforced as defined above, as well as eating, bathing, and sleeping. Sunday excursions to St. Xavier's to play soccer and basketball are also included.

Notes

Chapter One. Introduction: Hard Times, Goodness, and Visions of the Future

1. According to Wivell (1981:1), there were about thirty-five hundred Kairiru speakers, living both in the language area itself and elsewhere, in 1977. Wivell points out that Kairiru speakers who live on Kairiru island refer to their language in Kairiru as *Leiny Qairiru*. (I use Wivell's orthography here.) Other Kairiru speakers, however, use the term *Leiny Tau*, or Tau language. Tau is said to have been the common name for Kairiru prior to European contact, Kairiru then being only the name for the lake at the top of the mountain.

Melanesian Pidgin, called *Tok Pisin* in Pidgin, has grown out of the interactions among speakers of diverse languages, both indigenous Melanesian languages and those of English, German, Spanish, Portuguese, Malay, and Polynesian traders, explorers, sailors, and colonists. The preponderance of English speakers in recent Papua New Guinea history accounts for the large number of English cognates and false cognates in the Pidgin lexicon. With the suppression of indigenous warfare, the expansion of migrant labor, and the growth of towns and cities, Pidgin has become a more important and flexible language. Today one even can purchase newspapers and books, including the *New Testament*, printed in Pidgin. For more on Melanesian Pidgin, see Mihalic (1971).

2. A survey conducted by *The Times of Papua New Guinea* in 1987, on the occasion of the twelfth anniversary of national independence, indicates that Papua New Guineans in general agree that development of some kind is good for the nation (cited in Gewertz and Errington 1991:213).

3. Strathern (1988:164) makes a related point about work among the Hagen people of highlands Papua New Guinea. She writes: "Under a commodity regime, purposive activity results in artifacts. . . . Hagen work is also purposive activity but is directed toward effectiveness in relationships. Work includes making things, but things are instruments of relations. . . ." In Kragur, material productivity depends on the quality of relations, but it is also part of the basis of good relations, and material things are part of the substance of relations.

4. Domination, however, would take a different form in gift economies than in commodity economies. Strathern (1988:167) argues that in the latter, domination implies control over surplus product, while in the former, domination implies control over the process of forming social relations through the circulation of objects.

5. Strathern (1988:161) argues for a more categorical distinction between gift and commodity economies. See Thomas (1991:52–59) for a critique of her position.

6. See Carrier and Carrier (1989) for a discussion and critique of the concept

of articulation between capitalist and precapitalist political economies, particularly as it has been applied to Melanesia.

7. Thomas (1991:204) describes this as:

> the emergence of a neotraditional culture through oppositional practices: engagement with markets and wage relations has created difference in a domain which is represented as separate from, and anterior to, the world of money. Particularly when islanders have experienced these relations at a geographical distance from their homes, through engaging in indentured labor and migration, they have experienced another kind of exchange and economy and been able to recognize their own from an external vantage point. By making custom . . . explicit . . . islanders seem to have become more traditional than they could ever have been before. Ironically, the models which anthropology imagined for pristine societies have been approximated through acculturation.

8. Obviously being "on the ground" does not lead all anthropologists to this point of view. In my case, experience in the field was leavened by earlier exposure to one brand of actor-oriented political anthropology in studies with F. G. Bailey, and to a focus on process and event in studies with M. J. Swartz and Theodore Schwartz.

9. Sahlins (1981:vii) notes the kinship with Marxism of his approach to the history of the Sandwich islands, in that "it has the same minimum and sufficient premises: that men and women are suffering beings because they act at once in relationship to each other and in a world that has its own relationships." The relation of structure and autonomy or agency has been a major theme in recent anthropology and related social sciences (cf. Ortner 1984:152–160).

10. In Willis' (1977) analysis of the reproduction of the British working class, he argues that, in resisting authority in the schools, working-class youths develop attitudes and forms of behavior that, while they are expressions of protest against their lot, also preclude mobility within the class system and recreate existing class relations. Willis does not see this as planned, but as an unintentional product of the "dynamic" stability of capitalism "in its modern liberal democratic forms," which risks instability "by yielding relative freedom to circles of unintention in the hope of receiving back a minimum consent for rule" (175).

With reference to his own work concerning the reproduction of developed capitalist systems, Willis (1975:175) makes a methodological point that is also relevant to the issue I have posed. He writes:

> The profound—though not limitless—uncertainty at the heart of the system should also warn against too functionalist a view of class cultural process. Certainly, for instance, the circles of contradiction and unintention described in this book 'work' for capitalism at this point in time. But so must any system 'work' which is stable enough to be studied. There must always be a functional level of analysis in reproduction. But this must not be allowed to obscure the struggles which through uncertainties motor the working parts.

11. Willis (1977) also implies such historical variation.

12. Comaroff (1985:261) makes a related point, arguing that "if we confine our historical scrutiny to the zero-sum heroics of revolution successfully achieved, we discount the vast proportion of human social action which is played out, perforce, on a more humble scale" (cf. Thompson 1980:14).

13. Certain names are loosely associated with particular kinship and residence groups (see Chapter 2 on koyeng). Hence, Kragur people and other Kairiru islanders who know the village may be able to identify the actual actors or speakers; but they may be able to do so anyway simply from their knowledge of personalities and events. Except in the few cases of people whose reputations extend beyond the village and the island, the fictitious names used here will protect individuals' privacy from those who do not have an intimate knowledge of life in Kragur. My choice of fictitious names implies nothing about personality or status. I employ a slightly different convention for assigning pseudonyms to a few women who married into Kragur from other villages.

Chapter Two. The Setting: History and Geography, Kinship and Leadership, Food and Money

1. The Kragur trading circuit included the same stretch of mainland coast along which, according to Hogbin (1935), Wogeo people traded, as well as Wogeo itself. Although Hogbin does not mention that Wogeo people traded with any Kairiru village, Kragur people say that they did. It is significant that one of the large, named trading canoes from Kragur, Urim Tonukun, bore virtually the same name as one of the Wogeo canoes discussed by Hogbin (1935:382). I also was told that rights to one of the other Kragur trading canoes had been acquired from Wogeo.

2. Aside from published sources and Kragur villagers' oral histories, I am indebted for much historical information to Brother Patrick Howley, headmaster of St. Xavier's in 1976 and a resident of Kairiru for several years; Emil Brigil, son of the first catechist to visit Kragur and in 1976 head of the Copra Marketing Board in Wewak; and Father Francis Mihalic of the Society of the Divine Word.

3. See Huber (1988) for an extensive discussion of the activity of the Catholic Mission in the Sepik.

4. See Frank (1966) on the concepts of core and periphery and Wallerstein (1974) on the related concepts of metropolis and satellites.

5. The small village of Baru lies about half an hour or so away over a mountainside trail east of Kragur. Some Kragur villagers have close kin ties with Baru people, and some at times speak of Baru as though it were a part of Kragur. Baru people, however, do not take a full and regular part in events in Kragur, and for the most part they function as a separate community.

6. Dual organization of social relations and ritual functions is common in the Sepik. See Tuzin (1976; 1980) for an extensive analysis of dual organization among the Ilahita Arapesh.

7. The Pidgin term *kastom* (or *kastam*) has taken on broader, more politicized meanings in discussions of national identity among Melanesian elites. See Babadzan 1988; Foster 1992; Keesing and Tonkinson 1982; Lindstrom 1982; Philibert 1986.

8. Hogbin (1978:44–46) discusses the role of control of important magic in leadership on Wogeo and speculates on its significance in hereditary leadership throughout Melanesia.

9. Wivell (1981:89) translates *warap* (in his orthography, *worap*) simply as "feast." I have heard the term used only in connection with the commemorative feasts discussed here. Hogbin (1978:37) describes a "food festival" called a *warabwa,* given to mark succession to positions of hereditary leadership on Wogeo.

10. In contrast to Burridge (1969:42), who makes "a radical distinction between social orders which use money as a basic measure of man, and those which do not," Kahn (1986:154–155) points out a broad similarity between monetary societies and the nonmonetary society of the Wamira of Papua New Guinea. See Parry and Bloch (1989) for a discussion of the meanings of money in noncapitalist and capitalist societies and an analysis of how the variety of meanings has been construed, and perhaps oversimplified, in Western social thought. My interest here, however, is largely in how Kragur people see monetary society.

Chapter Three. Social Relations and Material Well-Being

1. Although villagers themselves translate *bak* into Pidgin as *ailan,* which translates to English as island, it might be more strictly accurate to translate it as "land mass." This would not necessarily contradict the contention that past generations thought of the world as made up primarily of islands, that is, small land masses like those with which they were most familiar.

2. This is not simply a belief in supernatural beings, a belief common in many large-scale, modern, industrial societies. Surveys in the United States, for example, have found that 42 percent of adults believe they have had contact with the dead, and 67 percent of teenagers say they believe in angels (Greeley 1986:49).

3. Ibor's immersion in Catholicism might lead him to bring God into the explanation. The pattern here, however, is classic suak, and most villagers probably would describe it so.

4. Not all illness is attributed to intervention of the dead on behalf of the living. That which is, is distinguished in part by its gravity and duration, although sorcery is another likely diagnosis for long and serious illness. One Kragur man old enough to remember told me that prior to the war sorcery was the most common diagnosis. Only after the war, he said, did people learn of *sik bilong graun*— which this man also spoke of as *sik bilong sol,* that is, illness caused by the souls of the dead—from people of Shagur village. He also noted, however, that sorcery and sik bilong sol were similar, because in both one's dead kin were the agents. Another informant, however, spoke of sik bilong sol as a postwar innovation but distinguished it from sik bilong graun. Still others seem to know nothing of these questions. In any event, sik bilong graun is presently a popular and credible diagnosis.

5. After the death of a person of importance there is often a prohibition on working in gardens, except for gathering food from mature gardens, of from one to several days. Some say this is so the ghost of the deceased, or ghosts of his or her kin, will not be angered that people have mourned so little and ruin the garden crops in retaliation. Others say there is a prohibition because living kin of the

deceased may in their grief use harmful magic, and going to the gardens might carry its effect to the crops.

6. See Hogbin (1978:46) on similar fear of leaders with magical powers on Wogeo. Hogbin writes: "The fact that a headman who is displeased may use his powers to cause famine is never far from the surface of people's consciousness. When events go against one of the leaders they begin voicing their alarm."

7. On at least one occasion, Ibor has also suggested making a large collective garden to produce taro for sale at the market in Wewak.

8. The staff at St. Xavier's High School provided me with this translation of van den Hemel's description of his visit to Chem, which was first printed in the *Steyler Missions Bote* and dated 1907/08. The remainder of the passage tells of Chem's other hardships at this time.

A year earlier many young boys had been recruited as laborers by the [German] New Guinea Company. [It is not clear if the author means a year before the raid or a year before his visit.] But they didn't like the work, they looked for the beach to try to get home. It was possible to do that but quite daring; because on the way home live many people who make short work of such defenseless fugitives, and so many died. On top of this there was disease. Six or seven had died already from pneumonia, and four were very sick. Of these soon three died. This explains the small number of people in the village.

9. It is important to note that sorcery is not necessarily condemned in Melanesian societies. In some, sorcery can be used legitimately against enemies outside the community or malefactors within the community (Bowden 1987; Chowning 1987). Those with power to kill with sorcery sometimes also have curative powers (Stephen 1987). Sorcery only came to my attention in Kragur in cases where its use was considered antisocial. Those most often accused of sorcery, however, are close patrikin of the leader with primary responsibility for many curing functions and sometimes are alleged to be able to influence sorcerers in other villages on behalf of Kragur people.

10. Given koyeng exogamy, the children of a man's sister will not be members of his patrilineally defined koyeng, but a tie between them and their mother's natal koyeng is recognized. They are sometimes referred to as the *nat moin* of the koyeng—literally, "children female."

11. Kahn (1986:150–155) argues convincingly that the Wamira find too much material abundance a threat to social harmony, and shows how this orientation is related to views of human nature common elsewhere in Melanesia. Fear of excessive material abundance, however, was not apparent in Kragur.

Chapter Four. The Supernatural: Old and New

1. The myth of two brothers appears throughout Papua New Guinea's north coast and among the nearby islands (Hogbin 1935; Lawrence 1964; 1988; Lipset 1991). While the basic themes remain the same, details vary, for example, the names of the brothers and the specific locales of the events. My concern is with the significance of variation within a single community, not variation across the region.

2. Some villagers themselves note problems with fitting Wankau into the image of God. One, for example, wonders where all the other people in the Wankau and Yabok story came from if Wankau was the first being. There is evidence, however, that on the nearby island of Wogeo a mythological being similar in name had many of the features of God. Dalle Gagin (1972) translates a "creation song" from the Wogeo language as follows:

> He is Wonka, the powerful spirit,
> The creator, the spirit of all spirits,
> The spirit of all things, ghosts and spirits,
> Plants, animals, and humans.

3. Villagers usually speak of encounters with ghosts as frightening, but they sometimes turn accounts of such frightening events into humorous stories. I once heard a young Kragur man tell of how, while bathing in the stream late one night, he looked up to see the ethereal and slightly luminous ghost of a recently deceased young Kragur woman watching him. The small group of men to whom he was telling the tale burst into laughter as he described how he panicked and bolted up the path to the village, leaving his bush knife lying by the stream, and trying to pull his pants on as he ran.

4. This seems to blur the distinction often made between magic and religion, the former involving direct action on the material world and the latter involving relations with supernatural beings.

5. Keesing (1982:36–37) discusses contradictions inherent in systems of male initiation in Papua New Guinea that may have contributed to their dissolution following the imposition of colonial rule and the suppression of indigenous warfare.

6. In contrast to demystification of men's cults, Tuzin (1980:123–128) describes a resurgence of the men's cult among the Ilahita Arapesh.

7. Just how successful the men were in actually fooling the women is another question (cf. Herdt 1982:86).

8. At least parts of the story of the Arai cult house may be of recent origin. Some villagers say that Moke's brother Lapim learned the story in a dream.

9. Although villagers often mention Jesus in prayers, sermons, and discussions of religion, I almost never heard them identify him with familiar indigenous supernaturals. Perhaps the fact that he is God's child—in Pidgin, *pikinini bilong God*—provides sufficient identity.

10. Accounts of premissionary encounters with God apparently are not uncommon in Papua New Guinea. Some Kragur villagers told me that the people of Walis island also claimed that God had visited them before the first missionaries arrived.

11. The table below compares several Kairiru villages by percentage of population that attended St. Xavier's High School from 1963 to 1976. Here I have used population figures taken from the 1976 Wewak Sub-District Office Population Register, which include both resident and nonresident villagers. The population figure for Kragur diverges considerably from the results of my own census. This is in part because the Sub-District Population Register groups the neighbor-

ing village of Baru with Kragur. Only two of the high school students attributed to Kragur, however, are from Baru. (Since St. Xavier's is a school for boys, this table does not show the relative educational accomplishments of Kairiru women. Very few women from Kragur or other Kairiru villages, however, have gone beyond primary school. This is part of a nationwide pattern that was also evident in the 1970s in the imbalance of male and female students at the University of Papua New Guinea.)

Students from Some Kairiru Villages at St. Xavier's High School, 1963–1976

VILLAGE	POPULATION	NUMBER OF STUDENTS AT ST. XAVIER'S HIGH SCHOOL	PERCENTAGE OF POPULATION
Kragur	419	23	5.49
Seraseng	136	6	4.41
Rumlal	153	6	3.92
Surai	105	4	3.81
Yuwun	171	5	2.92
Shagur	361	8	2.22
Brauniak	105	2	1.90
Yavik	127	1	.79

12. Allen (1976:82, cited in Huber 1988:90–91) illustrates the differences in attitudes toward indigenous magicoreligious practices to be found among Catholic missionaries in the Sepik.

Chapter Five. The Case of the *Konan*

1. According to some accounts, bones of dead ancestors were, or are, used in some indigenous subsistence magic.

2. Aside from the importance of focusing on the Virgin, villagers do not agree on the details of what following the way of Catholicism, or bilip, necessitates. One participant in these events told me simply that while the way of bilip required only a prohibition on anger, the indigenous way required customary leaders like Taunur to observe numerous weighty prohibitions, for example, on sexual relations, types of food, and such activities as using a knife or cutting firewood. Another man said that following the Catholic way did not require a prohibition on fishing with hook and line, but one must "putim pilaua," that is, display flowers on the Virgin's altar or statue. He also noted that, using Catholicism, schools of fish could come to spawn every day, but under indigenous methods they could come only every three of four days. As noted in this chapter, Ibor feels that both require prohibitions on fishing with hook and line and on anger.

3. Teachers at St. Xavier's who have conducted investigations of the biology of the lake say that it shows almost no signs of life of any kind, especially fish. Some Kragur people say there are eels in the lake, but indigenous islanders have not explored it thoroughly. Some regard it as a dangerous place because it is the alleged home of the masalai Kairiru.

4. Failure in subsistance ritual in any year probably would have aroused doubts about the moral capacity to cope with familiar problems. In contrast, ritual with less tangible ends is more likely to be reassuring. Tuzin (1990) writes of men's cult ritual among the Ilahita Arapesh that "usually it is successful, since its goals are intangible things such as species fertility, the masculinization' of youths or the rededicated patronage of cult spirits."

Chapter Six. Understanding Poverty: The Mundane, the Extraordinary, and the Moral Preoccupation

1. A report of an Australian government patrol to Kairiru and Mushu from July 1946 (Wewak Patrol Report, 1946–1947) discusses at some length a cargo cult said to have been led by a Mushu man named Lalau. Lalau is reported to have committed suicide in order to visit the ancestors and hasten delivery of the cargo. This report also asserts that cultists at first thought the ships of the Japanese invasion fleet were the ships of the ancestors bringing the cargo. Villagers on Kairiru, Mushu, and Yuo islands are said to have been involved in the cult.

2. Some villagers also find in traditional stories not only depictions of a vanished golden age of their own, but also reasons why contemporary whites enjoy a comparatively golden age from which most Papua New Guineans are excluded. The story of Wankau and Yabok is a common candidate for such reinterpretation. Some tellers cast one brother—the crafty one who seduces Moger and repeatedly escapes from his brother's assaults—as the ancestor or teacher of the whites, and the other brother as the ancestor or mentor of the Papua New Guineans. Taunur sometimes finishes his rendition of the story by speculating that eventually the two brothers parted ways and "one turned out like you people, the other turned out like us. Wankau worked the way the [Papua New Guineans] do, he made canoes. Yabok made boats [that is, European boats]. So now you Europeans have that kind of knowledge [and] Papua New Guineans make canoes." Brawaung makes the same point somewhat differently, saying that one of the brothers "didn't have knowledge, he worked with stone and shells." The other, however, "had plenty of knowledge, he could write and he worked with a chisel [that is, metal tools]." The knowledgeable brother "went to teach people all over, like Jesus, [but] he died in some other place. I think if he had come back, we would be just like you [whites]" (cf. Lawrence 1964).

3. To test my initial impression that this was the case, I selected three events in Kragur's past that villagers often speak of and asked a number of adult villagers to tell me in what order they had taken place. One of these events was a flood that allegedly destroyed a previous village site at the place called Kafow, about a half-hour walk from Kragur up the main trail over the mountain. Villages say this event came about when Kafow people angered the masalai Kairiru, and he and other masalai—recruited from Walis, Mushu, and other islands—first attacked Kafow with spears and then washed it away except for the narrow ridge that remains today. Some place this event within the span of genealogical time. Molap, for example, says it took place in the time of his grandparents' grandparents—in Pidgin, *tumbuna bilong tumbuna*—although he cannot name all the intervening ancestors. The second event I inquired about was a time of famine, called *yang* in the Kairiru language, when the ancestors of Kragur people scat-

tered not only from larger, centralized villages but also to other islands and the mainland. Kairiru people say that one can still see the places near the top of the mountain where their ancestors laid out the bodies of famine victims on large stones after they became too weak to bury them. Some older villagers can say where the ancestors of their koyeng went at the time of the famine. Although the genealogical links to the present are not always clear, it is at least apparent that the famine took place before the founding of Kragur. The third event in my inquiry was a time of darkness when the sun was blotted out for a period of several days, the *taim bilong tudak* as it is called in Pidgin. Some older villagers say they heard stories of the *tudak* from their parents, who they say were children when it took place.

I list these events here in what I think is the most likely order. Although villagers supplied me with enough information about these events and other aspects of their history to construct a plausible chronology, there is little agreement among villagers themselves about the sequence of such significant events prior to the past of living memory. Among those to whom I posed the question of the sequence of the flood, the famine, and the darkness—mostly middle-aged and older men— several said the darkness occurred in the time of their grandparents or when their parents were children. Some, however, were not certain if it had occurred before or after the famine, and some placed both the famine and the darkness before the flood. Some simply said they had no idea and declined to comment further. Most of those who did humor me with an answer acted as though this were a question they had seldom, if ever, considered before. Some who declined to attempt a chronology pointed out to me that there was no way they could know these things because they did not keep written records the way whites do.

4. Brison (1991), however, suggests that McDowell may place too much emphasis on expectations for "cataclysmic" change or *total* transformation.

5. Schwartz (1973) stresses the exaggeration in cults of Melanesian cultural patterns present in normal life. In a similar vein, Walter (1981:93) argues that cults should be understood in terms of "an inherent dynamism" of indigenous society and as "reactions against established indigenous social systems as well as endeavors to counter the apparent invincibility of the European culture."

6. Schwartz (1968:27) emphasizes the importance of essentially political factors in determining the distribution of cargo cults over wider areas than that with which I am concerned here. He writes:

> It is a typical Melanesian cultural reaction to respond antagonistically or competitively to what is going on among neighboring groups. In taking the wider view, the focus of explanation is shifted from an unwarranted assumption of differences in conditions and characteristics between cult and non-cult areas . . . with minor shifts in circumstances those who join cults and those who oppose them might have easily assumed reversed roles.

7. One among the many stories I heard about the magical or supernatural sources of European wealth suggests that such wealth can be obtained through collaboration with the forces of evil—specifically, a powerful figure identified as Satan. This suggests a parallel with Taussig's analysis of the importance of the

figure of the Devil in South American peasants' symbolic response to industrial capitalism (1980). This appears, however, to be a very minor theme in Kragur cargo lore.

8. Many villagers look to Catholic teachings for an explanation of the gulf that separates blacks and whites. Thus, Cain and Abel are said to be the Catholic version of Wankau and Yabok: one brother, the less favored by God, representing the heritage of Papua New Guineans, and the other representing the heritage of the whites, whom God has privileged. Says Mansu: "The two brothers made offerings to God. Cain gave produce from his garden, like us, and Abel gave a sheep. The smoke from Abel's offering went straight up, but God said that he didn't like Cain's offering. Cain killed Abel, and God punished Cain."

9. Schwartz (1968:51; 1973:157) focuses on the irrational element in the persistence of cults. Tuzin (1990) offers a contrasting interpretation of the persistence of cults in the face of contrary evidence. Tuzin writes of the emphasis on achieving social harmony found in cargo cults, as in the indigenous *tambaran* cult, and suggests that the cargo being sought signifies:

> an image of Self-Person unity amidst and in defiance of circumstances that are driving these elements of experience apart far more radically than traditional understandings and procedures are able to accommodate. That the Cargo is to be taken in a mythic rather than literal sense follows from the odd fact that, as the people themselves are somewhat aware, the preconditions set for its arrival are impossible to achieve. Given the indigenous recognition of the fractiousness and disorder which allegedly and, indeed, actually beset social life, is the attainment of perfect local or regional accord any less miraculous than the advent of the Cargo? The persistence of the idea that the Cargo will come might therefore be seen as an expression of the age-old hope that spiritual harmony . . . will be attained. In yearning for the Cargo, they yearn for themselves. And, since Cargo is not really what the cults are about, it is not surprising that sight-seeing tours by cultists to the factories of Australia and Japan have little effect on their (misunderstood) aspirations.

10. Tuzin (1990) suggests that among the Ilahita Arapesh the tambaran cult has been a functional alternative to cargo cults. His interpretation of the function of both types of cult in the contemporary context—the pursuit of "self-person unity" through achievement of collective harmony—is different from but not incompatible with my own.

11. See Tuzin (1990) for a complementary view of the function of ritual stressing social harmony.

12. Similarly, Taunur once told me of how a man from the south coast village of Chem had asked him what kind of ideas or knowledge I was giving the people of Kragur. He laughed at the Chem man's envy as he recounted the incident. "I think he's afraid. He thinks you and Ibor will put your heads together and Kragur will surpass all the other villages." The suspicion that I was imparting secret knowledge to Kragur people is also, of course, reminiscent of the suspicions of whites associated with cargo cults.

13. In many parts of Melanesia, indigenous people abandoned raiding and

warfare virtually voluntarily (Rodman 1983; Schwartz 1968; White 1983; Zelenietz 1983). Continuing peace, of course, depends on political and economic circumstances. In parts of Papua New Guinea, for example, land shortage contributed to a resurgence of warfare following national independence (Meggitt 1977).

14. Secular colonial suppression of indigenous violence and warfare at least was reinforced by Catholic teachings about anger and vengeance. While not everyone has taken such teachings completely to heart, the more devout make sure they are not forgotten. I once sat with a group of men who had recently returned from a visit to the south coast village of Brauniak where they had gone to discuss a sorcery allegation. They were grumbling that the Brauniak people had given them nothing to eat but coconuts, an insult as well as an inconvenience. One of the men declared that the next time people from Brauniak came to Kragur they should let them go hungry, and an older man sitting near me whispered to me that in the past they would have retaliated by magically destroying the Brauniak gardens so that they too would have had nothing to eat but coconuts. The mood was angry and vengeful; but Ibor spoke up, reminding the men that they were Catholics and should set a good example for others by treating the Brauniak people well despite what they had done.

15. By drawing such examples of obstacles to business success from elsewhere in Papua New Guinea, I do not wish to imply that all Papua New Guinea business ventures fail. The literature contains many accounts of Papua New Guineans enjoying comparative success in Western business. Standard works include Epstein (1968), Finney (1973), and Salisbury (1970). The authors of these accounts turn to differences in natural environments, colonial histories, and indigenous political economies to account for variations in success in Western business (cf. Thomas 1991:122–123).

Chapter Seven. Redefining Good Social Relations: Reciprocity vs the Commercial Spirit

1. In 1973, while a doctoral student at the University of California, San Diego, I spent three months in Manus Province as a research assistant to Theodore Schwartz. Edwin Hutchins and Geoffrey White were the other members of the research team.

2. At the time I do not believe I thought about why I made that distinction. In retrospect, I think I probably was equating gifts of cooked food with being invited to someone's home for dinner. In the urban and suburban West, one usually encounters raw food as an item of commerce.

3. When building a house for another villager, the food is assembled at the owner's present house or that of a kinsperson or friend. Once the new house has a floor and roof, the food is assembled there. In my case, some controversy arose over the appropriate place to assemble the food. Although I was living in Shewaratin, members of other koyeng had also helped organize the house building and assumed that they also should take part in the distribution of food. Some saw presiding over the distribution of food as a claim to leadership in this endeavor.

4. When the Village Development Fund was established, I did make a contribution, although I was in no position to contribute anything like the amount demanded by the young men in Port Moresby earlier that year.

5. Kathleen Barlow and David Lipset were both doing research in Darapap village.

6. Sahlins (1972:124–130) provides examples of similar contradictions of "an uncritical ideal of reciprocity" from several societies. Kahn (1986:42–46) discusses similar "strategies for deception" among the Wamira.

7. I was host at two of the village-wide events, both called for by local custom. One was a party to mark the completion of the house the villagers had built for me, and the other was a party just prior to my final departure.

8. A handful of younger men spoke openly of drinking methylated spirits. Interest in *spirit,* as it is called in Pidgin, is aroused by its capacity to render one *spak* (drunk), not by its significance as an item of prestation or display. Methylated spirits are not used in public drinking events, nor do they have the same associations with success in the postcontact society that legal commercial beverages do (cf. Lepowsky 1982).

9. Many villagers saw this as an important part of their performance at a competitive display of indigenous song and dance sponsored by St. Xavier's High School to celebrate the dedication of a new building. Although a large number of the Kragur contingent did last until just before sunrise, when rain ended everyone's efforts, some were not fully satisfied with the style and vigor of their performance. A few suggested that people from another village had used malign magic to sap their energy and enthusiasm.

10. There is no simple consistency in nonverbal behavior, either. In the midst of extravagant consumption, villagers are careful to preserve empty bottles and bottle caps, which they later return to the SP warehouse in Wewak for refunds.

11. See Smith (1982a:282–288) for a discussion of the relation of alcohol use to identity in Kragur and comments on the relevance of migration and urban life to drinking among Kragur people. Schwartz (1982:395) notes ambivalence about alcohol use among Manus villagers. He writes, "Many regular drinkers almost ritually deplore drinking, pointing out quite lucidly the adverse effects on economy, society, and health. 'But,' they say, 'we are hooked' *(mipela i laikim pinis)."* His points concerning the role alcohol plays in ceremonial exchange and the relation of such conspicuous accumulation and consumption to the general interest in material wealth are relevant to my argument.

12. Lawrence (1964:62–92) notes, with reference to other parts of Papua New Guinea, that some villagers adopted willing cooperation as a strategy for gaining parity with the Europeans, and that such a strategy often partook of the inflated expectations of cargo cults.

13. Gewertz and Errington (1991) make a similar point in their discussion of Chambri expectations of development. Noting that some Chambri have moved to town partly "to evade or buffer certain of their obligations to other Chambri, they had not repudiated the system that generated their entailments and therefore determined their identity" (124; cf. 146).

Chapter Eight. Redefining Good Social Relations:
Organizing Time and Work

1. I draw on Wivell (1981) as well as my own data for Kairiru time terms. Where our observations conflict, I rely on my own.

2. Wivell (1981:183) reports that the noun *puony* means "day" or "time" and is used to indicate "time when" or "contemporaneity of two events." It lacks, however, the sense of time as an entity.

3. I was not able to ascertain how the thirteen lunar months or *kareo* were kept synchronous with the seasonal cycle in the indigenous system. (Thirteen lunar months exceed the solar year by about nineteen days.)

A number of villagers observe that the moons pass faster now than when they were children. Some attribute this to the advent of schooling or to their own adult familiarity with Western days, weeks, and months. Mansu attributes differing perceptions of the passage of the moons to literacy. "Some can't read and write," he says, "and they think it's a long time. For those of us who can read and write the moons go fast." Such observations suggest that schooling and literacy affect perceptions of duration by directing attention to the progress of Western days and months (cf. Levy 1973:254).

4. Freedman (1980:292) warns against the assumption "that labor time can be compared across epochs and between cultures." He cautions that "measuring time and motion is a valuable and revealing strategy—but only where the . . . context of work and leisure is reasonably uniform, where one is examining relationships within a single social system, or where a concrete and specific task, say, gardening or cooking, is investigated cross-culturally."

5. Schieffelin (1976:132) gives a vivid example of a similar pattern among the Kaluli.

> When several men decide to work together at something, like building a fishing dam or clearing the stump of a large tree from the houseyard, they do not really function as a coordinated team but divide the job into a number of separate but parallel jobs. To remove a stump, for example, each man chooses a single root to work on and works at his own speed with a digging stick, resting when he feels like it regardless of what others are doing. Though the job gets done effectively, the performance does not project a coordinated effort. Even when there is a truly combined effort, as when men must pull together on a rope to rip the stump out and pull it over, there is no unified heave-ho. Everyone grabs the rope, and, whooping and stamping, pulls more or less together until the stump goes over.

6. My sample here included 19 of the 57 resident men above primary-school age and 19 of the 78 resident women above primary-school age. The unfamiliarity of the task with which I presented my informants, and the informal setting of the inquiries, made it impossible to elicit precisely the same comparisons in the same order from each informant. I often let informants follow their own inclinations in pairing activities for comparison. Although I encouraged them to give reasons for their judgments, I did not suggest any reasons. Although most judgments were explicitly comparative, in a few instances informants judged activities in isolation. I included the reasons given for these judgments as well. Only one informant asserted that it was impossible to judge activities in such a way, for they were all, he held, equally difficult. Villagers' judgments do not yield a neat hierarchy because tasks judged more difficult than others in one dimension were

sometimes judged easier in others. The point was to uncover the salient dimensions of comparison.

7. Waddell and Krinks (1968:175–176) report that among the Orokaiva the preferred "work routine" is one in which "one activity need not be pursued to the exclusion of others and each can be interrupted at will" (cf. Gostin 1986:151). Strathern (1975:311) shows how relative autonomy is associated with perceptions of "ease" in a different context. Speaking of Hagen migrants in Port Moresby, she writes:

> In all these jobs people say they get bored with routine. One hotel worker, commenting on how he thought all jobs in town were good ones with the exception of outside laboring which meant exposure to the sun, said: "In Moresby all the work is easy, none is hard. The employers do not force us to work—it is our own inclination and when we want to stop we leave it." The freedom of ordinary workers is compared favorably with the contracts which bind persons in the police or armed forces.

Here, of course, the comparison focuses on a dimension of autonomy outside the labor process itself. Strathern (1975:145) also speaks of the value Hagen migrants place on this kind of autonomy as an ideology facilitating adaption to the workers' "general powerlessness in the employment situation." She notes that the migrant can "exploit the ethic to turn against the work system in general, and act as though remaining in employment at all were simply a matter of personal whim."

8. Errington (1974:258) writes of perceptions of European "domesticity" elsewhere in Papua New Guinea.

9. Those, like Fisk (1964), who picture Papua New Guinea villagers making decisions about market participation by calculating the best use of time as a scarce resource overlook the fact that such economizing is possible only where people conceive of time as an entity that can be scarce (Smith 1982a).

10. Thompson (1967) and Rodgers (1978) each describe the significant contribution that religious institutions made to the growth of industrial capitalism in Europe and North America by promulgating new work habits and temporal values. Under the influence of Weber (1958 [1920]), we often think of Protestantism as the religious impetus behind the rationalization of activity patterns characteristic of capitalism. It is well to remember, however, that Catholic monasticism played a major role in the development of "the earnest regulation of time-sequences" and "the orderly punctual life" in the West (Mumford 1963 [1934]: 13–18). Comaroff and Comaroff (1986:12) contrast Catholic evangelism in seventeenth-century Mexico—which "relied heavily on collective ritual and dramatic spectacle, . . . often incorporating local populations in a depiction of their own subjection"—with Protestant missions, which "taught the unassuming 'arts of civilization' . . . , whose mundane logic worked upon the processes that more forcefully shaped the self and 'natural' reality." The Catholic mission in the Sepik, however, also placed great emphasis on the latter endeavor. From the standpoint of Kragur villagers, I suspect that all whites or Europeans look rather "Protestant" in their never-ending concern with time, order, and material efficiency.

11. A few villagers also question another dimension of the indigenous approach to work, the necessity for collective effort (in Pidgin, *wok bung*) in some endeavors. They say, for example, that often everyone's labor is not actually needed. Similarly, a few point to European individualism in business endeavors and question the village preference for wok bung in this sphere as well. Questioning and criticism of wok bung, however, is not nearly as common or public as discussion of the virtues of European temporal order in work and the deficiencies of indigenous temporal practices.

Chapter Nine. The Future, Hard Times, and Visions of Goodness

1. Most complaints about attrition focus on young men, but a few young women have also left Kragur, at least temporarily, to work on the mainland. Young women appear to have as many reasons as young men to leave the village, among them discontent with the system of arranged marriages and a desire for financial as well as romantic independence. However, they find it more difficult to leave than men do; they generally have less education, and they face greater dangers in town and much stronger parental opposition at home.

2. At the local level, while closer ties to the cash economy can lead to the "deterioration of preexisting relations of inequality" (Carrier and Carrier 1989: 28–29), they can also lead to new forms of inequality (Grossman 1983; Sexton 1983). There are signs that new and greater economic distinctions may be emerging within Kragur (Smith 1985:9–15).

3. If Kragur people continue to feel marginalized and embattled, this in itself could support the tendency to define harmonious and cooperative social relations in terms that are critical of individualistic endeavor and supportive of collective effort and unity of purpose. I have stressed the resonance of indigenous ideas about the interpenetration of social and material spheres with Catholicism under conditions of European domination in interpreting Kragur definitions of good social relations in the contemporary world. Schwartz (1972:21) argues that an emphasis on collectivist goals and "suppression of . . . individuation" is a common reaction "under conditions of perceived general threat to a society." Although in itself this observation does not account for the historical particulars of Kragur people's struggle with the issue of good social relations, it does appear applicable to their case.

4. Brison (n.d.) observes that among the Kwanga some have reacted to failure in development endeavors by eschewing ideals of harmonious and orderly cooperation and glorifying the "rough" contentiousness and aggressiveness perceived as characteristic of Papua New Guineans and antithetical to cooperation in business. This "roughness" is depicted as an indigenous form of strength that offers an alternative route to equality with Europeans. In 1981 Kragur's circumstances so far had discouraged such a reaction, although it is not impossible that something similar eventually could develop.

5. Gostin (1986) emphasizes the role of Catholicism as a major condition, "if not *the* major enabling condition" (147), of a transition to reliance on cash cropping among the Kuni people of Papua New Guinea's Central Province. She points out, however, the historically specific conditions of this role.

6. Carrier and Carrier (1989:238) argue that deeper capitalist incorporation

does not necessarily mean obvious displacement of indigenous social and economic forms. They suggest that the effects of capitalist involvement can appear in "transmuted" forms, which "do not mimic capitalism or preserve tradition, nor are they some average, some balance between the two." It does not appear, however, that the development of such "transmuted" forms is incompatible with conscious attempts to mimic capitalist forms or either conscious or inchoate processes of resistance to the incursion of capitalist forms.

Glossary

κ = Kairiru
MP = Melanesian Pidgin

beten (MP):	Catholic prayer or entreaties to dead kin
bikhet (MP):	To flout authority or disregard the common interest
bilip (MP):	Faith in Catholicism
bilum (MP):	A string bag
bisnis (MP):	Business
bos (κ):	A magical spell
divelopmen (MP):	Development
garamut (MP):	A log drum, hollowed out through a narrow opening along the side
gudpela fasin (MP):	Moral behavior by an individual or a group
harim tok (MP):	To obey authority or to pay due regard to the common interest
haus boi (MP):	A house where unmarried young men sleep and adult men gather
kaikrauap (κ):	A carved human figure used in indigenous magical procedures
kareo (κ):	The moon or one cycle of the moon
kastom (MP):	A village leader whose authority rests on traditional criteria, in particular, ownership of rights to important magic
kaunsil (MP):	An elected village leader under a system of elected local leadership first introduced by Australian colonial government
kif (MP):	A poisonous substance
komiti (MP):	Assistant to the *kaunsil* under the system of elected village leadership first established by Australian colonial government
konan (κ):	A long-bodied fish that inhabits Sepik coastal waters
koyeng (κ):	A residential and kinship division of the village
kundu (MP):	A hand-held wooden drum made in the shape of an hourglass
lo bilong waitman (MP):	White or European customs
luk (κ):	Sibling of the opposite sex
malolo (MP):	Leisure or rest

257

masalai (MP):   A dangerous spirit, usually associated with a particular
                    natural feature, such as a tree or rock
mol (K):   Work
pekato (MP):   Sin
poison (MP):   Sorcery
ramat walap (K):   A traditional leader or "big man"
singsing (MP):   A traditional song, sometimes accompanied by dance; a
                    performance of traditional song and dance; or a magical
                    spell
suak (K):   Failure of subsistence efforts—such as gardening, fishing, or
                    hunting—caused by the dead kin of angry living persons
taik (K):   Sibling of the same sex
taim (MP):   Time
tambaran (MP):   A tutelary spirit of the indigenous men's cult
tiptip (K):   Ownership of rights to make, possess, or use particular
                    kinds of material objects or particular kinds of knowl-
                    edge
ulai (K):   A traditional song, sometimes accompanied by dance
warap (K):   A feast given to commemorate a deceased leader and vali-
                    date his descendant's claims to authority
wok (MP):   Work

References Cited

Allen, Bryant J.
1976 "Information Flow and Innovation Diffusion in the East Sepik District, Papua New Guinea." Ph.D. dissertation, Australian National University, Canberra.

Amarshi, Azeem, Kenneth Good, and Rex Mortimer
1979 *Development and Dependency: The Political Economy of Papua New Guinea.* Oxford: Oxford University Press.

Anonymous
1968 *Buk bilong beten end* [sic] *sing sing bilong ol katolik/Prayer Book and Hymnal for Catholic Natives of New Guinea.* Westmead (Austral.?): Westmead Printing.

Apadurai, Arjun, ed.
1986 *The Social Life of Things: Commodities in Cultural Perspective.* Cambridge: Cambridge University Press.

Arbuckle, Gerald A.
1978 "The Impact of Vatican II on the Marists in Oceania." In *Mission, Church and Sect in Oceania,* James A. Boutillier, Daniel T. Hughes, and Sharon W. Tiffany, eds., pp. 275–299. Association for Social Anthropology in Oceania Monograph No. 6. Lanham, Md.: University Press of America.

Armstrong, M. Jocelyn
1990 "Christianity and Maori Ethnicity in the South Island of New Zealand." In *Christianity in Oceania: Ethnographic Perspectives,* John Barker, ed., pp. 237–258. Association for Social Anthropology in Oceania Monograph No. 12. Lanham, Md.: University Press of America.

Asad, Talal
1972 "Market Model, Class Structure and Consent: A Reconsideration of Swat Political Organization." *Man* 7(2):74–94.

Australian International Development Assistance Bureau
1989 *Papua New Guinea: Economic Situation and Outlook.* Canberra: Australian Government Publishing Service.

Babadzan, Alain
1988 "*Kastom* and Nation-Building in the South Pacific." In *Ethnicities and Nations,* Remo Guidieri, Francesco Pellizzi, and Stanley J. Tambiah, eds., pp. 198–228. Houston: Rothko Chapel and University of Texas Press.

Bailey, F. G.
1971 "The Management of Reputations and the Process of Change." In *Gifts and Poison,* F. G. Bailey, ed., pp. 281–301. New York: Schocken Books.

Barden, Garrett
1973 "Reflections on Time." *The Human Context* 5(2):331–344.
Bowden, Ross
1987 "Sorcery, Illness and Social Control in Kwoma Society." In *Sorcerer and Witch in Melanesia,* Michele Stephen, ed., pp. 183–208. New Brunswick, N.J.: Rutgers University Press.
Braverman, Harry
1974 *Labor and Monopoly Capital: The Degradation of Work in the Twentieth Century.* New York: Monthly Review Press.
Brison, Karen
1991 "Community and Prosperity: Social Movements among the Kwanga of Papua New Guinea." *The Contemporary Pacific* 3(2):325–355.
n.d. "Hegemony and Cultural Identity in the Pacific: A View from Rural Papua New Guinea." Unpublished manuscript.
Bureau of Statistics
1966 "Territory of Papua and New Guinea, Population Census 1966." Preliminary Bulletin No. 31: East Sepik District and Wewak Urban Area. Konedobu, Papua New Guinea: Bureau of Statistics.
Burridge, Kenelm
1960 *Mambu: A Melanesian Millennium.* London: Methuen and Co.
1969 *New Heaven, New Earth: A Study of Millenarian Activities.* Oxford: Basil Blackwell.
1978 "Introduction: Missionary Occasions." In *Mission, Church, and Sect in Oceania,* James A. Boutillier, Daniel T. Hughes, and Sharon W. Tiffany, eds., pp. 1–30. Association for Social Anthropology in Oceania Monograph No. 6. Lanham, Md.: University Press of America.
Carrier, Achsah H.
1982 "Alcohol Use on Ponam Island, Manus Province." In *Through a Glass Darkly: Beer and Modernization in Papua New Guinea.* Mac Marshall, ed., pp. 405–417. IASER Monograph 18, Boroko, Papua New Guinea: Institute of Applied Social and Economic Research.
Carrier, James G., and Achsah H. Carrier
1989 *Wage, Trade, and Exchange in Melanesia: A Manus Society in the Modern State.* Berkeley and Los Angeles: University of California Press.
Carrier, James G.
1992 "Occidentalism: The World Turned Upside-Down." *American Ethnologist* 19(2):195–212.
Chowning, Ann
1982 "Self-Esteem and Drinking in Kove, West New Britain." In *Through a Glass Darkly: Beer and Modernization in Papua New Guinea,* Mac Marshall, ed., pp. 365–378. IASER Monograph 18. Boroko, Papua New Guinea: Institute of Applied Social and Economic Research.
1987 "Sorcery and the Social Order in Kove." In *Sorcerer and Witch in Melanesia,* Michele Stephen, ed., pp. 149–182. New Brunswick, N.J.: Rutgers University Press.
Clarke, W. C.
1973 "Temporary Madness as Theatre: Wild Man Behavior in New Guinea." *Oceania* 43(3):183–214.

Clifford, James
1988 *The Predicament of Culture: Twentieth-Century Ethnography, Litera-ture, and Art.* Cambridge, Mass.: Harvard University Press.
Comaroff, Jean
1985 *Body of Power, Spirit of Resistance: The Culture and History of a South African People.* Chicago: University of Chicago Press.
Comaroff, Jean, and John Comaroff
1986 "Christianity and Colonialism in South Africa." *American Ethnologist* 13(1):1–22.
Dalle Gagin, Bernard
1972 "Some Wokeo Songs and Spells." *Oceania* 43(3):198–204.
Deming, W. Edwards
1982 *Out of the Crisis.* Cambridge, Mass.: MIT, Center for Advanced Engineering Study.
Diamond, Stanley
1974 *In Search of the Primitive: A Critique of Civilization.* New Brunswick, N.J.: Transaction Books.
Douglas, Mary, and Baron Isherwood
1979 *The World of Goods: Toward an Anthropology of Consumption.* New York: W. W. Norton and Company.
Edwards, Richard C.
1979 *Contested Terrain: The Transformation of the Workplace in the Twentieth Century.* New York: Basic Books.
Epstein, T. S.
1968 *Capitalism, Primitive and Modern: Some Aspects of Tolai Economic Growth.* East Lansing: Michigan State University Press.
1970 "Indigenous Entrepreneurs and Their Narrow Horizon." In *The Indigenous Role in Business Enterprise,* Marion W. Ward, ed., pp. 16–26. New Guinea Research Bulletin No. 35. Boroko and Canberra: New Guinea Research Unit/Australian National University.
Errington, Frederick
1974 "Indigenous Ideas of Order, Time, and Transition in a New Guinea Cargo Movement." *American Ethnologist* 1(2):255–267.
Errington, Frederick, and Deborah Gewertz
1987 *Cultural Alternatives and a Feminist Anthropology: An Analysis of Culturally Constructed Gender Interests in Papua New Guinea.* Cambridge: Cambridge University Press.
Finney, Ben R.
1973 *Big-Men and Business: Entrepreneurship and Economic Growth in the New Guinea Highlands.* Honolulu: The University Press of Hawaii.
Firth, Raymond
1967 *The Work of the Gods in Tikopia.* New York: Humanities Press.
Firth, Stewart
1975 "The Missions: From Chalmers to Indigenization." *Meanjin Quarterly* 34(3):342–350.
Fisk, E. K.
1964 "Planning in a Primitive Economy: From Pure Subsistence to the Production of a Market Surplus." *Economic Record* 40:156–174.

Fortune, R. F.
1932 *Sorcerers of Dobu: The Social Anthropology of the Dobu Islanders of the Western Pacific.* New York: E. P. Dutton and Company.
1965 [1935] *Manus Religion: An Ethnological Study of the Manus Natives of the Admirality Islands.* Lincoln: University of Nebraska Press.

Foster, Robert J.
1992 "Commoditization and the Emergence of *Kastam* as a Cultural Category: A New Ireland Case in Comparative Perspective." *Oceania* 62(4):284–294.

Frank, André Gunder
1966 "The Development of Underdevelopment." *Monthly Review* 18:17–31.

Freedman, Michael P.
1980 "Comment on 'Does Labor Time Decrease with Industrialization? A Survey of Time-Allocation Studies,' Wanda Minge-Klevana." *Current Anthropology* 21(3):291–292.

Geertz, Clifford
1966 *Person, Time, and Conduct in Bali: An Essay in Cultural Analysis.* New Haven, Conn.: Yale University Southeast Asian Studies.

Gewertz, Deborah, and Frederick Errington
1991 *Twisted Histories, Altered Contexts: Representing the Chambri in a World System.* Cambridge: Cambridge University Press.

Good, Kenneth
1986 *Papua New Guinea: A False Economy.* London: Anti-Slavery Society.

Goodman, Raymond, Charles Lepani, and David Morawetz
1985 *The Economy of Papua New Guinea: An Independent Review.* Canberra: National Centre for Development Studies, The Australian National University.

Gostin, Olga
1986 *Cash Cropping, Catholicism and Change: Resettlement among the Kuni of Papua.* Canberra: National Centre for Development Studies, The Australian National University.

Greeley, Andrew
1987 "Mysticism Goes Mainstream." *American Health,* January/February 1987, pp. 47–49.

Gregory, C. A.
1982 *Gifts and Commodities.* New York: Academic Press.

Grossman, Lawrence
1983 "Cattle, Rural Economic Differentation and Articulation in the Highlands of Papua New Guinea." *American Ethnologist* 10(1):59–76.

Gudeman, Stephen
1986 *Economics as Culture: Models and Metaphors of Livelihood.* Boston: Routledge and Kegan Paul.

Guilford, Virginia
1982 "Oksapmin Trade Stores." Paper presented at the Annual Meeting of the Association for Social Anthropology in Oceania, Hilton Head Island, South Carolina.

Gutman, Herbert G.
1973 "Work, Culture, and Society in Industralizing America, 1815–1919." *American Historical Review* 78(3):531–588.

Haantjens, H. A., E. Reiner, and R. G. Robbins
1968 "Land Systems of the Wewak-Lower Sepik Area." In *Lands of the Wewak-Lower Sepik Area, Territory of Papua New Guinea,* H. A. Haantjens, ed., pp. 15–48. Melbourne: Commonwealth Scientific and Industrial Research Organization.

Hallowell, A. Irving
1955 *Culture and Experience.* New York: Schocken Books.

Harris, Marvin
1975 *Cows, Pigs, Wars, and Witches: The Riddles of Culture.* New York: Vintage Books.

Herdt, Gilbert
1989 "Self and Culture: Contexts of Religious Experience in Melanesia." In *The Religious Imagination in New Guinea,* Gilbert Herdt and Michele Stephen, eds., pp. 15–40. New Brunswick, N.J.: Rutgers University Press.

Hogbin, H. Ian
1935 "Trading Expeditions in Northern New Guinea." *Oceania* 5(4):375–407.
1970 *The Island of Menstruating Men: Religion in Wogeo, New Guinea.* London: Chandler Publishing Company.
1978 *The Leaders and the Led: Social Control in Wogeo, New Guinea.* Melbourne, Austral.: Melbourne University Press.

Huber, Mary Taylor
1987 "Constituting the Church: Catholic Missionaries on the Sepik Frontier." *American Ethnologist* 14(1):107–125.
1988 *The Bishop's Progress: A Historical Ethnography of Catholic Missionary Experience on the Sepik Frontier.* Washington, D.C.: Smithsonian Institution Press.

Jackman, Harry
1977 "Some Thoughts on Entrepreneurship in Papua New Guinea." *Australian Outlook* 31(1):24–37.

Jones, William O.
1969 "The Demand for Food, Leisure and Economic Surpluses." In *Subsistence Agriculture and Economic Development,* Clifton R. Wharton, Jr., ed., pp. 275–283. Chicago: Aldine Publishing Company.

Kahn, Miriam
1986 *Always Hungry, Never Greedy: Food and the Expression of Gender in a Melanesian Society.* Cambridge: Cambridge University Press.

Katz, Michael B.
1989 *The Undeserving Poor.* New York: Pantheon Books.

Keesing, Roger M.
1982 "Introduction." In *Rituals of Manhood: Male Initiation in Papua New Guinea,* Gilbert H. Herdt, ed., pp. 1–43. Berkeley and Los Angeles: University of California Press.
1989 "Creating the Past: Custom and Identity in the Contemporary Pacific." *The Contemporary Pacific* 1(1/2):19–42.

Lawrence, Peter
1964 *Road Belong Cargo: A Study of the Cargo Movement in the Southern Madang District, New Guinea.* Manchester, Eng.: Manchester University Press.

1988 "Twenty Years After: A Reconsideration of Papua New Guinea Seaboard and Highlands Religions." *Oceania* 59(1):7–29.

Lawrence, Peter, and Mervyn Meggitt
1972 *Gods, Ghosts and Men in Melanesia: Some Religions of Australian New Guinea and the New Hebrides.* Melbourne, Austral.: Oxford University Press.

Lepowsky, Maria
1982 "A Comparison of Alcohol and Betelnut Use on Vanatinai (Sudest Island)." In *Through a Glass Darkly: Beer and Modernization in Papua New Guinea,* Mac Marshall, ed., pp. 325–342. IASER Monograph 18. Boroko, Papua New Guinea: Institute of Applied Social and Economic Research.

Levy, Marion J., Jr.
1966 *Modernization and the Structure of Societies: A Setting for International Affairs.* Vol. 1. Princeton, N.J.: Princeton University Press.

Levy, Robert I.
1973 *Tahitians: Mind and Experience in the Society Islands.* Chicago: University of Chicago Press.

Lindstrom, Lamont
1982 "*Leftemap Kastom:* The Political History of Tradition on Tanna, Vanuatu." *Mankind* 13(4):316–329.
1992 "*Pasin Tumbuna:* Cultural Traditions and National Identity in Papua New Guinea." Culture and Communication Working Papers. Honolulu: Institute of Culture and Communication, East-West Center.

Linnekin, Jocelyn
1983 "Defining Tradition: Variations on the Hawaiian Identity." *American Ethnologist* 10(2):241–252.
1990 "The Politics of Culture in the Pacific." In *Cultural Identity and Ethnicity in the Pacific,* Jocelyn Linnekin and Lyn Poyer, eds., pp. 149–173. Honolulu: University of Hawaii Press.

Lipset, David
1991 "Two Brothers: Concepts of the North Coast in Myth." Paper presented at the workshop "The North Coast of Papua New Guinea: Discourses of a Region and Regional Discourse," held at the University of Minnesota, Minneapolis.

MacAndrew, Craig, and Robert B. Edgerton, eds.
1969 *Drunken Comportment: A Social Explanation.* Chicago: Aldine Publishing Company.

McCracken, Grant
1988 *Culture and Consumption: New Approaches to the Symbolic Character of Consumer Goods and Activities.* Bloomington and Indianapolis: Indiana University Press.

McDowell, Nancy
1982 "Strength, Autonomy and Alcohol Use in Bun." In *Through a Glass Darkly: Beer and Modernization in Papua New Guinea,* Mac Marshall, ed., pp. 257–270. IASER Monograph 18. Boroko, Papua New Guinea: Institute of Applied Social and Economic Research.

1988 "A Note on Cargo Cults and Cultural Constructions of Change." *Pacific Studies* 11(2):121–134.

Malinowski, Bronislaw
1954 *Magic, Science, and Religion and Other Essays.* Garden City, N.Y.: Doubleday Anchor Books.

Marcus, George E., and Michael M. J. Fischer
1986 *Anthropology and Cultural Critique: An Experimental Moment in the Human Sciences.* Chicago: University of Chicago Press.

Marcuse, Herbert
1973 "Karl Popper and the Problem of Historical Laws." In *Studies in Critical Philosophy,* Joris De Bres, trans., pp. 191–208. Boston: Beacon Press.

Marshall, Mac, ed.
1979 *Beliefs, Behaviors, and Alcoholic Beverages: A Cross-Cultural Survey.* Ann Arbor: University of Michigan Press.

Marx, Karl
1959 [1844] Excerpt from "Toward the Critique of Hegel's Philosophy of Right." In *Marx and Engels: Basic Writings on Politics and Philosophy,* Lewis S. Feuer, ed., pp. 262–269. Garden City, N.Y.: Anchor Books.
1969 [1852] *The Eighteenth Brumaire of Louis Bonaparte.* New York: International Publishers.
1974 [1844] *Economic and Philosophic Manuscripts of 1844.* Moscow: Progress Publishers.

Mauss, Marcel
1967 [1925] *The Gift.* New York: W. W. Norton and Company.

May, R. J., and M. Spriggs, eds.
1990 *The Bougainville Crisis.* Bathurst (Austral.): Crawford House Press.

Meggitt, Mervyn
1977 *Blood Is Their Argument.* Palo Alto, Calif.: Mayfield Publishing Company.

Mihalic, Francis
1971 *The Jacaranda Dictionary and Grammar of Melanesian Pidgin.* Milton, Queensland, Austral.: The Jacaranda Press.

Moore, Wilbert E.
1963 *Man, Time, and Society.* New York: John Wiley and Sons.

Mumford, Lewis
1963 [1934] *Technics and Civilization.* New York: Harcourt, Brace and World.

O'Callaghan, Mary-Louise
1991 "State of Anarchy." *Far Eastern Economic Review* 151(6):23.

Oliver, Douglas L.
1967 [1955] *A Solomon Island Society: Kinship and Leadership among the Siuai of Bougainville.* Boston: Beacon Press.

Ortner, Sherry B.
1984 "Theory in Anthropology since the Sixties." *Comparative Studies in Society and History* 26(1):126–166.

Papua New Guinea Copra Marketing Board
1974–1976   *Price Directives.* Wewak, Papua New Guinea: Copra Marketing
       Board.
Papua New Guinea Office of Information
1976   *1976 Statistics: Economic Indicators. Hiri, February 12.* Konedobu:
       Papua New Guinea Office of Information.
Papua New Guinea Post-Courier
1976   "Collapse Faces Copra." May 1976 (more specific date could not be ascer-
       tained), p. 1.
Parry, Jonathan, and Maurice Bloch
1989   "Introduction: Money and the Morality of Exchange." In *Money and the
       Morality of Exchange,* Jonathan Parry and Maurice Bloch, eds., pp.
       1–32. Cambridge: Cambridge University Press.
Philibert, Jean-Marc
1986   "The Politics of Tradition: Toward a Generic Culture in Vanuatu." *Man-
       kind* 16(1):1–10.
Philpott, M. M., and Papua New Guinea Central Planning Office
1974   "East Sepik District Growth Center Study, Second Draft. January 1974."
       Papua New Guinea Central Planning Office.
Piven, Frances Fox, and Richard A. Cloward
1982   *The New Class War: Reagan's Attack on the Welfare State and Its Conse-
       quences.* New York: Pantheon Books.
Poole, Fitz John Porter
1982   "Cultural Significance of 'Drunken Comportment' in a Non-Drinking
       Society: The Bimin-Kuskusmin of the West Sepik." In *Through a Glass
       Darkly: Beer and Modernization in Papua New Guinea,* Mac Marshall,
       ed., pp. 189–210. IASER Monograph 18. Boroko, Papua New Guinea:
       Institute of Applied Social and Economic Research.
Power, Thomas Michael
1988   *The Economic Pursuit of Quality.* Armonk, N.Y.: M. E. Sharpe, Inc.
Reed, Stephen Winsor
1943   *The Making of Modern New Guinea.* Philadelphia: The American Philo-
       sophical Society.
Rodgers, Daniel T.
1978   *The Work Ethic in Industrial America, 1850–1920.* Chicago: University
       of Chicago Press.
Rodman, Margaret
1983   "Following Peace: Indigenous Pacification of a Northern New Hebri-
       dean Society." In *The Pacification of Melanesia,* Margaret Rodman and
       Matthew Cooper, eds., pp. 141–160. Association for Social Anthropol-
       ogy in Oceania Monograph No. 7. Lanham, Md.: University Press of
       America.
Rosch, Eleanor
1975   "Universals and Cultural Specifics in Human Categorization." In *Cross-
       Cultural Perspectives on Learning,* Richard W. Brislin, Stephen Bochner,
       and Walter J. Lonner, eds., pp. 177–206. New York: John Wiley and
       Sons.

Sack, P., and D. Clark
1979 *German New Guinea: The Annual Reports.* Canberra: Australian National University Press.

Sahlins, Marshall
1972 *Stone Age Economics.* Chicago: Aldine-Atherton.
1976 *Culture and Practical Reason.* Chicago: University of Chicago Press.
1981 *Historical Metaphors and Mythical Realities: Structure in the Early History of the Sandwich Islands Kingdom.* Ann Arbor: University of Michigan Press.
1991 "The Economics of 'Develop-man' in the Pacific." Sakamaki Lecture, 13th International Summer Institute for Semiotic and Structural Studies, University of Hawaii at Manoa.

Salisbury, Richard F.
1970 *Vunamami: Economic Transformation in a Traditional Society.* Berkeley and Los Angeles: University of California Press.

Scaglion, Richard
1986 "The Importance of Nighttime Observations in Time-Allocation Studies." *American Ethnologist* 13(3):537–545.

Schieffelin, Edward L.
1976 *The Sorrow of the Lonely and the Burning of the Dancers.* New York: St. Martin's Press.

Schwartz, Theodore
1968 "Cargo Cult: A Melanesian Type Response to Culture Contact." Paper presented at De Vos Conference on Psychological Adjustment and Adaptation to Culture Change, Hakone, Japan, 1968, and the 8th International Congress of Anthropological and Ethnological Sciences, Tokyo.
1972 "Distributive Models of Culture in Relation to Societal Scale." Paper prepared for Wenner-Gren Foundation for Anthropological Research Burg Wartenstein Symposium No. 55, July 31–August 8, 1972.
1973 "Cult and Context: The Paranoid Ethos in Melanesia." *Ethos* 1(2): 153–174.
1976 "Cultural Totemism: Ethnic Identity Primitive and Modern." In *Ethnic Identity: Cultural Continuities and Change,* George De Vos, ed., pp. 106–131. Palo Alto, Calif.: Mayfield.
1981 Remarks made at the Papua New Guinea Institute of Applied Social and Economic Research Conference on Alcohol Use and Abuse, Waigani, Papua New Guinea.
1982 "Alcohol Use in Manus Villages." In *Through a Glass Darkly: Beer and Modernization in Papua New Guinea.* Mac Marshall, ed., pp. 391–403. IASER Monograph 18. Boroko, Papua New Guinea: Institute of Applied Social and Economic Research.
n.d. "Spatial and Temporal Orientation in the Admiralty Islands." Unpublished manuscript.

Schwartz, Theodore, and Lola Romanucci-Ross
1974 "Drinking and Inebriate Behavior in the Admiralty Islands, Melanesia." *Ethos* 2(3):213–231.

Schwimmer, Eric
1979 "The Self and the Product: Concepts of Work in Comparative Perspective." In *Social Anthropology of Work,* Sandra Wallman, ed., pp. 287–315. New York: Academic Press.

Scott, James C.
1990 *Domination and the Arts of Resistance: Hidden Transcripts.* New Haven and London: Yale University Press.

Senge, Frank
1991 "Calendar of Fear." *Pacific Islands Monthly,* April, pp. 10–12.

Sennett, Richard, and Jonathan Cobb
1972 *The Hidden Injuries of Class.* New York: Vintage Books.

Sexton, Lorraine
1983 "Little Women and Big Men in Business: A Gorokan Development Project and Social Stratification." *Oceania* 54(2):133–150.

Smith, Michael French
1978 "Good Men Face Hard Times in Kragur: Ideology and Social Change in a New Guinea Village." Ph.D. dissertation, University of California, San Diego. Ann Arbor: University Microfilms.

1982a "Bloody Time and Bloody Scarcity: Capitalism, Authority, and the Transformation of Temporal Experience in a Papua New Guinea Village." *American Ethnologist* 9(3):503–518.

1982b "The Catholic Ethic and the Spirit of Alcohol Use in an East Sepik Province Village." In *Through a Glass Darkly: Beer and Modernization in Papua New Guinea,* Mac Marshall, ed., pp. 271–288. IASER Monograph 18. Boroko, Papua New Guinea: Institute of Applied Social and Economic Research.

1984 " 'Wild' Villagers and Capitalist Virtues: Perceptions of Western Work Habits in a Preindustrial Community." *Anthropological Quarterly* 57(4): 125–138.

1985 "White Man, Rich Man, Bureaucrat, Priest: Hierarchy, Inequality and Legitimacy in a Changing Papua New Guinea Village." *South Pacific Forum* 2(1):1–24.

1988 "From Heathen to Atheist on Kairiru Island." In *Culture and Christianity: The Dialectics of Transformation,* George Saunders, ed., pp. 33–46. Westport, Conn.: Greenwood Press.

1990 "Business and the Romance of Community Cooperation on Kairiru Island." In *Sepik Heritage: Tradition and Change in Papua New Guinea,* Nancy Lutkehaus, Christian Kaufman, William E. Mitchell, Douglas Newton, Lita Osmundsen, and Meinhard Schuster, eds., pp. 212–220. Durham, N.C.: Carolina Academic Press.

1990 "Catholicism, Capitalist Incorporation and Resistance in Kragur Village." In *The Ethnography of Christianity in the Pacific,* John Barker, ed., pp. 149–172. Association for Social Anthropology in Oceania Monograph No. 12. Lanham, Md.: University Press of America.

Stephen, Michele
1987 "Master of Souls: The Mekeo Sorcerer." In *Sorcerer and Witch in Melanesia,* Michele Stephen, ed., pp. 41–80. New Brunswick, N.J.: Rutgers University Press.

Strathern, Marilyn
1975 "No Money on Our Skins: Hagen Migrants in Moresby." New Guinea Research Bulletin No. 61. Port Moresby and Canberra: New Guinea Research Unit/Australian National University.
1988 *The Gender of the Gift: Problems with Women and Problems with Society in Melanesia.* Berkeley and Los Angeles: University of California Press.

Taussig, Michael
1980 *The Devil and Commodity Fetishism in South America.* Chapel Hill: University of North Carolina Press.

Terdiman, Richard
1985 *Discourse/Counter Discourse: The Theory and Practice of Symbolic Resistance in Nineteenth-Century France.* Ithaca and London: Cornell University Press.

Territory of Papua and New Guinea, Department of Agriculture, Stock and Fisheries
1969 "Wewak Sub-District Coconut Palms Per Capita." Typescript. Wewak, Papua New Guinea: Department of Agriculture, Stock and Fisheries.

Thomas, Nicholas
1990 "Regional Politics, Ethnicity, and Custom in Fiji." *The Contemporary Pacific* 2(1):131–146.
1991 *Entangled Objects: Exchange, Material Culture, and Colonialism in the Pacific.* Cambridge, Mass.: Harvard University Press.

Thompson, E. P.
1967 "Time, Work-Discipline, and Industrial Capitalism." *Past and Present* 38: 56–97.
1980 [1963] *The Making of the English Working Class.* London: Victor Gollancz.

Tiesler, Frank
1969–1970 *Die intertribalen Beziehungen an der Nordküste Neuguineas in Gebiet der Kleinen Schouten-Inseln. Abhandlungen und Berichte des Staatlichen Museums für Volkerkunde Dresden.* Vols. 30, 31. Berlin: Akademie-Verlag.

Tonkinson, Robert
1982 "*Kastom* in Melanesia: Introduction." In *Reinventing Traditional Culture: The Politics of Culture in Island Melanesia,* Roger M. Keesing and Robert Tonkinson, eds. *Mankind,* Special Issue, 13(4):302–305.

Townsend, Don
1980 "Disengagement and Incorporation: The Post-Colonial Reaction in the Rural Villages of Papua New Guinea." *Pacific Viewpoint* 21(1):1–25.

Tuzin, Donald F.
1976 *The Ilahita Arapesh: Dimensions of Unity.* Berkeley and Los Angeles: University of California Press.
1980 *The Voice of the Tambaran: Truth and Illusion in Ilahita Arapesh Religion.* Berkeley and Los Angeles: University of California Press.
1990 "Fighting For Their Lives: The Problem of Cultural Authenticity in Today's Sepik Region." In *Sepik Heritage: Tradition and Change in Papua New Guinea,* Nancy Lutkehaus, Christian Kaufman, William E. Mitchell,

Douglas Newton, Lita Osmundsen, and Meinhard Schuster, eds., pp. 364–369. Durham, N.C.: Carolina Academic Press.

Tylor, Edward B.
1873   *Primitive Culture.* London: John Murray.

van den Hemel, Konstantin
1907–1908   *Journal. Steyler Missions-Bote.* Translation provided by St. Xavier's High School, Kairiru Island, Papua New Guinea.

Vulliamy, Graham, and James Carrier
1985   "Sorcery and the SSCEP: The Cultural Context of an Educational Innovation." *British Journal of Sociology of Education* 6(1):17–33.

Waddell, E. W., and P. A. Krinks
1968   "The Organization of Production and Distribution among the Orokaiva: An Analysis of Work and Exchange in Two Communities Participating in Both the Subsistence and Monetary Sectors of the Economy." New Guinea Research Bulletin No. 24. Port Moresby and Canberra: New Guinea Research Unit / Australian National University.

Wagner, Roy
1981   *The Invention of Culture.* Chicago: University of Chicago Press.

Wallerstein, Immanuel
1974   *The Modern World-System: Capitalist Agriculture and the Origins of the European World Economy in the Sixteenth Century.* New York: Academic Press.

Wallman, Sandra
1977   "Introduction: Perceptions of Development." In *Perceptions of Development,* Sandra Wallman, ed., pp. 1–16. Cambridge: Cambridge University Press.

Walter, Michael A. H. B.
1981   "Cult Movements and Community Development Associations: Revolution and Evolution in the Papua New Guinea Countryside." In *Road Belong Development: Cargo Cults, Community Groups and Self-Help Movements in Papua New Guinea,* Rolf Gerritsen, R. J. May, and Michael A. H. B. Walter, eds., pp. 81–105. Working Paper No. 3, Department of Political and Social Change, Research School of Pacific Studies. Canberra: Australian National University.

Warry, Wayne
1982   "*Bia* and *Bisnis:* The Use of Beer in Chuave Ceremonies." In *Through a Glass Darkly: Beer and Modernization in Papua New Guinea,* Mac Marshall, ed., pp. 83–103. IASER Monograph 18. Boroko, Papua New Guinea: Institute of Applied Social and Economic Research.

Weber, Max
1958 [1920]   *The Protestant Ethic and the Spirit of Capitalism.* Translated by Talcott Parsons. New York: Charles Scribner's Sons.

Welsch, Robert L.
1989   "Context and Meaning of the A. B. Lewis Collection: An Example from the North Coast of New Guinea." Paper presented at Johns Hopkins University, Baltimore, Md., April 14–15.
1992   Personal communication.

Wesley-Smith, Terence
1991 "Papua New Guinea in 1990: A Year of Crisis." *Asian Survey* 31(2): 188–195.
Wewak Patrol Report
1946–1947 *Wewak Patrol Report No. 3*. Port Moresby: Papua New Guinea National Archives.
White, Geoffrey
1983 "War, Peace, and Piety in Santa Isabel, Solomon Islands." In *The Pacification of Melanesia,* Margaret Rodman and Matthew Cooper, eds., pp. 109–139. Association for Social Anthropology in Oceania Monograph No. 7. Lanham, Md.: University Press of America.
Willis, Paul
1977 *Learning to Labor: How Working-Class Kids Get Working-Class Jobs.* New York: Columbia University Press.
Wiltgen, Ralph M.
1969 "Catholic Mission Plantations in Mainland New Guinea: Their Origin and Purpose." In *The History of Melanesia,* K. S. Inglis, ed., pp. 329–362. Canberra and Port Moresby: Australian National University and University of Papua New Guinea.
Wivell, Richard
1981 "Kairiru Grammar." Master's thesis, University of Auckland, Auckland, New Zealand.
Worsley, Peter
1968 *The Trumpet Shall Sound*. New York: Schocken Books.
Young, R. E.
1975 "Papua New Guinea: The New Elite." *The Australian and New Zealand Journal of Sociology* 11(3):38–46.
Zelenietz, Martin
1983 "The End of Headhunting in New Georgia." In *The Pacification of Melanesia,* Margaret Rodman and Matthew Cooper, eds., pp. 91–108. Association for Social Anthropology in Oceania Monograph No. 7. Lanham, Md.: University Press of America.

Index